AF733284

The Suspect's Statement

What suspects tell the police may become a crucial piece of evidence when the case comes to court. But what happens to 'the suspect's statement' when it is written down by the police? Based on a unique set of data from over fifteen years' research, Martha Komter examines the trajectory of the suspect's statement from the police interrogation through to the trial. She shows how the suspect's statement is elicited and written down in the police report, how this police report both represents and differs from the original talk in the interrogation, and how it is quoted and referred to in court. The analyses cover interactions in multiple settings, with documents that link one interaction to the next, providing insights into the interactional and documentary foundations of the criminal process and, more generally, into the construction, character and uses of documents in institutional settings.

MARTHA KOMTER is research fellow at the Netherlands Institute for the Study of Crime and Law Enforcement (NSCR), Amsterdam. Her research interests include interaction in institutional settings, such as job interviews, courtroom interaction and police interrogations. She has published widely on these themes, and is author of *Conflict and Cooperation in Job Interviews: A Study of Talk, Tasks, and Ideas* (1991) and *Dilemmas in the Courtroom: A Study of Trials of Violent Crime in the Netherlands* (1998).

Studies in Interactional Sociolinguistics

Founding Editor
John J. Gumperz (1922–2013)

Editors
Paul Drew, Rebecca Clift, Lorenza Mondada, Marja-Leena Sorjonen

1 *Discourse Strategies* John J. Gumperz
2 *Language and Social Identity* edited by John J. Gumperz
3 *The Social Construction of Literacy* Jenny Cook-Gumperz
4 *Politeness: Some Universals in Language Usage* Penelope Brown and Stephen C. Levinson
5 *Discourse Markers* Deborah Schiffrin
6 *Talking Voices: Repetition, Dialogue, and Imagery in Conversational Discourse* Deborah Tannen
7 *Conducting Interaction: Patterns of Behaviour in Focused Encounters* Adam Kendon
8 *Talk at Work: Interaction in Institutional Settings* edited by Paul Drew and John Heritage
9 *Grammar in Interaction: Adverbial Clauses in American English Conversations* Cecilia E. Ford
10 *Crosstalk and Culture in Sino-American Communication* Linda W. L. Young (with foreword by John J. Gumperz)
11 *AIDS Counselling: Institutional Interaction and Clinical Practice* Anssi Perakyla
12 *Prosody in Conversation: Interactional Studies* edited by Elizabeth Couper-Kuhlen and Margret Selting
13 *Interaction and Grammar* edited by Elinor Ochs, Emanuel A. Schegloff and Sandra A. Thompson
14 *Credibility in Court: Communicative Practices in the Camorra Trials* Marco Jacquemet
15 *Interaction and the Development of Mind* A. J. Wootton
16 *The News Interview: Journalists and Public Figures on the Air* Steven Clayman and John Heritage
17 *Gender and Politeness* Sara Mills
18 *Laughter in Interaction* Philip Glenn
19 *Matters of Opinion: Talking about Public Issues* Greg Myers
20 *Communication in Medical Care: Interaction between Primary Care Physicians and Patients* edited by John Heritage and Douglas Maynard
21 *In Other Words: Variation in Reference and Narrative* Deborah Schiffrin
22 *Language in Late Modernity: Interaction in an Urban School* Ben Rampton
23 *Discourse and Identity* edited by Anna De Fina, Deborah Schiffrin and Michael Bamberg

24 *Reporting Talk: Reported Speech in Interaction* edited by Elizabeth Holt and Rebecca Clift
25 *The Social Construction of Literacy*, 2nd Edition edited by Jenny Cook-Gumperz
26 *Talking Voices*, 2nd Edition by Deborah Tannen
27 *Conversation Analysis* edited by Jack Sidnell
28 *Impoliteness: Using Language to Cause Offence* Jonathan Culpeper
29 *The Morality of Knowledge in Conversation* edited by Tanya Stivers, Lorenza Mondada and Jakob Steensig
30 *Conversational Repair and Human Understanding* edited by Makoto Hayashi, Geoffrey Raymond and Jack Sidnell
31 *Grammar and Everyday Talk: Building Responsive Actions* by Sandra A. Thompson, Barbara A. Fox, and Elizabeth Couper-Kuhlen
32 *Multimodal Conduct in the Law: Language, Gesture and Materiality in Legal Interaction* by Gregory Matoesian and Kristin Enola Gilbert
33 *The Suspect's Statement: Talk and Text in the Criminal Process* Martha Komter

The Suspect's Statement

Talk and Text in the Criminal Process

Martha Komter

Netherlands Institute for the Study of Crime and Law Enforcement (NSCR)

CAMBRIDGE
UNIVERSITY PRESS

CAMBRIDGE
UNIVERSITY PRESS

University Printing House, Cambridge CB2 8BS, United Kingdom

One Liberty Plaza, 20th Floor, New York, NY 10006, USA

477 Williamstown Road, Port Melbourne, VIC 3207, Australia

314–321, 3rd Floor, Plot 3, Splendor Forum, Jasola District Centre, New Delhi – 110025, India

79 Anson Road, #06–04/06, Singapore 079906

Cambridge University Press is part of the University of Cambridge.

It furthers the University's mission by disseminating knowledge in the pursuit of education, learning, and research at the highest international levels of excellence.

www.cambridge.org
Information on this title: www.cambridge.org/9781107059481
DOI: 10.1017/9781107445062

© Martha Komter 2019

This publication is in copyright. Subject to statutory exception and to the provisions of relevant collective licensing agreements, no reproduction of any part may take place without the written permission of Cambridge University Press.

First published 2019

Printed and bound in Great Britain by Clays Ltd, Elcograf S.p.A.

A catalogue record for this publication is available from the British Library.

Library of Congress Cataloging-in-Publication Data
Names: Komter, Martha, author.
Title: The suspect's statement : talk and text in the criminal process / Martha Komter, Netherlands Institute for the Study of Crime and Law Enforcement (NSCR).
Description: Cambridge, United Kingdom ; New York, NY : Cambridge Unviersity Press, 2018. | Series: Studies in interactional sociolinguistics | Includes bibliographical references and index.
Identifiers: LCCN 2018034115 | ISBN 9781107059481 (hardback : alk. paper)
Subjects: LCSH: Criminal procedure. | Criminal investigation. | Police questioning. | Due process of law.
Classification: LCC K5401 .K66 2018 | DDC 345/.052–dc23
LC record available at https://lccn.loc.gov/2018034115

ISBN 978-1-107-05948-1 Hardback

Cambridge University Press has no responsibility for the persistence or accuracy of URLs for external or third-party internet websites referred to in this publication and does not guarantee that any content on such websites is, or will remain, accurate or appropriate.

Contents

Acknowledgements

I am indebted to Paul Drew, Susan Ehrlich, Henk Elffers, Heimrich Kanis, Tom Koole, Marijke Malsch, Harrie Mazeland, Hedwig te Molder, Peter van der Laan, Annerie Smolders, Wilbert Spooren and Marigo Teeuwen, for their insightful comments on earlier versions of the chapters in this book; and to the anonymous suspects, police interrogators, defence lawyers, prosecutors and judges who gave permission for their talk to be recorded and their texts to be studied. And, finally, I am grateful to the NSCR for offering me this stimulating work environment.

This study has been supported by NWO, the Netherlands Organisation for Scientific Research (project 360-70-240).

Transcription Conventions

The transcription conventions depart from the standard Jeffersonian transcript notation for reasons of readability, and because the fragments are translated from Dutch (translation by the author). Those features of the standard transcript notation have been preserved that are compatible with the translation. For the original Dutch text, see Appendix B, which can be found online at www.cambridge.org

P	police interrogator/public prosecutor
P1	interrogating police officer
P2	reporting police officer
S	suspect
J	judge
D	defence lawyer
full stop.	falling intonation
comma,	slightly rising intonation
question mark?	rising intonation
underlining	emphasis
⌈brackets ⌊brackets	overlap
(3)	pause of three seconds etc.
dash-	sudden cut-off
. . . a few words omitted	
=	latched utterances
▲	gaze direction moving upward
▼	gaze direction moving down
::: colons	prolongation of prior sound
°yes°	spoken in a soft voice
( )	unclear utterance
((double brackets))	transcriber's note
shading	typing simultaneous to the talk
¦dotted line	editing simultaneous to the talk

bold	text of the police report
(13, N)	interrogation or trial number 13, of the 'new' (O = old) materials

Disclaimer

The names of the participants featuring in the excerpts (police officers, judges, prosecutors, defence lawyers, suspects, witnesses, etc.) and other identifying features (times, dates, places, etc.) have been changed.

1 Introduction

1.1 Introduction

When I started analysing the materials of courtroom interaction that I collected in the 1990s (Komter, 1998) I was struck by the ways judges referred to, or read from, the case file. They read sentences from police reports that were supposedly representing the suspect's 'own words' in the police interrogations; sentences that everyone could see would never have been spoken like that. This made me curious to find out what was really said in those interrogations, and to examine how these police reports came to look the way they did. Thus, when the courtroom study was completed, I collected a number of audio-recorded police interrogations and the reports made of these interrogations. The analyses of these materials made me aware of the complexities of the talk, the typing and the texts that emerged in and from the interrogations (Komter, 2001; 2002–3; 2003; 2005; 2006b). Then I realised that I could only understand the 'career' (cf. Cicourel, 1968; Meehan, 1986) of the suspect's statement if I followed cases from the police interrogation through to the trial. Therefore, new materials were collected, consisting of audio-recorded police interrogations, the reports made of these interrogations and video-recorded trials of the same cases. These materials formed the basis for studying how the talk in the police interrogation is transformed into the text of the 'suspect's statement', how this text is incorporated into the police report and becomes recognisable as an official piece of evidence, and how this police report is invoked by the professionals, especially the judges, in the courtroom. My main inspirations and tools for analysing these matters have been found in ethnomethodological and conversation analytic studies.

Although this book draws on my earlier research on trials and police interrogations, the combination and the interplay of the materials result in a synergy that affords the telling of a different, and in a sense more complete story. I shall illuminate the career of the suspect's statement by investigating its construction in the police interrogating room, its written character as part of the police report, and its uses in court by the professionals who deal with the case. I shall consider these foci of analysis in their particular settings, that is, the construction of the suspect's statement in the setting of the police interrogation, the character of the suspect's statement in the documentary 'settings' of the police report and the case file, and the invocation and use of the suspect's statement in the courtroom setting. These settings are not only separate entities with their own features and their own dynamics but they are also linked together by the various references to and invocations of the suspect's statement in the course of the process (Smith, 2001: 191).

It has been observed that 'following the career of a document through the various stages through which it goes will highlight the frameworks of organisational action as they are oriented to step by step, phase by phase, by organisational actors' (Harper, 1998: 44). The aim of this book is, by following the career of the suspect's statement from the police interrogation to the trial, to acquire insight into the interactional and documentary foundations of the Dutch criminal law process and, more generally, to understand the effects of the construction, character and use of documents in institutional settings. For medical settings, Heath and Luff (1996: 360) have noticed an absence of studies on 'the practices through which the document is written, read and used' (see also Cicourel, 1992; Raffel, 1979: 43–4. For the study of organisations, Llewellyn and Hindmarsh (2010: 19) have pointed to 'an absence of studies that are attentive to the situated integration of tools, documents, action and interaction'. This book can begin to fill the gap.

1.2 The Dutch Criminal Law Process

The Dutch criminal law process has been described as an 'audit model' of criminal adjudication, where the documented activities at each stage of the criminal law process are checked and reviewed by the legal professionals who use them in subsequent stages (Anderson, 1999: 50). In the Netherlands the criminal law process starts when someone is picked up by the police on the basis of a 'reasonable suspicion of guilt' (Code of Criminal Procedure, section 27.1), or when someone goes to the police station to report a crime or to press charges. Suspects or witnesses are then questioned by police officers, who make reports of these activities. These reports are checked and used by prosecutors as the basis for decisions about prosecution and about the involvement of the investigating judge (in the more serious cases) for the further implementation of the 'preliminary investigations'. The investigating judge is responsible for the means by which these 'preliminary investigations' should be carried out, and takes decisions for example on the suspect's custody and on means of detection, such as house searches and telephone taps.

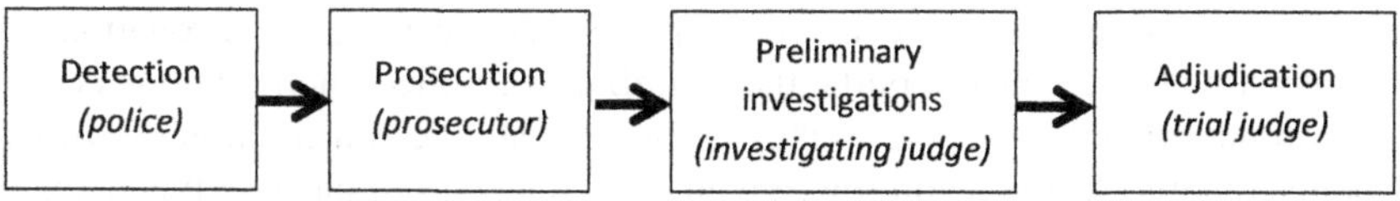

Figure 1 Phases in the criminal law process

During the 'preliminary investigations'[1] further evidence is collected that is necessary for adjudicating the case in court. When the prosecutor concludes that the case is sufficiently substantiated to obtain a conviction, the case file is considered complete and the case is brought to trial. Figure 1 shows the phases in the criminal law process and the professionals in charge. These phases accumulate, in the sense that police and prosecution remain involved in the preliminary investigations.

The Dutch criminal justice system can be described as mainly inquisitorial, with adversarial elements that come to the fore in the trial stage (Jörg et al., 1995). Features of an inquisitorial process are the emphasis on the pretrial investigations, the central role of the case file for the activities of the legal professionals, and the active involvement of the judge in the truth-finding process. The suspect remains an object of the investigations, and is called 'suspect' throughout the criminal law process. Although the prosecutor and the defence lawyer don't cross-examine suspects or witnesses in the same manner as in some adversarial systems, they do present their vision on the case in their closing statements, with the aim of influencing the outcome of the case (Komter and Malsch, 2012).

Recent developments show a mitigation of some of the more inquisitorial elements in the Dutch criminal law system. Under pressure from the European Court of Human Rights, Dutch courts are advised to depend less on documentary evidence and to question more witnesses in court, to improve the 'immediacy' of trials. Other changes in the system have been motivated by a series of miscarriages of justice in the first decade of this century. Between 2002 and 2010 four serious cases of wrongful convictions attracted a lot of media attention. As three of them were based on false confessions to the police (Brants, 2012: 1079), the need arose to achieve greater visibility of and control over the police detectives' activities in the interrogating room.

This resulted in the introduction in 2006 of mandatory audiovisual registration of police interrogations for the more serious offences (offences that carry a minimal punishment of twelve years in prison), and the introduction in 2016 of

[1] On 1 January 2013 the law concerning the preliminary investigations has been changed. Currently the investigating judge has a supervising function, and the prosecutor is in charge of the further investigations.

the suspect's right to have a lawyer present at the police interrogation. In contrast with the police reports, the recordings of police interrogations do not constitute official evidence, so they do not obviate the construction of written police reports. As the recordings are not, as a rule, part of the case file, defence lawyers who want to consult them before the trial have to do so at the police station where they were made. They are available to all the professionals who deal with the case, but in practice they are not consulted very often.[2] As it takes time, the professionals prefer the written police reports (Malsch et al., 2015; see also: Haworth, 2010: 169). Another change in the criminal law process is the digitisation of the criminal law process, which will be legislated in a new Code of Criminal Procedure (Kessler, 2016). This has been set in motion in an experimental phase since 2002–3 and is expected to be completed in 2019.

1.2.1 The Police Interrogation

The criminal law process can be seen as a series of events where a possibly criminal event in the real world is transformed into and treated as a legal entity, where a citizen in the civic world is transformed into and treated as a suspect, and where rules are applied that may be different from, or contradictory with, the rules of everyday life. This process starts as a citizen is picked up by the police on the suspicion of having committed an offence. People who are arrested by the police are immediately confronted with the world of the law: they are introduced (if they are first offenders) into a world they don't know, a world with different rules and a different language. They undergo a kind of 'rite of passage' that marks their transformation from being a citizen into being a suspect, during which they appear to have rights that they may not understand and that they may not know they had (Rock, 2007).

This is illustrated by an anecdote told to me by Peter, one of my informants at one of the police stations where I collected my materials. He was an experienced police detective, highly valued by his colleagues, especially for his skills in dealing with suspects. One of his colleagues had arrested a suspect and put him into custody. He informed the suspect of his right to silence and asked him whether he wished to make a statement. This the suspect refused to do. The police officer then consulted Peter and asked him if he perhaps could induce the suspect to talk. So, Peter went to the suspect's cell and said: 'I heard from my colleague that you refused to make a statement, is that so?' The suspect nodded. Then Peter added: 'But then you can perhaps just tell us what

[2] They may also be consulted by forensic psychologists who work as expert witnesses in the case. There are complaints about the poor quality of the recordings (Horselenberg et al., 2016)

happened?' To this the suspect agreed. So, he was brought to the interrogating room where he 'made a statement'.

A legal requirement for conducting a police interrogation in the Netherlands is that the police must inform suspects at the start of the interrogations that they are not obliged to answer questions.[3] The aim of this is not only to protect suspects against unacceptable pressure, but also to ensure the 'truth value' of a confession. A confession only counts as a confession if it is perceivedly voluntarily given (Watson, 1990: 287). The police interrogator must write down the delivery of the caution in the police report (Code of Criminal Procedure, section 29.3).

Before embarking on the interrogation proper, police interrogators often start with expressions of 'hospitality' such as offers of something to drink or, before the ban on smoking in the interrogating room, a cigarette.[4] Then they may start the 'social interrogation', which consists of talk about the suspect's personal circumstances, such as schooling, work, expectations and friends. This serves to get a general picture of what kind of person the suspect is, but also to make them feel at ease and thereby to increase their willingness to talk; the relatively 'harmless' information elicited at the start of the interrogation sets a more or less friendly tone that may defuse the antagonistic potential of the interrogation (Cicourel, 1968: 116). However, the 'social interrogation' may also contain information that might be of interest to interpret 'the facts', as for example a structural shortage of money may explain a suspect's motives for theft. In one interrogation the fact that the – denying – suspect had two daughters to support and little money, was adduced by the interrogator to express his understanding of people who would steal in such circumstances. The interrogator's insistent appeal to the suspect's personal circumstances eventually made her confess (Komter, 2003).

During the 'fact-related' phase of the interrogation the police must find the truth under the assumption of a non-partisan prosecution; so they must investigate all aspects of the case, not just the incriminating facts (Brants, 2012). As confessions are more easily believed than denials (Goffman, 1970: 111), interrogations with denying suspects involve more investigative or hostile questioning. My materials include three suspects who initially deny the charges and eventually confess; one of them in the course of the interrogation (Komter, 2003), the other two after the police did some additional investigative

[3] In the Netherlands this right is laid down in the Code of Criminal Procedure, section 29.1. The right to silence implies that suspects, in contrast to witnesses, are not required to swear an oath that they will speak the truth.

[4] When I collected my police materials in 1998–9 a standard attribute in interrogating rooms was a packet of tobacco from which suspects could roll their own cigarettes. Because of its value as a social lubricant, police detectives were not happy when smoking was banned from the interrogating room.

work. In many interrogations there is no clear division between denying and confessing suspects; most of the suspects confess to some degree, or to some of the charges (Komter, 1998; Wartna et al., 1999).

1.2.2 The Suspect's Statement, the Police Report and the Case File

In contrast to the general interest in the truth-seeking efforts of police interrogators, relatively little attention has been paid to another significant task: the drawing up of the suspect's statement. This is generally done on the spot by the interrogator or by one of the interrogators when they work as a pair. As a result of the importance of the police detectives' statement taking, the PC on which the police report is written has a prominent place in the interrogation, both visibly as object in the interrogating room and substantively as medium between the talk and the reporting of it. The suspect's statement is the core substance of the police report, and is surrounded by other texts that serve to transform the police report into an official piece of evidence. The evidential value of the reports is highlighted by the fact that they are written down by police functionaries who operate under their oath of office.

How police reports look and what information they contain appear to result largely from bureaucratic and practical considerations, as there are not many legal prerequisites for their format or substance. One of the few legal requirements of police reports is that police interrogators draw up the police report 'as much as possible in the suspect's own words' (Code of Criminal Procedure, section 29.3). At first sight this looks like an instruction to record verbatim what the suspect has said. In practice it appears that judges are satisfied with a police report that contains a 'factual representation' of what the suspect told the police (Franken, 2010: 406).

In the course of the past decade the format of police reports has changed. Until about a decade ago the monologue style was the style most commonly used for reporting police interrogations in the Netherlands (Komter, 2001; 2002–3). Presently, the question–answer (Q–A) style and the 'recontextualised monologue' (RM) style are used more frequently. The 'recontextualised monologue style' is composed of 'recontextualisation phrases'. These are descriptions of the interrogator's speech actions (mostly 'telling' and 'asking') that appear to be produced by the suspect (e.g. 'you tell me . . .', 'you ask me . . .', Komter, 2006c). Recontextualisation phrases are also used occasionally in monologue or question–answer-style police reports. Whatever the style of the police reports, they are always summaries of the talk in the interrogations.

The police report is only one record among the collection of documents in the case file or dossier. The case file contains statements of suspects and witnesses, reports of the investigative activities of the police, reports of the suspect's custodial situation, reports of procedural matters, the suspect's

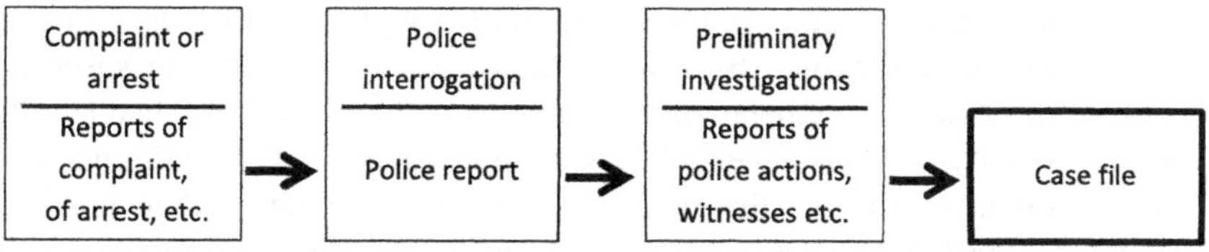

Figure 2 Compilation of the case file

criminal records and other pieces of evidence, such as photographs, audio or video recordings, letters and situation sketches. Documents in the case file may also be drawn up by 'external' professionals, such as psychiatrists, medical doctors, probation officers and forensic experts. Every document in the case file can serve as a piece of evidence.

Figure 2 gives an overview of the compilation of the case file through the successive stages of the criminal law process.[5]

The case file or dossier is meant to contain all the information gathered during the pretrial activities in the criminal process relevant for the adjudication of the case.

1.2.3 The Criminal Trial

The time spent on the pretrial investigations is one reason why Dutch trials last a relatively short period of time. Because most of the investigative work has already been done trials rarely take more than one day to be concluded; routine cases usually take no more than an hour. Another reason for the speedy dispatch of criminal cases is that most of the suspects confess to at least some of the charges, among other things because denying suspects may be filtered out of the system when there is not enough other evidence to build a case against them.

The documents in the case file form the basis for the legal professionals' management of their professional tasks in court (Komter, 1998; Malsch and Nijboer, 1999). Judges and defence lawyers receive the completed case file from the prosecutor's office around two weeks before the trial to give them the time to prepare it. Judges prepare the trial with the help of the clerks' summaries of and annotations to the important parts of the case file; they then check the clerks' work, mark what they consider to be the legally relevant passages and scribble notes on the documents (Van Oorschot, 2014a).

[5] 'Complaint' refers to the event that someone reports a crime to the police, files a complaint or presses charges.

The importance of the case file for the trial is highlighted by the fact that most cases are adjudicated by hearing no witnesses but only the suspects, because the written statements of witnesses as reported by the police can be used as evidence.[6] This potential lack of transparency of the criminal law process might undermine the suspect's right to a fair and public hearing. Therefore, the 'immediacy principle' of court proceedings requires that evidence should be presented in court in its most original form. When the judges rely on written evidence, they must read aloud or summarise this evidence if they want to use it for their verdict (Code of Criminal Procedure, section 301.4). Thus, in the course of their questioning the suspect, judges read aloud or summarise those passages from the case file that they consider pertinent for ratification as 'usable' evidence.[7] Moreover, judges review the evidence by mobilising the suspects' expressions of commitment to their earlier statements as reported by the police and by comparing their statements with the other evidence contained in the case file (Komter, 1998; 2002). Although this 'documentary method of interrogation' (Lynch and Bogen, 1996: 214) is by no means restricted to inquisitorial systems, it is one of the notable features of Dutch trials.

In contrast to the relatively passive role of judges in adversarial criminal justice systems, judges play a more active role in Dutch courtrooms.[8] Their main tasks are to preside over the court session, to decide on procedural correctness, to examine the suspect's involvement in the criminal offence of which he or she is accused and, if the suspect is found guilty, to decide on the appropriate kind and amount of punishment. A session in court consists of the following activities. The (presiding) judge opens the trial, verifies the suspect's personal details and informs them of their right to silence. Then the prosecutor presents the indictment, after which the (presiding) judge starts the 'main examinations'. These consist of questioning the suspect (and witnesses if any), first about 'the facts' in order to find out whether the suspects are guilty of the offences of which they are accused, and then about 'the person' in order to help judges decide on the appropriate measure of punishment. After that the prosecutor takes the floor for the closing arguments (the requisitory), which contain a summary of 'the facts' and of the measure of guilt of the suspect, and a demand for the kind and amount of punishment that the suspect should

[6] Even the presence of suspects in court is not required by law. Most suspects, however, do appear, as their defence lawyers cannot act on their behalf when they are absent.

[7] In studies of adversarial criminal law systems it has also been found that those passages are selected for quoting in court that are important for the evidence in the case (Ehrlich, 2012: 61–2; Philips, 1986: 154).

[8] Serious crimes (that carry a prison sentence of more than a year) are tried by a panel of three judges, of which one acts as presiding judge; simple cases are handled by a single judge (the 'police magistrate').

receive. Then the defence lawyer presents his or her arguments on behalf of the suspect. The two parties get the opportunity to respond to each other's closing arguments, after which the suspect gets the floor for his or her 'last word'. In the simple cases tried by the police magistrate the verdict is pronounced at the end of the trial; in the more serious cases the court generally passes judgment two weeks after the trial.

1.3 Research Approaches

The study of the 'career' of a suspect's statement from the police interrogation through to the trial involves the examination of different types of materials (audio and video recordings, police reports) in different settings (police interrogations and trials). These materials comprise a complex and interrelated collection of texts (suspects' statements), documents (police reports) and activities (e.g. talking, listening, typing, reading, truth finding, accusing and defending). As these materials cover a lot of ground, the research approaches must do justice to their variety and scope; on the other hand, in order to avoid losing sight of the focus of the project I had to confine myself to the essentials. As mentioned before, the main inspirations for analysing these materials derive from ethnomethodology and conversation analysis (CA). Although these approaches are related, each of them offers specific concepts and tools relevant for the analyses of my materials.

1.3.1 Ethnomethodology and Conversation Analysis

Ethnomethodologists and conversation analysts study what actors are actually doing in face-to-face interaction, and address how the actors themselves produce and make sense of the occasions they are involved in. An important contribution of ethnomethodology is the insights it offers into the ways in which people depend on taken-for-granted and shared knowledge for making sense of the world, into the practical circumstances that constrain and enable action, into the methods of practical reasoning that people employ for getting things done, and into the use of documents in organisations (Garfinkel, 1967c; Moore et al., 2010; Pollner 1987; Smith, 1974; 2001). These insights are particularly relevant for the study of legal practices, where the business of finding out 'what really happened' or 'who is to blame' is an overriding concern for those involved (Atkinson 1981; Dupret et al., 2015b; Garfinkel, 1967d; Manzo, 1997). The participants' reliance on the 'documentary method of interpretation' (Garfinkel, 1967c) for their truth-finding efforts is based on common-sense knowledge about the typical manner in which offences are committed, about the social characteristics of the persons who commit them, and about the features of the settings in which they occur (Sudnow, 1965: 259;

see also: Ericson, 1981; Sanders, 1977). Thus, police detectives gather information, physical evidence and witnesses' statements that are pieced together by reference to an imputed underlying pattern, which can lend coherence to the emerging 'discovery' of 'what happened'. The same methods are employed by the professionals in the courtroom – judges, prosecutors and defence lawyers – who monitor the suspects' and witnesses' narratives for coherence and consistency in order to decide on their truthfulness (Sacks, 1995 part I: 113–25).

A feature characteristic of institutional life is the production and use of documents. As a rule, these documents are considered as objective and factual accounts of prior events (Jönsson and Linell, 1991; Smith, 1974: 260; Zimmerman, 1969). Garfinkel's work on clinic records (1967e) drew attention to the fact that documents do not merely describe and represent an outside reality, but that they can be understood as objects in their own right and with their own dynamics, the purpose of which is to make available displays of justifiable work or 'correct procedures' (Benson and Drew, 1978; Harper, 1998; Smith, 1974; 1990a; 1990b; 2001; Watson, 2009; Zimmerman, 1969). Thus, police reports that are drawn up as representations of what suspects told the police in the interrogation room, are also constructed in anticipation of their prospective uses by professionals who deal with the case (Komter, 2001; 2002–3; 2006a; Linell and Jönsson 1995). This orientation to prospective uses anticipates the 'career' of the documents in an organisation as they are consulted or referred to on later occasions (Komter, 2012; Lynch, 2015; Meehan, 1986).

Conversation analysis focuses the attention on the sequential organisation of talk (Sacks et al., 1974). Each turn at talk displays the speaker's understanding of the previous turn and projects the range of activities available to the next speaker (Heritage, 1984a). This understanding is contingent on the sequential order of the talk. The smallest unit is the adjacency pair, where the first pair part anticipates a specific second pair part (for example a question projects an answer), so that if this second pair part is not forthcoming, it can be considered to be 'noticeably absent' (Sacks and Schegloff, 1973). It is not the analyst's interpretations or intuitions that count, but the interpretation of the participants themselves as shown in the sequential organisation of their talk, which can then be an important resource for the analyst.

Recent developments in CA have shown a growing interest in the role of the distribution of knowledge in the organisation of interaction (Heritage, 2012a; 2012b; Heritage and Raymond, 2005; Raymond and Heritage, 2006; Stivers et al., 2011; see also: Goodwin, 1981; Komter, 1995; Labov and Fanshel, 1977; Sacks, 1995). These studies have shown that the distribution of knowledge informs how participants in interaction produce and interpret their utterances, and on how they make their utterances recognisable as the actions they are. Especially in legal settings where the focus of the activities is on establishing 'what happened', the distribution of knowledge has an important impact on how the truth-finding efforts of police detectives, prosecutors, defence lawyers and judges are organised (Stivers et al., 2011: 8). Thus, the interaction in the police interrogating room and in court is informed by the suspect's alleged first-hand knowledge of 'the facts', the police interrogators' and the judges' knowledge of the investigations thus far, and the shared common-sense knowledge of typical conduct or typical situations (Garfinkel, 1967c).

Whereas ethnomethodologists have studied texts or documents in their own right, CA studies tend to approach texts or documents as integral parts of many types of talk-in-interaction, especially institutional interaction, rather than as objects for textual analysis (but see: Clayman, 1990; Drew, 2006). The construction and role of case notes in medical settings have been studied for their impact on doctor–patient interaction (e.g. Beach and LeBaron, 2002; Frers, 2009; Greatbatch et al., 1993; Heath and Luff, 1996; Sarangi and Brookes-Howell, 2006). Other studies have analysed the effect of questionnaires on survey interviews (Houtkoop-Steenstra, 2000; Maynard and Schaeffer, 2006), and the effect of precoded forms on the organisation of calls to the police or emergency services (Kameo and Whalen, 2015; Whalen, 1995; Zimmerman, 1992). A number of studies of legal settings has shown how documents inform, and are informed by, the talk (D'hondt, 2014; D'hondt and Van der Houwen, 2014; González Martínez, 2006; Halldorsdottir, 2006; Johnson, 2013; Jönsson and Linell, 1991; Komter, 2001; 2002; 2002–3; 2006b; 2012a; 2013; Licoppe, 2014; Lynch and Bogen, 1996; Maryns, 2013; Rock, 2001; 2013; Scheffer, 2006; 2010; Sneijder, 2014; Van der Houwen, 2013; Van Charldorp, 2011).

1.3.2 Entextualisation and Context

The transformation of talk into written text and the subsequent uses of this written text on other occasions has been described as a process of entextualisation. Entextualisation refers to 'the process of rendering discourse extractable, of making a stretch of linguistic production into a unit – a text – that can be lifted out of its interactional setting' (Bauman and Briggs, 1990: 73).[9] The entextualisation process involves decontextualisation and recontextualisation; decontextualisation refers to the extraction of a text from its original context of

9 This 'unit' need not necessarily be a written text (Blommaert, 2005: 47); it can encompass any kind of text or talk that is repeated and recycled from one context to another (Eades, 2008a: 157). It may be a bit of remembered talk that finds its way into a current conversation through quotation, or it may be an audio- or video-recorded witness statement to the police that is played in court as evidence.

production, recontextualisation to its subsequent insertion in a new setting through quotation, paraphrase, etc. (Blommaert, 2005).

When studying processes of de- and recontextualisation, we need to ask what aspects of context play a role in these processes. Roughly speaking, there are two main ways in which context can be perceived (Goodwin and Duranti, 1992). The traditional way of viewing context is to see it as part of larger social structures that 'surround' talk as an interpretive framework that 'exists' independently of the participants' communicative actions. For example, the context of the suspects' statements as they are elicited and written down by the police and eventually quoted by the judge, can be understood in the light of institutional requirements and operations of the criminal law process. In contrast, CA treats context as created in and through talk; in other words, context is not an external interpretive resource but it is 'endogenous' to the talk (Bauman and Briggs, 1990: 68; Heritage, 1984a: 283). This is a dynamic process in that 'context' is not just used by the participants as an interpretive resource, but also something that emerges out of the activities of the participants in the unfolding interaction, which creates new contexts for the actions to come (Drew and Heritage, 1992b). Thus, talk shapes context as much as context shapes talk (Goodwin and Duranti, 1992; Heritage, 1984a: 242).

As the production and uses of documents generally occur in institutional settings, processes of de- and recontextualisation are accomplished through institutional talk. Specific features of institutional talk are recognisable by: specific goal orientations of the participants, constraints on what will be treated as allowable contributions to the business at hand, and inferential frameworks and procedures particular to the specific context (Drew and Heritage, 1992b: 21–2). The participants themselves exhibit in their talk what aspects of context are relevant and, in so doing, create the contexts for the production and interpretation of further talk (Schegloff, 1987; 1991). Thus, instead of viewing institutions as existing prior to and independent of the participants' activities, they are 'talked into being' (Heritage, 1984a: 290).

As 'context' bestows meaning on utterances, de- and recontextualisations lead to changes in the meaning and interpretation of the talk in the course of the entextualisation process (Eades, 2010; 2012; Ehrlich, 2012; Linell, 1998: 144–5; Sarangi and Brookes-Howell, 2006). De- and recontextualisations involve the 'travelling' of documents through different contexts, moving between different participants with different orientations. Hence, what is relevant for the participants in the current interaction may not be relevant in later interactions, and what is not relevant for the participants now may become relevant later (Blommaert, 2005: 56; Ehrlich, 2012; Linell, 1998: 145; see also: Eades, 2010).

Entextualisation practices are central to institutional life (Linell, 1998; Park and Bucholtz, 2009). Hence the relevance of this study is not confined to providing insights into the operation of the Dutch criminal law process. The book can offer insights into the operation of talk, text and context in a range of other institutional settings where documents are produced in order to be consulted by practitioners in the field to serve as a basis for decision-making (e.g. Bucholtz, 2000; Linell, 1998; Matoesian, 2000; Ravotas and Berkenkotter, 1998; Sarangi, 2009).

1.4 Data and Transcription

The combination of my 'old' research materials on courtroom interaction and police interrogation with the 'new' materials of cases that could be followed throughout the criminal law process resulted in a unique body of materials that allowed for a detailed inspection of the relations between the talk in the police interrogation, the construction and character of the reports made of it, and the invocations of these reports in court. In the following sections I shall describe the research materials and the choices I made for their transcription.

1.4.1 Data

The materials for this study consist of thirty-four audio-recorded and transcribed police interrogations and the police reports made of those interrogations, and thirty-six audio- or video-recorded trials. These materials have been collected across three periods of time. In the early 1990s, I made audio recordings of thirty-one trials (Komter, 1998); before the turn of the century, I audio-recorded twenty police interrogations and collected the reports made of these interrogations (Komter, 2001; 2002; 2002–3; 2006b). In 2007 to 2009 the 'new' materials were collected to follow cases from the police interrogating room to the courtroom, resulting in fourteen audio-recorded police interrogations, the reports that were made of those interrogations and five video-recorded trials.[10] Although these materials afford an opportunity to study the career of a suspect's statement through the criminal law process, they cover only a fraction of the activities on which the criminal law process is built, as the police report is only one among many other documents in the completed case file, and the police interrogation and the trial only cover part of the activities in the criminal law process.

Practical circumstances of the criminal law process affect the chances that a specific police report of a police interrogation will be invoked by the judge in court. Suspects are often interrogated by the police more than once; prosecutors may drop the case because of a lack of evidence or because prosecution is

[10] The police materials were collected by Tessa van Charldorp, the courtroom materials by Petra Sneijder and Fleur van der Houwen.

not 'in the public interest' ('principle of prosecutorial discretion', Code of Criminal Procedure, sections 167, 242); suspects may be tried together with their alleged accomplices, and they may be tried for more than one offence in one court session. The result of this is that in the new materials, of the fourteen suspects whose police interrogations were recorded seven eventually had to appear in court; the statements of only three of them could be traced from the police interrogation room through to the courtroom.

One of the features of this research setting is that in the first stages of the criminal law process the 'supply' of criminal cases is very diverse, depending, among other things, on the location of the police station and on the specialisation of the police area team. Another constraint on the collection of the materials is the willingness of the police detectives to offer researchers a look behind the scenes of their daily work. We did not get access to interrogations for the more serious types of crime because, as one police officer formulated it, there is a chance that 'a clever lawyer would say that the interrogation was recorded and could therefore be used in court' (Van Charldorp, 2011: 45); another police officer joked to me about the possibility that he would be brought to justice because it was 'on record' how he had induced an initially denying suspect to confess (Komter, 2003). Police officers are aware of the risks of their job, risks that may involve putting unacceptable pressure on suspects to confess. Thus, most of the police interrogations that we were allowed to record concern common street crimes such as drugs dealing, robbery or theft. This could be considered a weakness of these materials, because it is in the serious cases that the police will be more tempted to put the suspect under pressure to confess, and it is in the serious cases that miscarriages of justice may be spotted. On the other hand, it can be argued that the less serious offences are a lot more common than those that receive media attention, and that these materials exhibit the workings of the criminal law process equally well, irrespective of the seriousness of the crimes. It could even be thought of as a strength, because the analyst is less likely to be impressed by the heinousness of the crimes and therefore more likely to approach the materials with an open mind (Lynch, 2015: 167).

The collection of the materials has not been easy. Although in general the professionals on the 'work floor' (police detectives, prosecutors, defence lawyers and judges) were not unwilling to cooperate, the sensitive nature of the research materials, and the hierarchical nature of the criminal justice apparatus made it necessary to ask the permission of the officials at the highest ranks (the Attorney General for making audio recordings of police interrogations and the Council for the Judiciary[11] for making audio or video recordings of trials). After the required conditions were agreed upon and the permission to collect the materials was

[11] In Dutch: 'het College van Procureurs-Generaal' and 'de Raad voor de Rechtspraak'.

granted, the regional courts and prosecution offices and the professionals on the 'work floor' could be approached. As recordings could only be made with the cooperation of all the people involved, this meant that for recording a police interrogation the permission was needed from the regional prosecutor's office, from the chiefs of the police area teams, from the interrogating police officers and from the suspect; in order to film or audio-record a trial, the cooperation had to be sought of the president of the district court and of the participants in the trial: the judge, the prosecutor, the defence lawyer and the suspect.

The type of data chosen conditions what is available for observation, and therefore affects and constrains the possibilities for analysis. My choice of what materials to use (audio and video recordings of the talk, and the texts of the police reports) was motivated by my foci of analysis and research approaches as well as by practical considerations. The decision to audio-record rather than video-record police interrogations was mainly prompted by practical considerations. To avoid intruding too much on the business of the police detectives, I used a small audio recorder. I put this small audio recorder on the table at which the interrogator(s) and suspect were sitting, while I tried to make myself invisible in a corner of the interrogating room (cf. Van Charldorp, 2011: 38–57). For the 'new' courtroom materials I decided that video recordings were more appropriate because I expected that visual information would reveal more about the professionals' handling of the documents in court.

The duration of the period of time in which the materials were collected may raise questions about the changes in the operation of the criminal law process that may affect the consistency and pertinence of these materials. As mentioned before, a series of miscarriages of justice drew attention to the vulnerabilities of the system in the first stages of the criminal law process. This resulted in a preference for two police interrogators instead of one, and for question–answer rather than monologue-style police reports. The 'old' police interrogations were more often conducted by a single interrogator (sixteen out of twenty) than the more recent ones (nine out of fourteen). A more distinct difference is that, in the police interrogations conducted by two interrogators, only the new materials show a division of labour between the two, in the sense that one officer did the interrogating and the other the reporting on a PC. As mentioned before, the past decade has shown a shift from predominantly monologue-style police reports to a more varied stylistic repertoire. All of the 'old' police reports are written in the monologue style, sometimes formulated as 'recontextualisation phrases' (Komter, 2006c). One of the fourteen more recent reports is written up as a monologue, five are written predominantly as question–answer-style reports, six are written up in the recontextualised monologue style and two reports start off as monologue style and continue in the recontextualised monologue style.

It is noticeable that the parts of the reports that represent the 'social interrogation' are all written in the monologue style. This may be related to the relatively harmless nature of the information asked for in the introductory stages of the interrogations. When asked, police detectives mentioned that they prefer the question–answer style for the more complex interrogations (i.e. with denying suspects) and the monologue style for the simple ones (Malsch et al., 2012). An example of this in our materials is a case of an initially denying suspect. The report of the first interrogation, in which the suspect denied the accusations, is written in the Q–A style. After the interrogation the suspect was brought back to his cell where one of the interrogators paid him a visit and persuaded him to confess. After this the suspect was interrogated a second time and his confession was written down in the monologue style. Thus, the writing style of police reports is not only related to the period in time when they were written but also to the topic and the suspect's position in the interrogation.[12] In spite of these differences between the 'old' and the 'new' materials, the professionals' concern with finding out 'what happened' has not changed, nor has the nature of their truth-finding efforts.

In the course of my analyses of the police interrogations, it became clear how important the activity of the typing is for the management of the interrogation. If I had known that beforehand, I would have tried to install some kind of a text-tracking device through a connection between the audio recorder and the PC that would enable me to trace exactly what was typed when. Because the audio recordings made it possible to hear the talk and the typing sounds, a comparison with the text of the police report enabled me to approximately reconstruct what was typed when, but that became difficult in those instances when there was continuous overlap between the talk and the typing (when one of the police officers was asking the questions and the other was typing up the talk), and in those cases where there was some editing done at the end of the interrogation. It is sometimes easier to make an informed choice about what kind of data is needed when they have already been collected and studied.

1.4.2 Transcription

Transcriptions of recordings of naturally occurring interactions are the basic tools for conversation analysis, both for making the recordings more easily accessible for the researcher and for presenting the research materials for publication.[13] The aim of transcription is to get as much of the original sound in the transcripts as possible, while still retaining readability (Sacks et al.,

[12] The proposal for the legislation of the new Code of Criminal Procedure contains the advice to write the police report of suspect interrogations 'as much as possible in the question–answer style' (Kessler, 2016: 12)

[13] Although it is now possible to put sound clips of transcriptions of published articles on the internet, see: www.sscnet.ucla.edu/soc/faculty/schegloff/new-clips/word-repeats-as.html# http://comminfo.rutgers.edu/~gbolden/RussianCA/publications/bolden2003.pdf

1974: 734). Although transcription is meant to represent the original talk in some way it is always selective and never to be seen as the ultimate representation. It is an evolving and flexible object as the researcher may return at any moment to the original recordings to check and revise it (Mondada, 2007: 810).

What is transcribed depends on the research questions and analytic perspective (Hepburn and Bolden, 2012: 71). However, when embarking on a research project the research questions may not be fully crystallised but will materialise in the course of the researcher's growing familiarity with the data. In the course of my analyses I was confronted by the need to make choices about the degree of detail of the transcripts, about the transcription of the police officers' typing activities,[14] about the presentation of the text of the emerging police report, and about the transcription of the visual courtroom materials.

Transcriptions, no matter how detailed, show only a fraction of what is going on. So the analyst is inevitably confronted with the compromise between the transcription of phonetic detail and readability: the more readability, the greater the chance that you are missing something essential (Jefferson, 1983). In the present study a constraint on the transcription of phonetic detail is that the 'transcriptions' presented here are translations, which can never represent the phonetic details of the original talk. The usual way to present translated transcriptions to an English-speaking readership is a three-line transcription, where the first line is the original transcript, the second line a word-by-word translation into English, and the third line an idiomatic translation that is meant to capture the conversational style of the talk (Hepburn and Bolden, 2012: 68–9). For my purpose this turned out to be impractical, as I also chose to transcribe the typing and present the translation of the emerging text in one and the same excerpt. Another constraint on the transcription is that the Jeffersonian transcription notations only cover talk; for the other activities such as typing or activities that are visible on the video recordings of the 'new' courtroom materials, I had to improvise.[15] Hence, I have made use of the Jeffersonian transcription notations as much as I thought I needed, and added some of my own when I thought I needed them.[16]

[14] There is no standard way of transcribing keystrokes. Zimmerman (1992) uses dashes to indicate keyboard activity, and Whalen (1995) and Van Charldorp (2011; 2014) xxxx symbols. Besides, Whalen's transcription distinguishes between the use of keys other than the letter keys and the number keys (space bar, tab, back tab, return, cursor and arrow keys) and Van Charldorp distinguishes between louder (X) and softer (x) keystrokes. Greatbatch et al. (1995a) use symbols that differentiate between keystrokes, keystrokes that are pressed with greater force than normal, and return keystrokes.

[15] For more information about transcribing visual data, see Heath and Luff, 2012.

[16] See Transcription Conventions, at the beginning of the book.

As I became more familiar with my materials and realised how important the typing was for the organisation of the interrogation, I retranscribed parts of the data. I initially transcribed the typing as a transcriber's note, for example: ((types, 20 seconds)) (cf. Jönsson and Linell, 1991: 427–8). Close attention to the coordination of the talk and the typing revealed that often there was some, and sometimes substantial overlap. Further analysis made it clear to me that there was something systematic in the places where the interrogator started the typing. Thus, the typing acquired properties of a turn at talk in that the typing onsets could be analysed as 'typing relevance places' (Komter, 2006b: 209; cf. Sacks, Schegloff and Jefferson, 1974) that exhibit the reporting officer's interpretation of prior talk as legally relevant and 'recordable' (Komter, 2002–3: 210). Therefore I started to transcribe the typing sounds as separate objects (as: ####) and used overlap symbols to indicate at what point in the talk the typing overlapped (Komter, 2006b). The problem with this notation is that it creates the impression that it is possible to hear and transcribe every single keystroke separately.

When I familiarised myself with the 'new' materials, I found that in the police interrogations conducted by two police officers (of which one asked the questions and the other typed up the talk) the overlap between the talk and the typing became almost continuous some of the time. I then decided to transcribe the talk and the typing not as two different lines but as one, the typing marked by a shade of grey covering the transcribed talk, as a better and more direct way to accentuate the simultaneity of the two different activities.

Once I made the choice to transcribe the typing so as to highlight the simultaneity of overlapping talk and typing, I faced the choice of whether or not to indicate what was being typed. I decided to present the transcribed talk and the text typed up in two columns, on the left the transcribed talk, and on the right (in bold type) the corresponding text (Komter, 2006b). This would make it easy to inspect differences and similarities between the talk and the text of the police report, for example (see Chapter 5, excerpts 19a and 1):

(1)

1. P[1]: Can you yourself tell what happened,	**You ask me if I want to tell**
2. that e- that afternoon, that evening?	**something about it.**
3. S: No.	**No I do not want that.**
4. P[1]: No? (3)	

This is an example from an interrogation where the police officers work as a team: one of them asks the questions and the other types up the talk. As most of the talk is overlapped by the typing, I had to reconstruct at what moments in the talk what text was typed. Although this example shows the differences and similarities between the transcribed talk and the text written in the police report, it does not give information about the timing of the typing. Excerpt (2) shows a longer version of excerpt (1) and includes transcription of the typing during the ongoing talk and a presentation of the text at the approximate moments when it was typed (the typing in overlap with lines 1–3 concerns prior talk):

(2)

1.	P[1]:	Can you yourself tell what happened,	
2.		that e- that afternoon, that evening?	
3.	S:	No.	
4.	P[1]:	No? (3)	**You ask me**
5.		According to Dan uh you were with uh	**if I want**
6.		(1) a number of other boys	**to tell**
7.		amongst whom Jairo, (1)	**something**
8.		shopping centre Bloemhof in Liemen. (2)	**about it.**
9.		There uh there was a boy, (1)	**No I do**
10.		he was addressed first by Jairo, (2)	**not want**
11.		and uh (1) then uh (1) at a certain moment	**that.**

As stated above, the placement of the texts typed simultaneously with the talk is an approximation. The reconstruction of the moments when the texts were typed is based on an inspection of the following elements:

- the correspondence between the talk and the text;
- the differential pace between the talk and the text;
- the text follows the talk;
- typing onset may signify recordability of prior talk;
- break off of typing may signify a completion of the text thus far.

For the problematic episodes I have 'try-typed' the Dutch text and compared its duration with the duration of the talk in the audio recording of the episode. These ways of reconstructing what was typed when shows that in these circumstances the text lags considerably behind the talk.

The collection of video-recorded materials resulted in such an abundance of visual information that choices had to be made about how and how much of the interaction should be transcribed. The focus of Chapter 4 and part of Chapter 5 is on the judges' management of the documents in the case file. A global inspection of the materials showed that, in the course of their questioning the suspect, judges continually shift their attention between the documents and the suspect, reading aloud texts from the case file and questioning the suspect about them, or questioning the suspect and turning to the case file to consult the documents. Hence I decided to transcribe only the shifts in gaze direction of the judges (upward from the documents to the suspect ▲, and downward from the suspect to the documents ▼, cf. Glenn and LeBaron, 2011) in order to capture their effects on the suspect's participation (cf. Lerner, 2003).

1.5 Foci of Analysis

The tracking of the suspect's statement through the criminal law process comprises an examination of talk, text and context. It involves an inspection of talk-in-interaction in two different work settings (the police interrogation and the trial) and an examination of texts in their documentary settings (the suspect's statement as part of the police report, the police report as part of the case file). To cover the activities involved in the career of the suspect's statement the analysis will deal with the talk and with the coordination of talk and the typing in the police interrogation, with the text of the police report and the relations between the text and the talk it is meant to represent, and with the ways in which the legal professionals, especially judges, invoke the case file in court. Only the 'fact-related' parts of the materials will be analysed; the 'social interrogation' in the police interrogating room, and the discussions about 'the person' of the suspect and about legal points in the courtroom, will not be considered here.

1.5.1 The Talk

It has been observed that there is no sharp division line between 'ordinary' conversation and institutional talk because many institutional encounters contain conversational episodes, but that 'conversation' is the fundamental form of talk-in-interaction from which institutional talk is derived (Drew and Heritage, 1992b). Typical features of institutional talk are the pre-allocation of turns and the question–answer organisation (Sacks et al., 1974). That is, the institutional functionary asks the questions and the individual participant gives the answers. This question–answer format is the basic organisation for both police interrogations and the examinations in court. In police interrogations this structure may be extended by the reporting officer's typing (Komter, 2002–3; 2006b). In both police interrogations and trials the slot after the suspect's answer may be used to evaluate or reject this answer. An examination of these conversational structures is meant to reveal the participants' understandings of prior actions, their production of current actions and their orientations to next actions. For example, the typing may occur at the moment when the interrogator accepts the suspect's answer, whereas a different 'third-position action' may occur when the interrogator rejects the suspect's answer (Komter, 2006b).

Goffman's deconstruction of the speaker's role as expounded in 'footing' (1981) will be an analytic tool for describing the practices of the judges' recontextualisations of the suspect's statement and for illuminating their relationship with the texts they utter in court. Goffman describes 'footing' as the alignment of an individual to a particular utterance (1981: 128). Speakers may draw attention to their involvement in the events as animator, author and principal. The animator is the speaker who utters words and sentences, like a 'sounding box'; the author is the speaker who is seen as originator of the utterance; the principal is the speaker whose viewpoint or position is being expressed. Thus, judges who quote or read aloud a suspect's statement as written down in the police report display that it is not their own text they are reading but the suspect's. Or, in Goffman's terms, the judge is the animator and the suspect is the author and the principal of the text read aloud. At the same time the interactional organisation of the judges' references to the case file will be taken into account as recognition of the fact that the suspect is not merely a person whose talk is being reported but also an active participant who may respond to the judge's quotations, or whose talk may be the judge's incentive to start quoting from the documents (cf. Goodwin, 2007).

1.5.2 The Text

Police reports can be studied as 'self-explicating documents', in that they offer readers implicit 'instructions' for how to read them. Readers are able to recognise what these instructions are because they are familiar with the settings in which those documents have a place (Harper, 1998: 38). Smith (1990a) has shown how a text can be analysed by taking into account the perspective of the writer. As mentioned above, Goffman's concept of 'footing' (1981) can describe the recontextualisation practices of judges in court but it can also be useful for an analysis of written text. The recontextualisation of the suspect's statement as a written text and part of the police report involves a 'writer' (the reporting officer) and a reported 'speaker' (the suspect). This 'writer' does not only report what the suspect has said, but also includes other texts in the report that show his or her adherence to legal rules and bureaucratic routines. For distinguishing between the roles of speakers and writers I reserve the term '*author*' for describing the 'footing' of a speaker who is producing his or her own utterances, and I use the term '*writer-author*' for describing the alignment of a writer to his or her own text. Hence, police reports will be studied by considering how they show the administrative or bureaucratic routines that highlight the 'officialness' of the police report, how they show the alignments of the reporting officers to their own texts, and how they show the reporting officers' representations of the words attributed to the suspect.

As mentioned before, there is a distinction between the written text of the suspect's statement, the document in which it is embedded (the police report) and the collection of documents that contains all the evidence for adjudicating the case (the case file). So, whereas the text of the suspect's statement can be studied in its own right, it does not stand alone: as part of the police report it becomes understandable and available as an official piece of evidence, and as part of the case file it becomes understandable and available as one piece of evidence among many others. Hence, the suspects' written statement will be examined by analysing both text-external elements (the texts surrounding it in the police report) and text-internal elements (the sequential organisation of the sentences it contains). The basis for the sequential analysis of written texts is the idea that this can be grounded in findings from conversation-analytic studies of talk, because readers can understand interactional moves and narrative coherence in a text in a similar way as the participants do in face-to-face interaction (Clayman, 1990: 83).

The text of the suspect's statement is meant to give the reader insight into what was said in the police interrogation and, depending on the writing style of the police report, into the interactional organisation of the original talk. A comparison of the suspect's statement with the original talk in the interrogation yields insight into the transparency of the suspect's statement for those readers who have no access to the original talk. My concern is not to present an ironic contrast between the talk and the document that is supposed to represent it, but to show how the texts in the police report have acquired new meanings within their new textual environments or contexts that may not be discernible by readers of the police reports. How the professionals have read and understood the texts of the police will be shown by an analysis of their quotations from and references to these texts in court (Watson 2009: 28–9).

1.5.3 The Context

The dual view of context as described above affects the ways in which de- and recontextualisations can be analysed. The traditional way of understanding the operation of entextualisation is to say that the transformation of the talk in the police interrogation into the text of the police report enables it to be decontextualised from the setting of the police interrogation and to be recontextualised into the setting of the trial by way of quoting or paraphrasing. In this view two 'contexts' are in play: the police interrogation and the trial.

The CA perspective of an endogenous context, created in and through the talk, affords insights into how the participants themselves produce and interpret the activities they are involved in. When the talk in the police interrogation is written down in the police report it is decontextualised from its interactional environment and recontextualised as a written document. The context of the details of the suspect's statement can then be discovered by inspecting the sequential organisation of the words and sentences (Clayman, 1990: 83). For example, because a question can be understood as a context for the answer, the representation of a question–answer sequence as a monologue-style statement in the police report decontextualises the suspect's talk by leaving out its interactional embedding and recontextualises it as a text that reads as a series of volunteered assertions (Komter, 2001; 2002–3; 2012a). In addition to the *sequential* context, based on the immediate contiguity of turns, we can distinguish an *interactional* context, based on the kind of actions that are performed. For example, an accusation projects a defence, such as a denial, justification, counter-accusation and so on (Atkinson and Drew, 1979: 49–50). And conversely, when a speaker produces a defensive utterance it can be taken as a display of the fact that the prior utterance has been interpreted as an accusation.

The wider contexts of the suspect's written statement can be found in the surrounding texts that identify the document as a police report and that make the police report into an official piece of evidence. Moreover, the other documents in the case file can be seen as contexts of the suspect's statement, as they offer the professionals in court opportunities for comparison and evaluation.

The recontextualisation of the police report and the case file in court by way of quoting or summarising reintroduces talk and interaction as contexts for the activities of the professionals and the suspect. How and what the professionals quote or summarise from the case file exhibits how they have read it. As 'context' offers an interpretive framework for an understanding of what is going on, and as recontextualisations change the meaning and interpretation of the talk and the text, I shall inspect the changes of meaning in the suspect's statement to discover what aspects of context are made relevant at what moments.

1.6 Overview of the Book

This book more or less follows the chronological order of the phases in the criminal law process: the police interrogation, the police report and the trial. Although the police report is not a 'phase' in the technical sense, it can be located in the space between the police interrogation and the trial as a link between these two settings. The final analytic chapter is based on one criminal case that is followed through these phases as a specimen of 'the career of the suspect's statement'.

Chapter 2 starts with an investigation of the two institutional tasks of police officers: interrogating and statement taking. The fact that these activities are usually performed contemporaneously means that police interrogators have to find a way to integrate the talk in the interrogation with the typing of the police report. There are several practical circumstances that affect the coordination of the talk and the typing, such as the adversarial or routine character of the particular episode in the interrogation, the number of police interrogators and the differential pace of the talk and the typing. The aim of this chapter is to show how these practical circumstances affect both the talk in the interrogation and the text of the police report.

The aim of Chapter 3 is to acquire insight into the nature of the transformations that the suspect's statement has undergone, and into the transparency of the reports for readers who are unacquainted with the original interaction on which the police reports are based. First, the texts surrounding 'the suspect's written statement' will be examined for the ways in which reporting officers show their adherence to the appropriate bureaucratic and institutional requirements, through which they convert the suspect's statement into an official piece of evidence. Then the core of the document, the suspect's statement, will be investigated for the understandings it affords those readers who have no access to the original talk, after which more detailed analyses will be made of the different writing styles of the reports in comparison with the original interaction in the interrogations.

How the legal professionals in court have read the text of the police report is shown in Chapter 4, where I analyse how prosecutors, defence lawyers and especially judges, refer to or quote from the texts in the case file. These professionals deploy their 'professional reading' of the case file for the performance of their institutional tasks in court. The case file is their main source of knowledge, apart from their common-sense knowledge about the plausibility of the different versions of the events. Most of the references to the case file in court are made by the judges as they are required by law to read from or summarise those passages from the case file that they may base their verdict on. As this task is combined with the judges' questioning of the suspect, they have to divide their attention between the case file and the suspect, displaying their double task of ratifying the evidence and finding the truth. The analysis will show the effects of the judges' management of this dual commitment on the suspects' opportunities for participation.

In Chapter 5 I trace a suspect's statement through successive stages of the criminal law process in one criminal case. The chapter contains the same elements as those analysed in prior chapters: the step-by-step examination of the construction of the report of the police interrogation, the inspection of the text of the police report for transparency, and the study of the professionals' references to the case file in court. The fact that it concerns one criminal case allows me to analyse the concrete details of the entextualisation process and to detect the changes of meaning that the suspect's statement undergoes as it moves from one setting to the next. Thus, by examining the moment-by-moment flow of institutional work new insights are generated about the unnoticed and unintended effects of the routine practices of the legal professionals who deal with the case.

2 The Police Interrogation

The Talk, the Typing and the Text

2.1 Introduction

The two most important institutional tasks of police interrogators are truth finding and statement taking. Because these activities are usually performed contemporaneously, the talk in the interrogation must be coordinated with the typing of the police report (Komter, 2002–3; 2006b). The aim of this chapter is to show how these practical circumstances affect both the talk in the interrogation and the text of the police report.

One of the features of the interrogators' *truth-finding* activities is the fact that they have to discover the truth from suspects who are not legally required to tell it, and who may not be willing to tell it. As a result, the interrogators exhibit their 'investigative stance': a hard-headed commitment to establishing the 'facts of the matter' against the 'mere claims' of the suspect (Zimmerman, 1969: 331). The degree of adversarialness of the interrogations varies with the complexity of the case, the suspect's stance, the availability of other evidence, and the nature of the information to be discussed. Simple cases, confessing suspects, or uncontroversial topics tend to lead to routine questioning practices in the interrogations. Yet, almost all the interrogations in my materials contain episodes where the suspect's version of the events is – explicitly or implicitly – called into doubt or contested by the interrogators.

The *statement-taking* activities of the interrogators involve both the 'typeability' and the 'recordability' of the talk. To achieve 'typability' interrogators design their questions and organise the interaction so as to be able to coordinate the talk and the typing (Komter, 2002–3; 2006b). That is, the typing must be practicable and fit in the ongoing interaction (Greatbatch et al., 1995a; 1995b; Heath & Luff, 1996; Whalen, 1995; Zimmerman, 1992). The police officers' concern for the 'recordability' of the talk involves a prospective orientation to the text of the report: the police report must contain those items that contribute to its legal adequacy, so that it may serve as a piece of evidence. Thus, the police report looks backward, as a representation of what was said in the interrogation, and it looks forward in anticipation of the scrutiny of the legal professionals in the criminal law process (Jönsson and Linell, 1991: 436;

Komter, 2002–3: 203; cf. Frankel, 1989; Houtkoop-Steenstra, 2000: 107–27; Iversen, 2012: 694).

Another practical circumstance that affects the truth-finding and statement-taking activities of the interrogators is the number of interrogators (one or two).[1] The decision about the number of interrogators is related to the seriousness of the case. The more serious the case, the more likely it is that the interrogation will be conducted by two interrogators (Malsch et al., 2012). When interrogators work in pairs the usual division of labour is that one officer asks the questions and the other types up the talk on a PC. In these interrogations there is more room for overlap between the talk and the typing, which results in a sequential organisation of the talk and the typing different from the organisation of 'solo' interrogations. I shall therefore discuss the management of 'duo' interrogations separately.

In this chapter I shall first investigate how, in the 'solo' interrogations, the interrogators implement their truth-finding and statement-taking activities and organise the talk and the typing. I then show how the interrogators manage their dual commitment to the suspect and to the screen through their coordination of and their switches between the talk and the typing. Next, I shall examine the ways in which the interrogators organise the talk so as to anticipate a legally appropriate text for the record. And finally I examine how these orientations to the talk, the typing and the text are realised in the 'duo' interrogations.

2.2 Talk and Typing

A number of interrogations in my materials begin with the interrogators asking the suspect to tell them what happened. This is typically meant to elicit a narrative told from the suspect's position of first-hand knowledge of the events (Kidwell, 2009). In some of these initial stages of the interrogations the interrogators listen to what the suspects have to say without writing it down. After a while they start out anew and 'recycle' the suspects' version (Holt and Johnson, 2006; Van Charldorp, 2011), this time in combination with their further questioning and their typing. The interrogators' further questioning retrospectively reveals that they have listened to the suspects' narrative as a source of selecting the elements to be developed further for ascertaining its truth or plausibility. Thus, the suspect is first invited to tell a more or less 'free' story, after which the interrogators ask further questions that are geared to eliciting a recordable story for the police report (Van Charldorp, 2014: 22).

In the 'solo' interrogations the reporting of the interrogators' truth-finding activities varies with the degree of adversarialness of the interaction. In the following sections I shall discuss how the interrogators' statement-taking

[1] I shall call them 'solo' interrogations and 'duo' interrogations.

activities are organised as question–answer-typing sequences in the routine episodes of the interrogations, how interrogators deal with overlap between the talk and the typing, and how they suspend their typing in the more adversarial moments of the interrogations.

2.2.1 Question–Answer-Typing Sequences

The most elementary organisation of the typing and the talk in 'solo' interrogations is the question–answer-typing (Q–A-T) sequence. These stretches of talk consist minimally of one question–answer exchange, but usually a series of questions and answers is produced before it is written down (Komter, 2001; 2002–3; 2006b: 204). Excerpt (1) is an example of the basic structure:

(1)
1. P: Do you realise that it is forbidden in the Netherlands to uh have cocaine on you,
2. or to deal in it?
3. S: ((nods))
4. P: ((types, 24 seconds))
I know that it is forbidden in the Netherlands to possess cocaine or to deal in it.
5. P: What did you get for that cocaine. For a balloon.[2]
6. S: Fifty.
7. P: ((types, 16 seconds))
I received the amount of *f* 50, – a balloon.
8. P: And to what kind of people did you sell that cocaine?
9. Did you know those people?
10. S: No I don't know them.
11. P: ((types, 43 seconds))
I don't know the persons that I sold the cocaine to, I have not seen them before.
(19, O)

This is a simple example of a Q–A-T sequence: the interrogator asks a question and starts typing after what can count as an answer (such as the nod, line 3). The question–answer-typing sequence is accomplished by a piecemeal elicitation of 'chunks' of information and by writing them down step by step. The typing is accompanied by a temporary shift from a mutual focus on the interaction to divergence, where the attention of the interrogator is directed towards the screen of his PC.

The fact that the typing interrogator is visibly occupied elsewhere discourages suspects from volunteering additional turn components. This organisation of the talk and the typing occasions periods of non-talk (lines 4, 7 and 11) while the suspect waits for the interrogator to finish the typing. This shows that the typing can be treated as a proper response, which suspects do not interrupt (Greatbatch et al., 1995a: 206). The typing can then be seen as a third-turn receipt object, in the

[2] A 'balloon' is the name for the packaging of cocaine and heroin sold on the street.

sense that it retrospectively suggests that the suspect's prior answer has been good enough to be recorded (Komter, 2006b: 205). The turn after the typing is for the interrogator to ask a new question, which recycles the Q–A-T sequence.

We can see that the text of the report is put together by collapsing the words of the police interrogator's questions with those of the suspect's answers, and by reformulating these as the suspect's first-person narrative. For example, the suspect's nodding (line 3) results in the following entry in the report: 'I know that it is forbidden in the Netherlands to possess cocaine or to deal in it'. If we look at the correspondence of the two reported sentences with the talk in the interrogation we can conclude that the contributions of the suspect have undergone a drastic transformation in the report. All the items that are included are told at P's request, whereas the monologue style creates the impression that the story is volunteered rather than invited. Through this reorganisation of the text the activities of the interrogator have become invisible, which results in a 'blurring of source distinctions': one cannot know from reading the reports under what conditions a given piece of information has been introduced (Jönsson and Linell, 1991: 434).

In the question–answer (Q–A)-style reports and the recontextualised monologue (RM)-style reports the question–answer-typing organisation is also found, but there is more variation as the interrogator may start typing not just after the answer, but also after the question (Van Charldorp, 2013: 230). Excerpt (2) shows that P starts typing after his question and acknowledgement of S's incipient talk (lines 3–4). The text written simultaneously is presented in the right-hand column; the shaded areas indicate simultaneous typing (see Transcription Conventions, at the beginning of the book). The text is written in the recontextualised monologue style:

(2)

1.	P: Okay u::h (2)	
2.	if I'd ask you what that uh young man looked like	
3.	S: Hm yes it is an	
4.	P: Yes,	
5.	S: uh an uh yes a white man	**If you ask me**
6.	P: Just a moment,	
7.	(14)	**what this man looked like**
8.	( )	**I describe him as follows:**
9.	P: So it is an- a man.	
10.	S: Hm hm.	
11.	P: Was it an uh an a white man, a negroid man,	
12.	S: No a white man.	
13.	P: A white man.	
14.	(3)	**A white man,**
15.	P: Yes, how old was he roughly do you think?	

(4, O)

P asks an 'open question' in the sense that it only asks for a person description, and does not further circumscribe the domain within which the answer should be confined. When P starts typing (line 5) the suspect has not yet produced anything like an answer. The typing of recontextualised monologue is obviously more cumbersome than that of monologue-style texts; before P can write down the suspect's answer he has to type: 'if you ask me what this man looked like I describe him as follows'. As a result, the typing lags behind, and P cannot type fast enough to catch up with the talk. Besides, P has another practical problem: open questions generate undirected answers that may be too long to remember and write down in one go (Komter, 2002–3: 205). Thus, the interrogator has two imminent projects: writing down his recontextualised question and listening to whatever description the suspect is giving.

We see here that the simultaneous requirements of typing and listening can create task performance problems. P's absorption in typing his sentence-under-construction apparently prevents him from listening to the suspect's answer (Whalen, 1995: 203–4). So, while he is typing up his recontextualised question, P asks S to withhold his further answer (line 6). P apparently has not heard the suspect's answer (line 5) as, after having stopped the typing, he elicits the person description item by item, beginning with the person's gender (line 9), proceeding with his ethnicity (line 11) and his age (line 15). In this way the Q–A-T organisation is resumed, as P elicits recordable answers that can be written down bit by bit (Komter, 2001; 2002–3).

2.2.2 *Overlap of Talk and Typing*

Periods of overlap of the typing and the talk are relatively common in my materials. As discussed earlier, typing may reflect on previous talk in that it can display interrogators' assessments of suspects' answers as 'recordable'. From this perspective, overlap of the typing and the talk can be analysed in the same way as conversational overlap, in that the overlapping talk or the overlapping typing may be inspected for the sort of reaction it gets or for the stance it embodies relative to preceding talk or typing (Schegloff, 2000: 20). That is, the typing onset may be related to interrogators' acknowledgement or acceptance of the preceding answer, and the typing termination to the completeness of the information that has been typed, or to the problems resulting from the simultaneity of the typing and the talk.

In the more routine moments of the interrogations, interrogators sometimes start typing when the suspect has not yet provided any answer:

(3)

1.	P: How old is Clive roughly.	
2.	(2)	
3.	S: Hm around thirty.	**Clive is**
4.	(6)	**around thirty years old.**

(15, O)

After P's question there is a two-second pause (line 1). Then P starts typing at the same time as S starts answering, and after the answer is finished he goes on typing for another six seconds. We might wonder what there is to type when the suspect has not answered yet. This puzzle is solved when we look at the practice in monologue-style reports of collapsing the interrogator's question and the suspect's answer. P starts with the subject and the verb of the sentence to be written: Clive is . . . As he is typing this, the suspect provides him with the information that he can write down next. Thus, when P starts typing he orients to what he is about to write and to what S is about to say (Zimmerman, 1992: 429), making use of the syntactic structure of Dutch sentences.

Experienced police officers are – to some extent – capable of typing and listening at the same time:

(4)

1.	P: And uh on what floor do those friends live?	
2.	S: Uh one lives	
3.	two- two friends I have	**You ask me**
4.	that I know that live there. (3)	**what floor my**
5.	(sometimes I go chilling)	**friends**
6.	One lives at (1) three, forty-five, (1)	**live.**
7.	three forty-five, and the other (1)	**One lives**
8.	the other lives on the first floor.	**at 345,**
9.	First floor or second floor.	**that is the**
10.	Second floor. (8)	**third floor and the other**
11.	P: So three forty-five is the number right?	
12.	S: Yes.	
13.	P: And the other on the first floor.	
14.	S: Yes.	
15.	P: °Okay°.	
16.	(7)	**lives on the first floor.**

(6, N)

P starts writing before S has produced something that could count as a proper answer (line 3). As in excerpt (3) the interrogator begins writing in overlap with the suspect's incipient answer. After he has written down the recontextualised question (right-hand column, lines **3–6**) he continues typing up part of the suspect's answer in overlap with the talk until eight seconds after the end of the suspect's talk (line 10). Then he stops the typing in order to verify whether he has correctly 'copied' that talk. His requests for verification (lines 11 and 13) may result from the difficulty of listening and typing at the same time. P may not have heard the suspect's repair of his original answer ('first floor . . . second floor', lines 8–10) but, as the suspect agrees with his suggestion 'first floor' (lines 13–14) he writes that down after his soft-spoken pre-typing 'okay' (lines 15–16).

A comparison of the talk with the text shows that the interrogator adds an item in the report ('that is the third floor', lines **9–10**) that has no origin in the suspect's talk, but that 'fits in' with the reported question ('what floor . . .' line 1 and right-hand column, line 4). The interrogator leaves out those contributions of the suspect that are not direct answers to his question (lines 3–5). This suggests that the nature of the reported question has an effect on the reporting of the answer. The interrogator's orientation to the coherence of the text temporarily appears to overrule his attention to the suspect's contributions.

Excerpts (3) and (4) show how interrogators start typing before suspects have produced recognisable answers. In anticipation of suspects' answers, typing onset can be brought forward by taking into account the syntactic structure of the planned sentence. The interrogator's use of a 'recontextualisation phrase' can cause problems because there is a lot of text to be written down before the suspect's answer can be reported (see also excerpt 2). However, the occurrence of periods of prolonged overlap shows that some interrogators can – for some time – manage the task of typing and listening simultaneously.

As mentioned before, the most common location of typing onset is after a suspect's answer. Although suspects usually wait during the typing, it is not uncommon for them to 'answer more than the question' (Komter, 2006b: 210–12; Stivers and Heritage, 2001) in overlap with the typing. The following excerpt is from a case where the suspect has been arrested by two police officers, one of whom allegedly saw him throw away some drugs into a canal on their way to the police station:

(5)

1.	P: So you deny having thrown something away.	
2.	S: I have thrown nothing away.	
3.	P: (3)	**I deny**
4.	S: I uh I swear it I have thrown nothing	**having**
5.	I have thrown nothing away.	**thrown**
6.	I had to make way,	**something**
7.	(8)	**away. I swear it,**
8.	S: Ask those officers themselves	**I have**
9.	there just came an oncoming car	**thrown**
10.	and we had to-	**nothing**
11.	the one went that way and I went this way,	
12.	the other one kept standing behind it.	**away.**
13.	And he suddenly says like yes he	**I had to**
14.	has thrown something away.	**make way**
15.	(4)	**for the car.**
16.	P: So why do you think that officer says that.	

(20, O)

This episode starts out as a 'proper' question–answer typing sequence, in the form of a formulation–agreement-typing action sequence; that is, P produces a formulation (line 1), listens to the suspect's agreement (line 3) and starts typing. After three seconds of P's typing the suspect starts elaborating on his answer (line 4). The information provided by the suspect is not solicited by the interrogator who is, at this point, engaged in typing up the suspect's answer (Stivers and Heritage, 2001: 159). The suspect first adds some emphasis ('I swear', stress on 'nothing', repetition of 'I have thrown nothing', lines 4–5) to his previous answer, which he then follows with an account (lines 6–12). His line of reasoning is that the police officer could not have seen that he threw something away, because he stepped aside for an oncoming car and was standing behind a car. His denial, his dramatisation of innocence and his subsequent account are defensive actions designed to pre-empt the accusatory implications of P's question (Stivers and Heritage, 2001: 164).

The text of the report shows that P first writes down the monologue-style version of his formulation (right-hand column, lines **3–7**), and then almost literally copies the suspect's talk (right-hand column, lines **7–14**) until 'I had to make way' (line 6). When the suspect continues his defensive expressions after the eight-second pause (line 7), P is still in the process of writing down S's earlier talk. Perhaps because P's typing lags behind, the suspect's further elaborations (lines 8–14) are not reported, with the exception of the word 'car' (line 9). With this word and the addition of 'for the...' P can then finish his sentence-under-construction (right-hand column, lines **13–15**).

It is noticeable that the suspect's elaborations do not lead the interrogator to stop the typing and yield the floor. This may be due to the circumstance that P's formulation (line 1) is oriented to getting a specific text on paper. Thus, when the suspect starts adding defensive turn components (line 4) P is in the process of writing down his anticipated text. As excerpts (3) and (4) have also shown, the interrogator's planned text may take precedence over the suspect's overlapping contributions.

Let us now observe the simultaneous production of the talk and the typing in the following excerpt:

(6)

1.		(..)	**William bought**
2.	P:	<Two (0.5) CDs, (1) >	**two CDs.**
3.		or three?	
4.	S:	Yes I don't remember how many there were two or three	
5.		or one or I don't remember exactly how	**Two or three,**
6.		many there were. (2)	**I don't remember**
7.		And I wasn't uh I wasn't with him I was uh	**exactly how many**
8.		CDs- looking at CDs.	**there were.**
9.		(18)	**I was not with him.**
10.		( )	**I was looking at**
11.	P:	Yes? (1)	**CDs.**
12.	S:	And then we left.=	

(10, O)

The interrogator is finishing typing up what the suspect said earlier (lines 1–2), and produces a 'next' question in partial overlap with his typing (lines 2–3). He waits with the typing of the answer until the first point where the suspect's talk contains evidence of a recordable answer (line 4; cf. Maynard and Schaeffer, 2006: 21). While P is typing, the suspect continues answering, adding defensive turn components by repeating her uncertainty about the number of CDs (lines 4–6), after which she adds an account for her lack of knowledge (lines 7–8). During this period P does not stop typing. The suspect ends her elaborations and then waits for the interrogator to finish the typing (line 9).

A common feature in my materials is that interrogators do not suspend their typing when suspects start expanding their answers (Komter, 2006b: 212). The interrogators' continued typing in spite of the suspects' expansions, and the suspects' expansions in spite of the typing, could be illuminated by examining the participants' local commitments. Periods of prolonged overlap between the talk and the typing result from the interrogator's orientation to completing his planned text rather than yielding the floor to the suspect's expansions. The fact that the suspects offer their expansions in overlap with the typing instead of after the conclusion of the typing, could be explained first by the fact that the question–answer-typing format provides for a 'next' turn for the interrogator, after the typing. S does not know what P is typing, nor when the typing will be finished. Consequently, there appears to be no other slot for S's defensive activities than in this sequential position, in overlap with the typing (Komter, 2006b: 211). Second, the suspects' overlapping contributions could be responsive to the activity of the typing itself. The typing 'fixes' their prior utterances for the record, making them permanent and preserving them in 'black and white'. This may encourage the suspects' defensiveness and the urgency of expressing it.

2.2.3 *Suspension of Typing*

One of the noticeable features of the reporting of interrogators' truth-finding activities is an orientation to the 'recordability' of suspects' answers. In the following excerpt the suspect has just told the interrogator that she bit a market stall assistant who tried to apprehend her on the suspicion of having stolen jewellery from the stall. P starts writing it down and continues:

(7)

1. P: ((types, 10 seconds))
Subsequently I bit the lady,
2. And which of the two ladies did you bite,
3. S: The one from the stall.
4. P: The one from the stall.
5. ((types, 2 seconds))

from the
6. P: where you had bought that brooch.
7. S: Yes.
8. P: ((types, 20 seconds))
market stall where I had bought the brooch,
(15, O)

We see here that the interrogator is in the process of constructing a sentence bit by bit, where each entry is a result of his queries for more details. It shows how the writing down of the beginning of a sentence creates the relevance of eliciting the information that could make up the rest of the sentence. However, this sequential organisation changes after S's answer to his next question:

(8)
9. P: Where did you bite her,
10. S: In her hand. ((she points at her wrist))
11. P: Her hand,
12. S: Yes here.
13. P: You pointed here ((he points at his wrist))
14. S: Yes I've bitten her here. ((she points at her wrist))
15. P: That's her wrist.
16. S: Yes well yes here. ((she points at her wrist))
17. P: Yes.
18. ((types, 6 seconds))
in her wrist.

As the interrogator notices a discrepancy between the suspect's answer ('in her hand', line 10) and her action of pointing at her wrist, he suspends the typing during the time they are involved in clearing up this problem. His orientation to the 'recordability' of the suspect's answer leads him to write down the outcome of the discussion rather than his own input in reaching this outcome.

The following two examples are from a case of credit card theft and fraud (Komter, 2006b). The suspect has been arrested together with her boyfriend William. The suspect's account is that they went shopping, and that she was not fully aware that William paid with a credit card that did not belong to him. They first went to a CD shop called 'Fame' where William bought some CDs. S has been telling P that she was not aware of her boyfriend's activities as she was looking at CDs in another part of the shop. Up to this moment P has been typing up the suspect's answers to his questions. He invites S to continue her narrative while he is still typing (see also excerpt 6):

(9)

1. P: Yes? (1)
2. S: And then we left.=
3. P: =Yes no, but he pays,
4. S: Yes I wasn't- I tell you I wasn't there I don't know
((two lines omitted))

5. P: William, he told me something different yesterday.
6. S: Yes that has- that
7. [might be so
8. P: [That you got frightened.
9. That you got frightened because he paid with a credit card.
10. S: No because he took his own card first, (0.5) to pay.
11. And then I went to the back.
12. I went where- it's quite a big- yes where all those CDs are,
13. then I went to the back.
14. P: hm hm,

(10, O)

The suspect's answer 'And then we left' (line 2) displays her understanding of P's 'Yes?' (line 1) as a prompt to continue with the temporal progression of the events to be told (Sacks, 1978: 252). This answer could then provide P with the information to be typed up next. However, P's immediate response (line 3) indicates that this is not the answer he is waiting for. The suspension of P's typing activities is responsive to and indicative of the perceived insufficiency of S's answer. P concludes on this insufficiency on the basis of an inconsistency between the suspect's version and what everybody knows (that people pay for the things they buy before leaving the shop) and what he knows himself from what her boyfriend told him (that she got frightened). P shows that he is not just listening for a text to write down, but also for a complete story. On that basis he can hear that something is 'missing' (Kidwell, 2009: 39).

The suspect clarifies her position by reiterating her stance of non-involvement (line 4). This time, P brings into play his own knowledge of the case; he explicitly confronts her with contradictions between her position and what her boyfriend told him the day before (lines 5, 8–9). The suspect responds by elaborating on her earlier account that she did not see what happened because she was standing in the back of the shop (lines 11–13). In the episode that follows she tells some more details about William's use of the credit card. In response, P recapitulates and reformulates her version thus far:

(10)

1.	P: William wanted to pay with his own card	
2.	and that did not work?	
3.	S: No because the	
4.	already uh yes the limit had been reached	**In the shop William wanted to**
5.	or something, maximum been reached.	**pay with his own card but that**
6.	(24)	**did not work, because his limit**
7.	( )	**had been reached or something.**

The suspect's confirmation of P's proposal (line 3) activates the resumption of his typing (lines **4–6**). Note that P first writes down what he has summarised (lines 1–2) and then what the suspect adds in overlap with the typing ('his limit has been reached or something').

The interrogator's talk and the suspension of his typing treat the suspect's answers as incomplete and as inaccurate, and the resumption of the typing marks the shift from 'talk for the truth' to 'talk for the text'. This construction can be found frequently in my materials: the suspect gives an answer that is treated as inadequate, the interrogator probes further without writing anything down, and eventually steers the suspect towards something that can count as a 'recordable' answer (Van Charldorp, 2013: 231), after which he resumes typing. Thus, only the results of the negotiations about a recordable text tend to be shown in the police report, not the police officer's efforts to get there.

In the more adversarial episodes of the interrogations the interrogators may bring their common-sense knowledge or their knowledge about the case into play (Kidwell, 2009: 32). Because suspects are considered to be unreliable sources of information, police officers are oriented to confronting them with counter versions or with inconsistencies in their stories in their efforts to get them to tell the truth. Direct, contemporaneous reporting of such confrontations does not occur very often.

The set of examples to be discussed below comes from a case where the suspect is accused of having stolen a display case from a market stall (Komter, 2003). Her version is that Clive, an acquaintance of hers, stole the case, asked her to keep it for him until he would come back, and then left. The suspect waited on a cafe terrace with her two daughters, with the display case hidden in her shopping bag. Then the market stall assistant, who was looking for the thief, spotted her. With some help from a friend she tried to apprehend the suspect and called the police.

Up to this point the interrogator has typed up the suspect's responses to his questioning. However, after a discussion about the suspect's confrontation with the market stall assistant the interrogator stops typing and tells the suspect that he does not believe her:

(11)
1 P: Tell me the truth for once. (3)
2 And look at me now. (3)
3 For I really think you're lying to me.
4 S: How so?
5 P: How so, because it all hangs together on on coincidences.
6 S: Well but it is no coincidence I met him
(15, O)

P's emphatic request to tell him the truth is followed by a three-second pause. His subsequent instruction to look at him is followed by another three-second pause, after which he accuses the suspect of lying (line 3). This does occasion a response, but not a denial or an account, the responses usually associated with an accusation (Atkinson and Drew, 1979). Instead, the suspect replies with a query after the interpretive basis on which P founds his accusation ('How so?'). As a response, P exhibits an analysis of the story as implausible, because it 'all hangs together on coincidences'. As events are assumed to have some kind of 'logical' connection, P concludes that the suspect's story is false (Garfinkel, 1967c; Kidwell, 2009).

This is followed by an episode in which the interrogator suggests that the suspect stole the display case herself, which she denies. After P expresses his moral disapproval of the fact that the suspect's daughters were witness to her actions, he returns to the previous topic:

(12)
1. P: So everything that you told me is just honest.
2. S: Yes that sure is honest yes.
3. P: Why can't you just look at me then when you say that. (2)
4. S: I <u>did</u> look at you.
5. P: No you did <u>not</u> look at me. (2)
6.   You looked at that handkerchief that you have in your hand. (3)
7.   Look people who are honest, they look one another straight in the eyes.
8.   ((they look one another in the eyes for eight seconds))

The basis for P's show of distrust is the background knowledge available to assess the credibility of the suspect's stance. In excerpt (11) P questions S's truthfulness by analysing it on the basis of common-sense notions of plausible events; here he accounts for his doubts by analysing her behaviour on the basis of common-sense notions of nonverbal expressions of sincerity (line 3). Again she disputes his analysis. In fact, she appears to demonstrate on the spot that he is wrong, by looking him in the eyes. As everyone knows that nonverbal behaviour cannot be assessed as sincere if it is produced on command, his question about her honesty and his comments on her gaze direction renew the issue of her lying and keep it alive (lines 5–7). The renewed orientation to the suspect's honesty reveals P's continued 'investigative' listening and his reliance on his common-sense knowledge for disputing the suspect's version (Garfinkel, 1967c; Kidwell, 2009; Watson, 1990). In the exchanges that follow, P recapitulates the suspect's story, stressing her responsibility for what happened and the effect this may have on her daughters.

Now let us pick up the interaction some time later. The interrogator has recapitulated the events as told by the suspect, emphasising the presence of her two young daughters at the scene of the offence, and he continues:

(13)
1. P: So what do you think of that. (1)
2. S: Not good of course. (5)
3. P: Why do you <u>do</u> it then. (9)
4.   Give me <u>one</u> reason why you have done this. (2)
5. S: I don't know. (2)
6. P: For that single bra- bracelet that you wanted to have?

7. S: Yes. (1)
8. P: Yes was <u>that</u> it.
9. S: I think that- that was it yes. (6)
10. P: Don't you think it's ridiculous. (1)
11. S: Yes it's ridiculous.°
12. P: Sorry?
13. S: Yes it's ridiculous. (15)
14. P: How uh (2) do you see your daughters' future.

P asks for the suspect's evaluation of her actions (line 1), for an account of her actions (line 3) followed by an invitation to condemn her own actions (line 10). This episode is noteworthy for the number and length of the silences (Atkinson and Drew 1979: 198, 260). The meaning and effect of silences depend on their sequential positions. After a number of S's answers, especially those that express self-blame, P leaves pauses of increasing duration (lines 2, 9, 13). The longest silence (line 13) occurs when S has confirmed P's analysis of the account of her actions ('it's ridiculous'). This pause appears to give special weight to the suspect's expression of self-blame (Atkinson and Drew, 1979: 68). The relatively long silences after the suspect's answers accentuate the incongruity and the lack of credibility of her story (Drew, 1992: 514; Matoesian, 1993).

Excerpts (11)–(13) show that P is building up tension by, among other things, non-verbal means such as intense looking and leaving silences. An obvious explanation for the absence of typing would be that these actions are typically not the substance of a written text. More importantly perhaps, an activity such as typing would defuse the tension and thus interfere with the interrogator's further truth-seeking actions. And, as shown before, the interrogator can indicate his dissatisfaction with the suspect's contributions by not writing them down. Another reason for not reporting this episode could be that he may be reluctant to put his adversarial actions on display.

In the interaction that follows the interrogator gradually steers the suspect towards admitting that she has not told the truth (Komter, 2003). For more than half an hour the interrogator has stopped writing down entries in the report, as he directs his attention solely to interrogating the suspect. Then he shows an orientation to the report again, and to the recording of what she will be telling him:

(14)
1. P: Right.
2. ((types, 8 seconds))

I have not told

3. I now put 'I haven't told the whole truth, but I shall tell you the truth now'.
4. Okay?
5. ((types, 21 seconds))

the whole truth, but I shall tell you the truth now.

P spells out what was only implied before: the suspect's admission to not having told the truth carries with it the obligation to start telling it now, on the assumption that her 'truth' will be a confession (Komter, 2003: 462; 2006b: 215). P starts typing, announces what he is reporting, and appears to get her tacit permission to do so. P's typing displays that the narrative that the suspect is going to tell now is fit to be written up. It identifies his activities to come as 'taking down the suspect's statement', in contrast with his earlier orientation to 'truth finding'.

2.3 Achieving Coherence

A consequence of the Q–A-T organisation is that there are 'conversational gaps' during the typing that last much longer than do the usual conversational pauses. During that time the interrogator is busy writing down a text in the report, while the suspect is waiting. The setting is 'partially opaque' (Goodwin, 2000: 1508), in the sense that the suspect does not know what the interrogator is writing, nor how long the typing will last. It could be expected that relatively long periods of typing may interrupt the flow of the conversation. In the following sections I shall consider the ways in which interrogators coordinate the talk and the typing. I shall first discuss how they bridge the gap occasioned by the typing, after which I investigate how the transitions between the talk and the typing are managed.

2.3.1 Bridging the Gaps

A special kind of 'bridging the gaps' is what I have called 'typing aloud' (Komter, 2006b; cf. Houtkoop-Steenstra 2000: 59). The interrogator talks and types at the same time and at the same pace (González Martínez, 2006). The following excerpt is an example:

(15)

1.	P: Okay, (2) did you hit her?	
2.	S: No.	
3.	P: No?	
4.	(5)	**Q:**
5.	<did. you. hit. her.>	**Did you hit her?**
6.	<answer. No..>	**A: No**
7.	<I. did. not. hit. her.>	**I did not hit her.**
8.	Nor threaten her or something,	
9.	aggressive,	
10.	S: °Noho° ((laughing))	

(15, N)

P vocalises the words as he is writing them, as if he is dictating the text to himself (lines 5–7). In doing this, he creates transparency about the text he is writing. Typing aloud makes available to the suspect the substance of the interrogator's typing, and allows the interrogator to assume a total occupation of the floor (Komter, 2006b: 208).

The following two excerpts show how interrogators can retain topical coherence, in spite of the gaps caused by the typing. In an interrogation about a shoplifting the following sentence has been constructed in the course of a number of question–answer-typing sequences: **On the ground floor I took a T-shirt worth Fl. 15, – from a rack and put it under my coat** (Komter, 2001). When the interrogator has completed writing down this sentence he continues:

(16)

1. P: Well you put that shirt under your coat and you left the store without paying.
2. S: Yes.
3. P: And were- were you stopped outside or or
4. [uh
5. S: [Yes.
6. P: in in the doorway or after the gates where exactly was that?
7. S: Outside.
8. P: In the street.
9. S: Yes.
10. P: ((types, 20 seconds))

Then I walked out of the store without paying. Outside I was stopped
(17, O)

Interrogators sometimes solve the problem of returning to the interrogation after their typing by reiterating some of the information that has just been reported. The last phrase P has typed before he resumes the talk is then transformed into the formulation (Heritage and Watson, 1979): 'Well you put that shirt under your coat' (line 1). Among other things, formulations can work to minimise breaks in the flow of topical talk (Heritage and Watson, 1979: 152). This makes them appropriate objects to shift the attention from the typing back to the interrogation, and to resume the topic of the interrogation.[3] P immediately follows this with another formulation: 'you left the shop without paying'. It can be seen as a 'candidate recordable' even though, after the suspect's confirmation (line 2), P does not yet write it down immediately.

This shows a distinction between formulations uttered after, and those uttered before, the typing. P's utterance in line 1 starts with a post-typing formulation ('... you put that shirt under your coat') that repeats the text just written down, and continues with a pre-typing formulation ('you left the store without paying') and a pre-typing question ('were you stopped outside', line 3) that prospectively mobilise the suspect's agreement with the text to write next.

[3] For more work on formulations in Dutch police interrogations, see Sliedrecht (2013).

Thus, the text just written down in the police report is used as a resource to carry on the interrogation, and the talk in the interrogation is produced as a resource to construct a text in the police report.

The interrogation continues:

(17)
10. P: ((types, 20 seconds))
Then I walked out of the store without paying. Outside I was stopped
11. P: And outside you were stopped by a by a man or a woman of security?
12. S: Two.
13. P: Two persons. Man and woman?
14. S: Two men.
15. P: ((reads in report of arrest, 20 seconds)) Hm.
16. ((types, 7 seconds))
by two security men.
(17, O)

Here again, P uses his last phrase ('outside I was stopped') as a way of bridging the gap in the conversation and shifting the attention after the typing back to the interrogation. Moreover, the report shows that P orients to the phrase 'outside I was stopped' as unfinished until he gets the information about the persons who stopped S. After the suspect's answer (line 14) he checks its veracity with the help of the documents he has in front of him. These documents are visible evidence that the suspect's first-hand knowledge of the events may be compared with the information already available from the documents.

Because the interrogators are attentive to the screen in front of them, they are informed of the report thus far and may thus base their 'next' question on the text just written down. Interrogators' actions of 'typing aloud' or of reading the text from the screen, give suspects some insight into the substance of the emerging text on the screen and, by implication, illuminate the rationale of the 'next' question. P's formulations and questions display the momentum of the events thus far for the story to be reported. First S took a T-shirt, then he put it under his coat, then he left the store without paying, and then he was stopped by two security men; this is the order in which these events are to be told and reported. Pre- and post-tying formulations are the interrogator's conversational tools for maintaining narrative and conversational coherence, in spite of the duration of the 'gaps' occasioned by the typing.

2.3.2 *Transition Devices*

The examples above have shown how interrogators pick up the thread of the conversation by formulating what has just been written, and how formulations anticipate a next entry in the report. These pre-typing formulations mark the shift from the talk to the typing (Beach and Dixson, 2001: 30; Heritage and Watson, 1979: 151; Komter, 2001). The following excerpt is an example:

(18)
1. P: So you said to one of those officers I haven't done anything, or or
2. S: Yes I just said truthfully I haven't done anything.
3. P: ((types, 13 seconds))
I said to one of the officers: "I haven't done anything".
4. P: Do you remember what date it was?
(3, O)

The interrogator summarises the suspect's prior talk (line 1), proffering a text which, after the suspect has agreed with it (line 2), is written down. (Komter, 2006b: 215). We see that the Q–A-T format has been realised as a formulation–agreement-typing action sequence. The turn after the typing is, as in the Q–A-T format, the interrogator's next question.

As there is a preference for agreeing with formulations (Heritage and Watson, 1979: 143), they can be used as understanding checks by the interrogators in order to move towards an agreed-upon version of events (Holt and Johnson, 2006) that they can then write down in the police report:

(19)
1. P: So there was nobody there I understand.=
2. S: =No.
3. P: <So. therefore.>
4. <so. there. was. nobody. (2) there>. **So there was nobody there.**
5. Okay.
(15, N)

The suspect's response to the interrogator's understanding check (lines 1–2) is taken up by P as a token of agreement with the wording of the formulation; he simultaneously repeats it in a 'dictating voice' and writes it down (line 4). Thus, the formulation looks backward and forward; it looks backward as recapitulating what has just been said, and it looks forward as a candidate entry in the police report (Komter, 2006b: 215). The transition between the typing and the interrogator's next turn is marked by his 'okay' (line 5).

'Okay' is another device frequently used for managing transitions between the talk and the typing. The use of 'okay' has been described as occurring at moments of transition between turns at talk but also between 'activity shifts' (Beach, 1993: 326) such as initiating the closure of a telephone conversation (Beach, 1995: 134–9). In my materials the 'okays' occur both before and after the interrogator's typing activities. 'Okays' occur more frequently after the typing than they do before the typing, and they are usually followed by a 'next' question:

(20)

1. P: You explain to him that you like that bracelet,
2. S: Yes,
3. P: So what is the aim of that then? (2)
4. S: That he goes and gets the bracelet.
5. P: Yes yes.
6. ((types and edits, 59 seconds))

So I wanted Clive to steal that bracelet for me.

7. P: Okay and and Clive he goes in there, (2)
8. S: and then he took (that box with the) bracelet,

(15, O)

(21)

1. S: They went after him the four of them (three or four police)
2. P: ((types, 19 seconds))

I saw that three or four police officers were running after him.

3. P: Okay and then.
4. S: Yes then he was arrested.

(4, O)

The 'okays' introducing new questions after the typing mark the end of the typing and signal a 'state of readiness' for moving to next-positioned matters (Beach, 1995: 143). For the interrogators they mark a shift in attention from the screen back to the suspect. The 'okays' are directed to the suspects and initiate the request to continue their narrative as displayed by the use of 'and then' (excerpt 20, line 7; excerpt 21, line 3), which accomplishes a movement to the next event in the narrative. For the suspects, who have been 'waiting' for some time (59 seconds in excerpt 20, line 6; 19 seconds in excerpt 21, line 2), the 'okays' signal a 'return to business'.

'Okays' before the typing accompany the interrogator's shift of attention from the talk to the typing. It is noticeable that these 'okays' are often spoken in a soft voice:

(22)

1. P: You wait until someone comes out of the entrance hall.
2. S: Yes out of the entrance hall
3. [yes.
4. P: [Out of the apartment building yes,
5. [and then you walk in.
6. S: [then I go yes.
7. P: And then you take the elevator.
8. S: Yes.
9. P: °Okay.°
10. ((types, 29 seconds))

I wait until someone comes out of the entrance hall, for my friends' bell does not work. Then I take the elevator up.

(6, N)

(23)
1. P: And how many scooters or mo- mopeds or things were there.
2. S: Three.
3. P: °Okay.°
4. ((types,7 seconds))
There were also a few mopeds.
(8, N)

The low volume of these 'okays' may be explained by the direction of the shift of activity. As mentioned before, the post-typing 'okays' in excerpts (20) and (21) are directed to the suspect; in excerpts (22) and (23) the interrogators' soft-spoken 'okays' could be the 'self-talk' of people whose attention is going to be caught up by their activities on the PC. They introduce a spate of activity in which the suspect does not participate. Thus, the interrogators' uses of transition devices such as formulations and 'okays' before and after the typing display their management of the dual orientation to the suspect and to the screen.

2.4 Achieving Recordability

Some of the talk in the interrogations can be understood by considering the projected 'career' of the report in the further criminal law process (Meehan, 1986). Interrogators are likely to ask suspects questions or to suggest candidate recordables, the responses to which may be important to be 'on the record' for building a case. At the same time, the police report is supposed to reflect an account of the events by suspects who are not likely to volunteer the information necessary for building a case. Thus, the interrogators' actions may be understood as directed towards getting a certain text on paper that is considered to be useful for future readers of the reports (Garfinkel, 1967e; Komter, 2002; 2002–3; Meehan, 1986; Zimmerman, 1969). The following sections deal with the forward-looking features of the talk.

2.4.1 Questions for Building a Case

Conspicuous examples of narratives that are elicited 'for the record' are the episodes when interrogators ask 'silly questions' (Stokoe and Edwards, 2008):

(24)
1. P: Simon that sounds a bit stupid all these kind of questions,
2. but you had that that that T-shirt was not yours
3. and you had no permission to take it away right?
4. S: ((shakes his head))
5. P: That's right isn't it?

6. S: Yes.
7. P: ((types, 25 seconds))
The T-shirt was not mine and I had no permission to take it away.
I wanted to have it for myself.
(17, O)

P distances himself from the 'silliness' of the question by expressing his awareness of it, as if to indicate that he is 'only doing his job' (line 1). The interrogator anticipates the judge's task of achieving certainty about all the elements of the crime description as laid down in the Criminal Code. What has to be established in this case of theft then is that the T-shirt belongs to someone else, and that S took it unlawfully. The 'for the record' nature of this question–answer sequence is demonstrated on the spot when P starts typing. The strangeness of the question and of the text in the report becomes understandable when we consider the projected use of the report by the legal professionals in the further criminal law process.

Prosecutors have to include information in their indictment about the place and the time of the alleged crime so that judges will be able to identify the events as 'this particular crime'. Interrogators show that they take this into account when questioning the suspect:

(25)
1. P: So this morning you walked uh (3) just let's have a look,
2. ((leafs through documents, 9 seconds))
3. Yes at twenty uh that time could be about right? Twenty to six?
4. S: Yes that could be about right.
5. P: Sint Anthoniestraat here,
6. ... ((types, 43 seconds))
Today, Saturday the 8th of May 1999 at around twenty to six I walked in the Sint Anthoniestraat in Amsterdam.
(5, O)

The interrogator turns to the documents in front of him (line 2, probably the report of the suspect's arrest) and asks the suspect to confirm the details about the time of the events, which the suspect half-heartedly does (line 4). The interrogator's questions are not meant to elicit 'new' information, but to mobilise the suspect's contribution so that he can write it down as part of 'the suspect's statement'. The text of the report reveals that the interrogator has also added details that were not talked about ('**Saturday the 8th of May**'; '**in Amsterdam**'). In a conversational storytelling 'today' or 'this morning' (line 1) would have been sufficient description for the time of the events. To add the day of the week, the date, the year and the approximate time could be heard as redundant, as people do not ordinarily go into such detail (Schegloff, 1972). It is clear that these details are only relevant to future readers of the report (Jönsson and Linell, 1991; Shuy, 1998).

The next example shows how reporting officers deal with instances where, when asked, the suspect does not remember or know the time of the events. The interrogator has just been typing: **This afternoon I went to the Bijenkorf[4] in order to commit shoplifting** and continues:

(26)

1. P: Do you remember what time it was roughly?
2. S: Yes, uh around uh half past twelve.
3. P: And if it was around twenty to three could that be right too?
4. S: (Yes that's possible)
5. P: It says here that it was around twenty to three that you-
6. that you went through the gates just after twenty to three.
7. S: Oh no that's right [then yes (now that you say it)
8. P: [at twenty to three the alarm went off,
9. S: Oh yes yes yes. It was later than two o'clock.
10. P: ((types, 15 seconds))

You tell me that that was at around 14.40 hrs. That is possible.
(8, O)

The suspect gives a 'wrong' answer to the interrogator's question about the time of the events (lines 1–2). As in excerpt (25) the interrogator already knows the time of the suspect's arrest. The inclusion of the recontextualisation phrase '**you tell me**' in the report shows that the information about the time of the criminal events was provided by the reporting officer. This construction may then be a solution to the police officer's problem of how to include information in a monologue-style police report that should be included for the benefit of future readership but that cannot be ascribed to the suspect.

These examples exhibit the 'double duty' of the police report: it is presumed to describe what suspects tell interrogators, but many of the details are meant for future readers of the report. This 'double duty' involves a 'multiple recipiency' for the interrogator, but not for the suspect: the suspect talks only to the interrogator, while the interrogator also 'talks' to those readers of the report who will deal with the case in the further stages of the process (Haworth, 2010: 177–8).

2.4.2 *Candidate Recordables*

Formulations are versatile conversational objects. Earlier I have shown them to be devices that accompany the shift between the talk and the typing. A feature of this type of transition device is the twofold manner in which they work: preparing both for the typing and for the text. I shall now highlight the role of

[4] The Bijenkorf (beehive) is a well-known department store in the centre of Amsterdam.

formulations for inserting a desired text in the police report. Let us reconsider excerpt (18), reproduced here as excerpt (27):

(27)

1. P: So you said to one of those two officers I've done nothing, or or-
2. S: Yes I have just said truthfully I've done nothing.
3. P: ((types, 13 seconds))

I said to one of the officers: 'I have done nothing'.

4. P: Do you remember what date it was?

(3, O)

It is noticeable that the suspect does not just confirm the interrogator's proposal with 'yes', but he also offers some additions: 'just' and 'truthfully', underlining his stance of innocence. However, the text that is written down shows that the interrogator ignores the suspect's additions and writes down his own original formulation (line 1) in the monologue-style version. It could be suggested that his production of a formulation-in-anticipation-of-the-text-to-be-typed encourages the interrogator to listen for the suspect's agreement rather than for the extra information.

Excerpt (28) is another example where the wording of the interrogator's formulation appears to take precedence over the suspect's additions:

(28)

1. P: So you first pointed out that stall to Clive,
2. [do I understand that correctly?
3. S: [Yes,
4. and then I went uh to stand further away.
5. P: Yes yes.
6. ((types, 36 seconds))

I pointed out to Clive the market stall where I had bought the brooch.

7. P: And what did you like about that uh that display case.

(15, O)

Here again the suspect does not just agree with the interrogators' formulations, but she also adds some further – defensive – turn components that are not written down (line 4). Moreover, the interrogator adds some text that completes and supplements the sentence ('**where I had bought the brooch**'). Thus, the police interrogator shows a tendency to listen for the suspect's confirmation of his formulation and to show an orientation to building a complete text, rather than to attend to the suspect's defensive turn additions.

Formulations may also be produced with a specific future readership in mind. For the establishment of the suspect's 'punishability' or *mens rea*, interrogators sometimes produce formulations, the responses to which may then function as explicating the suspect's frame of mind at the time of the events. The following excerpt concerns a case in which the suspect has admitted to having sold methadone pills on the 'pill bridge' in Amsterdam:[5]

(29)

1. P: But you do- you know that it is forbidden.
2. S: Yes, of course.
3. ((P types, 31 seconds))

Of course I know that it is forbidden to sell methadone pills.
I know that methadone pills are equivalent to hard drugs.
(2, O)

The interrogator's question states the obvious: everybody who frequents the 'pill bridge' knows that it is forbidden to sell methadone pills. The suspect's answer 'of course' (line 2) orients to this feature (Stokoe and Edwards, 2008: 100). This answer then allows the reporting officer to explicate the suspect's *mens rea* for the report: the suspect is fully aware of the illegality of his actions. The suspect's agreement then can be understood as his having endorsed the formulation as a recordable text. Moreover, a sentence is added that confirms and highlights the suspect's knowledge, although it does not correspond with the original talk in the interrogation.

2.5 Division of Labour

Thus far we have seen how the talk and the typing are sequentially organised in 'solo' interrogations. In 'duo' interrogations the interactional organisation of the event is different: it affords opportunities for a division of labour between the two police officers and it provides for different forms of speakership and recipiency. The interactional organisation of the talk is more complex than in the 'solo' interrogations as there is also room for interaction between the two police officers and between the reporting officer and the suspect.

The usual division of labour in 'duo' interrogations is that one of the police officers does the typing and the other does (most of) the questioning. This allows for the simultaneous production of the talk and the typing, and for an orientation to interrogating and statement taking as appropriate simultaneous activities. In the following sections I shall examine the effects of the division of labour between the two police officers on talk, typing and (constructing a) text.

2.5.1 Teamwork

In his study on Thai courtroom interaction Moerman found that, as it was part of the judge's task to write down what was said, the lawyer's actions took the

[5] A bridge in Amsterdam, the scene of a flourishing drugs trade, especially pills.

judge's writing into account. That is, the lawyer left pauses for the judge to write, repeated the suspect's answers, and produced candidate recordables for the judge to write down (1988: 52–4). Similar features can be found in my data of police interrogations.

There are various ways in which the interrogating officers encourage and inform the reporting officers' writing tasks. For example, interrogators sometimes explicitly instruct reporting officers on what to write, and in some cases they slow down their talk and articulate it as if dictating a text to the reporting officer. At a more implicit level, the interrogating officers may show an awareness of the reporting officers' tasks at hand by producing utterances that could facilitate the typing, for example repeats of the suspects' answers.

Repeats have been described as similar to formulations in that they are summaries, but also as different in that they preserve not only the gist of former talk, but also the exact wording (Holt and Johnson, 2006). In this way, repeats make the suspects' answers visible for the report writing (Puchta et al., 2004: 302):

(30)

1.	P^1:	I just want to talk about those fake	
2.		drugs right? (2)	
3.		How did you come by them. (1)	
4.	S:	I made them myself	
5.	P^1:	You made them yourself.=	**Question:**
6.	S:	=Yes. With what?	**how did**
7.	P^1	Yes that is the next question. Okay.	**you come**
8.	S:	With wheat flour and salt,	**by those**
9.	P^1:	Wheat flour and salt. (3)	**fake drugs?**
10.		And where did you make that.	**Answer:**
11.	S:	At home.	**I made**
12.	P^1:	Where is home.	**them myself**
13.	S:	In the kitchen.	**with wheat**
14.	P^1:	No, what do you mean with home. (2)	**flour and salt,**
15.	S:	At my uncle's house.=	**at home.**
16.	P^1:	=At your uncle's house.	**With that**
17.		(8)	**I mean in the kitchen of my**
18.		Was your uncle at home too,	**uncle's**
19.		when you did that.	**house.**

(7, N)

There are three repeats in this fragment (lines 5, 9 and 16). The first repeat is followed immediately by the suspect's confirmation and by his production of what would be the next logical question (line 6). The suspect's answer to this question is then followed by the second repeat (line 9). This time the interrogating officer (P^1) is in the position to leave a pause after the repeat (line 9), as the suspect appears to wait for the next question. P^1's next question (line 10) does not at first receive what he considers to be a complete answer, as is evidenced by his further questioning about the meaning of the suspect's answer 'at home' (line 11). The suspect's final answer 'at my uncle's house' (line 15) is then accepted by P^1 with a repeat followed by an eight-second pause (lines 16–17).

The combination of repeats and pauses attends both to the 'typeability' and to the 'recordability' of the talk. P^1's choice of repeats suggests the recordability of the substance of the text to be written down and his leaving pauses promotes the 'typeability' of this text (cf. Moerman, 1988: 54). The inclusion of the pauses is not P^1's decision alone, as S takes the opportunity to respond to P^1's first repeat (lines 5–6). Although the pauses facilitate the typing, they are shorter than the 'typing turns' in the 'solo' interrogations. The excerpt shows that the reporting officer (P^2) does not have enough time to complete the 'typing turn', for when P^1 asks the next question P^2 is still typing (lines 18–19). P^1 apparently relies on P^2's capacity to listen and type at the same time.

In 'duo' interrogations the typing may become just a background noise (Van Charldorp, 2013: 234). As P^2 is almost continually occupied with the typing, this makes it difficult to ascertain what P^2 writes at what moment. In the beginning of excerpt (30) P^2 is still typing up the answer to a previous question when P^1 proceeds with a next question, in overlap with the typing (lines 1–3). P^2 finishes her typing (line 4) and then starts typing up the question just asked (line 5). The text of the report shows both how P^2 listens to the substance of the talk, and how she deals with the limited amount of time available for the writing. She writes down the first question and the suspect's answers to the series of next questions but does not write down the follow-up questions (lines 6–7, 10, 12, 14). She collapses these questions and answers into a more 'writer-friendly' monologue style account (right-hand column, lines **11–17**), so that the suspect's contribution appears to be produced as an answer to the first question

The following excerpt is from the same interrogation. The police officers have made an 'interrogation plan' and have written down some of the questions beforehand.[6]

(31)

1.	P^1:	How long have you had the number.	
2.	P^2:	¦((types, edits, 3 seconds))	**Question:**
3.	S:	¦This was my old SIM card.	
4.	P^1:	¦But how long have you had it. (3)	
5.	S:	¦Perhaps a year and a half.	
6.	P^1:	¦°A year and a half. Okay°	**How long**
7.		¦She just has to type it up.	
8.		¦(7)	
9.	S:	¦It was my cousin's card,	**have you had**

[6] The vertical dotted lines indicate that during the talk in that line the sounds of editing can be heard.

10.	then he gave it to me,	
11.	°then I used it°.	
12.	P^1: ¡What is your cousin called.	
13.	S: What do you say?	
14.	P^1: What is your cousin called.	**that number?**
15.	S: ¡My cousin. David.	
16.	P^1: David.	
17.	¡And his surname? (2)	
18.	S: I'm not going to tell his surname.	**Answer:**
19.	P^1: O::kay, suit yourself.	
20.	((to P^2:))	
21.	He's had it for a year and a half.	**I've had it**
22.	And before that (1) it belonged to his	**for a year**
23.	cousin, Da- David.	**and a half,**
24.	S: Yes.	
25.	P^2: ((types, 24 seconds:))	

before that the number belonged to my cousin, he is called David, I do not want to tell the surname.

26. P^1: Okay.

(7, N)

After the interrogating officer's (P^1) question (line 1), there are editing sounds, as the reporting officer (P^2) copies and pastes the prepared question in the police report (lines 2–17) (Van Charldorp, 2013: 235). The suspect responds but does not answer the question (line 3), which leads P^1 to ask it once more (line 4). In response to the suspect's subsequent answer (line 5) P^1 draws attention to it by repeating it (however, without the qualification 'perhaps'). His subsequent 'okay' highlights the correctness and completeness of the suspect's answer as candidate recordable (line 6). The sequence is rounded off by P^1 explicating the typing task of P^2 (line 7) and by his leaving a pause for her to write (line 8).

Lines 6–8 illuminate how the interrogating officer takes into account the reporting officer's tasks at hand. The interrogating officer steers the reporting officer towards the typing of the desired text first by rejecting the suspect's initial answer (line 4), then by repeating part of the suspect's 'improved' answer (line 6), by confirming his repetition with the transition marker 'okay' (line 6), by explicating what the reporting officer has to do (line 7), and finally by leaving a pause (line 8). After her editing activities the reporting officer starts typing in overlap with the suspect's refusal to reveal his cousin's surname (line 18). Then P^1 turns towards P^2 (line 20) perhaps because he has seen that she has not yet written down the answer. This time he spells it out for her (lines 21–3) and leaves her enough time to write it down (line 25). When P^2 has finished the typing, P^1 produces an 'okay' receipt to restore the interaction with the suspect in anticipation of the next question (line 26).

As in excerpt (30) the 'teamwork' of the two police officers is displayed by P²'s reliance on P¹'s typing-facilitating actions. P¹ helps P² construct the text by repeating or summarising the suspect's answers, and he facilitates the typing by leaving pauses. As the typing lags behind the talk (what the suspect answers in line 5 is written down in overlap with lines 21–3), P² simplifies the typing task by leaving out some of P¹'s follow-up questions and by reporting that interaction in the monologue style.

2.5.2 *Typing Problems*

Typing and listening simultaneously may present problems for reporting officers, as is illustrated by the following excerpts. Excerpt (32) shows the beginning of an interrogation; the suspect has already told the interrogator that he was present when his friend Elmer committed the offence (taking some money out of a boy's coat pocket, see Chapter 5), but that he left because he did not want to get involved. The interrogator asks the suspect whether he knows what happened:

(32)

1.	P¹:	But, do you know what <u>did</u> happen then, (1)	
2.	S:	Not really.	
3.	P¹:	No. (2)	**You ask**
4.		He says, they're standing with seven of them,	**me if I**
5.		at a certain moment. Around me. (2)	**know what**
6.		He'd put his keys and his money in his	**happened.**
7.		coat pocket (2) and	**I don't really**
8.		then uh (4) Elmer he goes to-	
9.		he walks toward him	**know it.**
10.		and starts feeling in his coat pocket. (1)	
11.		Well if you're standing around him, the seven of you, (1)	
12.	S:	I did no- did not	
13.		[go and stand around him	**You read**
14.	P¹:	[then you must surely have seen it?	
15.	S:	I did not stand around him	**to me that**
16.		I don't understand why he says that.	**a group of**
17.	P¹:	You did <u>not</u> go and stand around him.	**7 boys**
18.	S:	No.	**stood**
19.		(7)	**around the victim.**
20.	P¹:	Well, you're very good friends	**I do not**
21.		with Elmer right?	**understand**
22.		((30 lines omitted))	**what he said.**

(9, N)

After the suspect has claimed his relative ignorance of the events (line 2) P¹ recapitulates the case by reading and summarising the report of the statement of Dan, the alleged victim (lines 4–10). His next utterance (lines 11 and 14) shows that he strategically uses this information (that S was part of a group of boys that stood around Dan) to undermine the suspect's claim that he did not really know what happened. The suspect contradicts the basis of this conclusion both by denying that he was part of that group (lines 12–13) and by stating that he does not understand why Dan should have said that he was (line 16). S's denial is emphatically repeated by P^1, who leaves a pause after the suspect's confirmation (lines 18–19).

Most of the typing here is done in overlap with the talk. As P^2 starts typing after the question–answer sequence (line 3), it is reasonable to assume that the 'you ask me . . .' question and its answer were typed from that moment on, in overlap with P^1's consultation and summary of the alleged victim's statement (lines 3–9). The periods of non-typing (lines 8, 10–12) suggest completion of the reporting of the question–answer sequence. So the reporting of this information (**you read to me ...** right-hand column lines **13–19**) is likely to start in overlap with the talk transcribed as lines 13–22). P^1's emphatic repetition of the suspect's answer, the suspect's confirmation and the subsequent seven-second pause (lines 17–19) could be taken as facilitating the typing and suggesting a text to be typed.

We can see that the text written by P^2 lags considerably behind, partly due to the 'writer-unfriendliness' of the recontextualised monologue writing style. The representation of the talk in lines 1–2 is probably written down in overlap with the talk in lines 3–9, the reporting of the talk in lines 3–5 is likely to have been written in overlap with lines 13–19, and the talk in line 16 is represented as lines **20–2**. The rest of the talk is not reported. It can be noted that P^2 misses the point of P^1's recapitulation of the alleged victim's statement (that S must have seen what happened, line 14) and the suspect's defensive response (that he did not stand around Dan, line 15), in spite of P^1's repetition of it and the pause he leaves after S's confirmation (lines 17–18). P^2 also misrepresents the suspect's account in line 16 ('why he says that' is written down as '**what he said**', line **22**). These troubles can be a result of the unwieldy format of the recontextualised monologue style, in combination with the differential pace of talking and typing, and the relative shortness of the pauses.

In the episode that follows P^1 asks the suspect how much he knows, and tells him that Dan has pointed out Elmer, the suspect's friend, as the perpetrator of the theft. This information is not written down, probably because P^2 is still in the process of reporting previous talk. P^2 then interrupts the talk and addresses the suspect:

(33)

52. P^2: Can I just break in for I sort of missed that,	
53. you were all standing around him.	
54. S: That's what he says	
55. [( )	
56. P^1: [Dan says that yes.	
57. P^1: [Seven of them.	
58. P^2: [But it's not true.	
59. S: No.	
60. P^2: But what's it then according to you?	
61. S: Uh I don't know	
62. it could be that they stood around him	**That is not true.**
63. but I walked away, so.	**I did not go and**
64. (6)	**stand around Dan.**
65. P^2: You walked away at once.	
66. S: Yes.	**I walked**
67. But I stood in front of a shop,	**away at once.**

(9, N)

P^2 recapitulates part of the exchanges shown in excerpt (32) (lines 52–3), to which S replies that this is the alleged victim's version, which P^1 confirms. P^2 then formulates a conclusion ('it's not true', line 58) and, after S's agreement asks him for his version of the events (line 60). She starts typing shortly after the start of S's non-committal answer (line 61). The pause in line 64 is a 'typing pause', as in the 'solo' interrogations with a Q–A-T structure: the suspect has finished his answer, and P^2 first completes the typing before she asks a next question, while S waits. The next question is another formulation (line 65), based on the final item of S's answer (line 63).

The text P^2 writes down is based on her three formulations in lines 53, 58 and 65. As shown before, formulations are used in 'solo' interrogations in anticipation of the text to be written down. Excerpt (33) is an example of how these formulations may serve at the same time as understanding checks and as candidate recordables. As in the monologue-style reports of 'solo' interrogations, P^2's formulations are reported as utterances volunteered by the suspect (lines **62–67**).

Thus, the difficulties encountered in the simultaneous talk-typing constellation as shown in excerpts (32) and (33) are partly solved by P^2's falling back on the kind of coordination of talking and typing that is typical of 'solo' interrogations and monologue-style reports. What is not resolved is the reporting officer's mishearing of the suspect's defensive response (excerpt 32, line 16), while her selection of recordables can be assumed to have suffered from the pressures of her multitasking.

2.6 Conclusion

The police interrogators' two institutional tasks, truth finding and statement taking, are deeply interconnected, as is shown in the interrelationships between talk, typing and (constructing a) text. Practical circumstances that affect these interrelationships are: the number of interrogators, the degree of 'adversarialness' of the interaction, the differential pace of talking and typing, and the writing style of the police report.

In 'solo' interrogations, the interrogators' statement-taking activities are contingent on the routine or adversarial nature of their truth-finding efforts. The elementary organisation of the talk and the typing is the question–answer-typing sequence, where the typing can be seen as a 'third-turn receipt object' that conveys the interrogator's provisional acceptance of the answer as appropriate and 'recordable'. As the question–answer-typing organisation does not allow for suspect contributions other than answering questions, suspects may use the periods of non-talk during the typing to produce additional – defensive – turn components. Although interrogators can, to some extent, type and listen to the suspect's answer at the same time, the suspects' talk in overlap with the typing tends to be underreported. That the interrogators generally do not yield the floor to the suspects' overlapping talk but continue typing shows that there is more tolerance for overlap in these circumstances than in 'ordinary' talk.

The more adversarial the interaction, the more incompatible it is with the typing. This is first due to the fact that interrogators may find investigative questioning difficult to combine with the typing, as their attention to the screen would reduce the intensity of the questioning. Second, interrogators can display their dissatisfaction with the suspect's answer by not writing it down, as typing can be interpreted as an acceptance of the suspect's talk. And, third, police interrogators may be reluctant to put their more adversarial actions on display. As a result, the more adversarial moments in the interrogations are less likely to be reported than the routine episodes.

The interrogators coordinate their dual orientation to the suspect and the screen through their management of the transitions between the talk and the typing. The fact that they are visibly occupied elsewhere discourages the suspect's contributions. Although the resulting periods of non-talk might disrupt the flow of the interrogation, the emerging text on the screen provides for topical continuity, as what has been written down last may serve as the substance of a next question. This shows that the report is not merely a document in which what is said is laid down, but that it actively informs and directs the interrogation. The interrogators' switches of attention between the suspect and the screen are exhibited not just through their gaze movements but also by way of transition devices such as 'okays' and formulations. These transition devices do not just demarcate stretches of talk and typing, they also coordinate the shifts between the participants' joint involvement in the interrogations on the one hand, and the interrogators' intermittent solo-performances on the other.

The interrogators' orientation to the text of the report reflects their task of producing a police report that can serve as official legal evidence in the further criminal law process. This forward-looking character of police reports has an effect on the talk as it may lead interrogators to design their questions to generate a specific text that can accommodate the demands of future readers of the reports. More specifically, they may formulate a text, a 'candidate recordable', for inclusion in the police report after the suspect's agreement; the suspects' agreement with the formulations then serves both as a confirmation of the 'correctness' of the formulation and as agreement with the reporting of this text. This makes the use of formulations instrumental for controlling the substance of the police report.

In 'duo' interrogations the typing has a less prominent position: it does not completely occupy the floor, and the moments of typing onset or typing completion have less sequential relevance for the talk. These interrogations show various degrees of 'teamwork'. Interrogators may facilitate the writing by highlighting or explicating the text to be reported, by repeating an answer and by leaving pauses for the typing, or they may follow their own plan and leave it up to the reporting officer to decide what to write. Reporting officers are dependent on the interrogating officers for allowing them the time to write, and interrogating officers depend on the reporting officers' skill in keeping up with the talk and selecting the relevant items for the report. The simultaneity and the differential pace of the talk and the typing affect the typing more than in the 'solo' interrogations; it may result in mishearings, in a more selective reporting and in a 'monologisation' of Q–A and RM-style reports. Reporting officers may then fall back on the more writer-friendly monologue style and the simpler interactional structure of 'solo' interrogations.

3 The Police Report

The Document, the Text and the Talk

3.1 Introduction

Chapter 2 has shown how the emergent and transitory nature of the talk in the interrogation is transformed into a fixed and stable document that can stand on its own, regardless of the circumstances of its production. What has now become 'the suspect's statement' has been decontextualised from its original habitat, and recontextualised as a material object, as a document that can be photocopied and distributed among the professionals who will deal with the case in the further criminal law process (Bauman and Briggs, 1990: 74). Thus, the suspect's statement has acquired a new context, a new textual environment within which it will be read and understood. In this chapter I shall explore this new environment, in order to acquire insight into the nature of the transformations that the suspect's statement has undergone, and into the transparency of the police reports for readers who have no access to the original interaction on which they are based.

Appendix A shows the police report on which this chapter is based. It is a document that contains not just the report of the police interrogation ('the suspect's statement') but also a great deal of introductory information and some concluding sentences. A closer inspection of the document reveals that the report of the suspect's statement is embedded within quotation marks and the sentences: *"I understand that you wish to hear me and that I am not obliged to answer questions . . . I have nothing further to state."* These sentences seem to be produced by the suspect, to introduce and conclude his statement. The texts before and after these sentences are written from the reporting officers' perspective. Thus, the core of the police report, 'the suspect's statement', is embedded within other texts, which may have an impact on how it can or should be understood. Just as a turn at talk can be analysed in relation to what is said immediately before and after the turn, the textual items of the suspect's statement can be understood on the basis of their surrounding texts (Clayman, 1990: 83).

I shall first discuss how the bureaucratic and institutional features of the police report may affect its understanding or interpretation (Smith, 1974; 1990a). Second, I consider the substantive cores of the reports: the suspects' statements. I shall examine the transparency of the texts by inspecting them for the understandings they may afford readers who have no knowledge of how they have come about, and by comparing the texts in the reports with the original talk which the reports are meant to represent. As the transparency of the text is related to the writing style in which the report is drawn up, I shall then examine for each writing style to what extent readers are offered insights into the original interactional organisation of the interrogation.

3.2 Bureaucratic and Institutional Perspectives

The document examined here as a typical example is the police report of the case analysed further in Chapter 5 (see Appendix A). A global inspection of the police report shows that the suspect's statement, which is the core of the document, is surrounded by other, more or less standard texts. These surrounding texts represent two different perspectives (Smith, 1990a): an anonymous, bureaucratic perspective, exhibited by a type of text that could have been written by anyone in a position to do so (Atkinson and Coffey, 2004: 70), and the reporting officers'[1] perspective displaying their personal commitments to their institutional tasks; this perspective is distinguishable by the use of first-person pronouns that identify the police detectives as the 'writer-authors' (see Chapter 1) of the text. The suspect's statement is distinguishable from the other texts, among other things, by quotation marks at the beginning and the end of it, introduced by: 'he stated' and closed by 'I have nothing further to state'. In the following sections I shall zoom in on the suspect's statement by first examining the texts surrounding it.

3.2.1 The Bureaucratic Perspective

Many of the items in the police report are preprogrammed. At the start of the interrogation the reporting officer enters the special police computer system to which all computers in the police station have access, which opens a form-filling screen where items automatically appear as the officer fills in the required information in the slots. On this screen there are a number of blank fields that must be filled in by the officer before he or she can print the document (Van Charldorp, 2011: 81).

Bureaucratic features of the police report come to the fore in the headings. Let us consider these items step by step, beginning with the top left-hand corner:[2]

[1] I use the phrase 'reporting officer' to highlight the interrogator's task of reporting; when I describe the police officers' questioning actions in the interrogations I call them 'interrogators'. In many cases they are one and the same person.

[2] Throughout this chapter I shall use the font of the original police reports (Courier) for their representation.

```
POLICE AMSTERDAM - AMSTELLAND
DISTRICT 7
AREA TEAM Fledder Laan



Police report nr. : 2008123456-3
```

P O L I C E   R E P O R T
of suspect interrogation

This introductory section places the report within a bureaucratic and organisational frame. It consists of different types of information such as the location of the interrogation, the area team and the police report number. The identification of the area team where the report was drawn up locates the team within the bigger units of which it forms a part. This is a reflection of the regional structure of the police organisation: the document begins with the biggest unit, the larger region of Amsterdam and its surroundings, then zooms in on the smaller one (the district) and finally on the police station where the activities have actually taken place (the location of the area team).

This information is succeeded by the police report number that begins with the year in which the report was written (2008), followed by a longer number with a dash before the last number. It is a unique number that identifies the case as 'this particular case', of which there are no others. The police report number is essential for its identification and its bureaucratic management: it allows the document to be referred to by its bureaucratic identification – for filing and subsequent recovery. The police report number also involves limited accessibility: the police report has a restricted readership and will be archived in a storage space that is inaccessible to outsiders.

Whereas the numbers before the dash identify the case, the number 3 after the dash displays this document as the third in a series. This number shows that the document is part of a case file under construction that already contains two police reports (such as reports of the arrest, witness statements, etc.). It makes the report 'the next one', in relation to the report preceding it, and 'a previous one' with respect to the documents still to come. As a result, this report can be read to confirm, contradict or complement previous reports, and it can contain information that will affect the reading and writing of next reports.

Then the text moves from the left-hand corner to the middle of the page, highlighting this as the heading for everything that follows. In bold typescript, it is a display of what kind of object this is: a police report of a suspect interrogation. First the generic name is given in capital letters (**POLICE**

REPORT) then, in smaller letters, the name of the specific type of police report (**of suspect interrogation**).

In sum, the heading of the police report consists of the specific, bureaucratic designation of the location, the identification number and the character of the document. It designates what kind of document it is, and anticipates what it promises to be: a 'police report of suspect interrogation'. These features allow the reader to know what area team is accountable for the document, in what archives and under what numbers to store or to find it, and what type of information will be contained in the document.

3.2.2 The Reporting Officers' Perspective

Underneath the identification of the nature of this document there is a line, after which the margin moves to the right. This separates the introductory information in the headings from the texts to come. It introduces a new element into the report: the identification of the reporting officers. The preceding text was prompted by activating the computer system and could have been written by any ratified employee of the area team, but from this moment on the reporting officers' professional identities are brought into play:

Reporting officer 1
Henk Walter Bloem, (12345), police sergeant, district 7 detection office and
Reporting officer 2
Fiona Balken, (67890), senior police officer, area team Fledder Laan

---

The police officers identify themselves first by their current task: drawing up a police report. Although it is unlikely that two police officers are both typing up the suspect's statement, and although an important task of at least one of the officers is to interrogate the suspect, the officers identify themselves as 'reporting officers', not as 'interrogating officers' nor as 'police detectives'. Moreover, they do not mention which of them is the interrogator and which the reporter. Thus, these self-descriptions show that the 'authorship' of the text to follow is the joint responsibility of the two police detectives. They are then identified by their names, ID numbers, ranks and area teams. The importance of the officers' ID numbers and rank is characteristic of the hierarchical organisation of the police. It is a feature of their institutional identity that distinguishes them on the one hand from other criminal law professionals, and on the other from 'citizens' (van Charldorp, 2011: 46).

The line underneath this professional identification closes off the current item and marks its separation from the following text:[3]

```
On Wednesday the 4th of March 2008, at around 12.00 hrs, we, reporting
officers, questioned a man, in the police station Fledder Laan 48 in
Amsterdam, as suspected of violation of section 312/2/2 Criminal Code
juncto section 310 Criminal Code.
The suspect stated to us to be named:
```

This is where the reporting officers begin their account of the interrogation. It marks a change with the texts above it, insofar as the actions of the reporting officers become visible. From now on the reader is invited to observe the creation of the police report from the perspective of the reporting officers. It is a first-person narrative that shows some of their professional requirements: indicating the date, time, and location of the interrogation, their professional actions ('we questioned'), a provisional description of the suspect ('a man') and the nature of the suspicion according to the relevant sections of the Criminal Code. The use of the first-person pronoun 'we' displays a change of 'footing'. By using the personal pronoun 'we' the reporting officers indicate that they are the 'writer-authors' of the text in two ways: the text to come is of their devising (Goffmann, 1981: 128) and they are the 'writers' of it. They do not just state that they are the reporting officers, as in the passage before, they now demonstrate it.

This text is oriented to the legal professionals in later stages of the criminal process: the reference to the sections of the offences as laid down in the Criminal Code reveals a system of categorisation that is alien to outsiders. If we consider the criminal law process as a transformation of the fluidity and indefiniteness of events in the real world into the fixed legal categories that are required for the business at hand, this is where it starts. Sections 310 (simple theft) and 312/2/2 (violent theft by two or more persons) may apply in a variety of circumstances and may refer to a variety of actions. From a legal point of view, these differences do not matter as yet. What is relevant now is to apply the relevant legal categories to answer the question whether a theft has been committed, whether violence has been used, and whether the suspect was in the company of others.

A noticeable feature of this text is that it is expressed with different degrees of certainty. There are concrete references to what is held to be certain and indisputable: the date, the address, the police station, and the participants (the two reporting officers and the suspect). Other pieces of information are written down with some degree of uncertainty. The time is not 12.00 hrs, but 'at around 12.00 hrs'. This type of 'approximation marker' in references to the time of the

[3] I have translated the 'legalese' features of the original text into a similar type of stilted English. The Latin term 'juncto' has been preserved.

police interrogation is a common feature of police reports.[4] Another type of 'open-endedness' can be seen in the references to the crime descriptions of the Criminal Code. The concrete and detailed mentioning of the relevant sections in the Criminal Code is at odds with the vagueness of the term 'juncto' (used in the sense of 'in relation to'). This term refers to the fact that the suspect is not charged with two separate offences, but that the two qualifications of theft are offered simultaneously, in anticipation of what may happen in the further criminal process, and as 'inoculation' against possible future attacks from the defence. It means in practice that, if the violence or the complicity of others in the theft cannot be proved, the suspect can still be convicted for a simple theft.

This open-endedness, in combination with the two crime-descriptions (312/2/2 and 310), can be explained by the early stage of the investigations. When a suspect is brought in for questioning not much may be known yet about the offence that the suspect is alleged to have committed. At this stage, the exact type of offence may yet have to be established by, among other things, the interrogation to come. Thus, this open-endedness is a pre-emptive action to ensure it will cover what the suspect may later turn out to have done according to the evidence then available.

The report continues with an enumeration of the suspect's personal details:[5]

```
The suspect stated to us to be named:

Name                              : Martina (man)
Christian names                   : Elmer
Place of birth                    : Amsterdam
Date of birth                     : 03/05/1991
Country of birth                  : The Netherlands
Nationality                       : Dutch
Address                           : West Dreef 18
Place                             : 1002 BK Liemen
Telephone number                  : 061234567
ID in accordance with             : register of residents
Age                               : 16
School                            : vocational education
Name school                       : Regional Education College
____________________________________________________________
The suspect stated that the address given by him is also the postal
address for announcements in criminal cases.

After we informed the suspect that he was not obliged to answer
questions and about what we wished to question him he stated: "

"I understand that you wish to question me and that I am not obliged
to answer questions.
```

[4] This is comparable with the prosecutors' formulations in the indictment. The events invariably seem to have taken place 'at or around' a certain moment in time.

[5] The materials invariably show two quotation marks, one after 'he stated' and another at the beginning of the initial sentence. The first quotation mark is probably part of the form-filling items and the second is then entered by hand.

Listing the suspect's personal details is a routine way to identify a person, characteristic of many kinds of institutional settings.[6] In contrast with the information that the police officers have given about their professional selves (name, number, rank, area team), the information about the suspect describes his individual self. It is a reflection of the fact that the police report represents interaction between professionals who act on behalf of the organisation and a layperson who acts on behalf of himself.

For the first time the suspect is presented here as a source of information and as speaker. The suspect's speech is reported in three different ways. In the first place the suspect is reported as having 'stated . . . to be named', which is followed by a list of personal details, not only containing his name but a lot of other details as well; this makes this section of the police report recognisable as a prearranged set of routine items. The form of the second reported instance of the suspect's speech is 'indirect reported speech' ('the suspect stated that the address . . .'). And finally, after the delivery of his right to silence, the announcement 'he stated' is followed by a colon and by the opening of quotation marks.[7] This creates the slot for the substance of the suspect's statement.

The sentence reporting the interrogator's expression of the suspect's right to silence (the caution) has been programmed in the computer, and the reporting officer has to fill in a prompt during the form-filling after which the sentence automatically appears on the screen (Van Charldorp, 2011: 84). Thus, the report of the caution features in every police report, and in every police interrogation in our corpus the caution is given. This is the last item of the form-filling procedure before the report of the substance of the suspect's statement (to be discussed in next sections). The phrase 'he stated', the colon and the opening of the quotation marks introduce a text in the direct reported speech style, and shows a change of 'speakership' in that it yields the 'floor' to the suspect.

Let us now consider the final sections of the police report. The suspect's statement is rounded off by his assertion the he has nothing further to state. When the interrogation is completed the police officer prints the report, invites the suspect to read it (or reads it aloud himself) and, when the suspect has approved of it, to sign it. Then the police officers sign the report. This is exhibited in the following text:[8]

[6] This suspect is underage. Reports for adult suspects do not contain the last three items.

[7] Note that the choice of the term 'stated' does not specify whether the information was volunteered or elicited.

[8] In Dutch: 'volhardde hij daarbij'. It is a routine phrase used to conclude the suspect's statement.

```
I have nothing further to state."

After the suspect had read his statement, he stood by it¹ and
signed it.

                                                  Elmer Martina

                                                      (suspect)

This report has been drawn up by us on oath of office and promise of
office respectively, finalised and signed in Amsterdam on the 4th of
March 2008.

The reporting officers,

Henk Bloem (12345) (oath)

F. Balken (67890) (promise)
```

These are the last entries in the report. The suspect and the reporting officers sign the document: the suspect on the right of the page, then the reporting officers underneath their printed names on the left. The reference to their oath and promise of office[9] is meant to convey the truthfulness of the reporting officers and, when ratified through their signatures, the validity of the document is established. As the printing of the document changes a virtual text on a screen into a material object, it becomes physically 'detachable' from its setting (Bauman and Briggs, 1990). This prospectively enables the police officer and his superiors to ship it off to other desks and other places and to serve the purposes of those professionals who will be dealing with the case.

When documents are drawn up to serve as representations of something else, in our case of police interrogations, the question invariably arises as to their *authenticity* and *accuracy* (Drew, 2006: 64). The *authenticity* of a police report relates to its form, and is based on the correspondence of the document with what it claims to be: a genuine police report and, by implication, a valid piece of evidence; the *accuracy* of the document relates to its content, and is based on the correspondence of the text of the suspect's statement with what it claims to represent: the talk in the interrogation. These two features are displayed in the two different sentences that introduce the signing of the document. These sentences reveal that the

[9] Police officers take their oath or promise of office when they are installed. The difference between the promise and the oath is that in the oath God is invoked, in the promise it is not.

suspect and the police officers sign for different things: the suspect signs for the accuracy of his or her statement, and the reporting officers for the authenticity of the report. In combination with the entries in the beginning of the document these texts frame the suspect's statement as embedded in the appropriate legal and institutional procedures. The visibility of this underlines the authoritative and factual character of the document (Benson and Drew, 1978: 89).

The texts considered thus far show various shifts of footing by the reporting officers (Goffman, 1981). The first occurs when, after the introductory bureaucratic texts, they introduce themselves and describe their activities; this shift is recognisable in the layout of the document and in their use of the personal pronouns 'we' and 'us'. A next shift of footing occurs when they start reporting the suspect's talk; this can be recognised by the opening of quotation marks and by the use of the personal pronoun 'I' as standing for the suspect. The completion of the suspect's reported talk is marked by another shift of footing, where the reporting officers return to their own text, and where the 'I' representing the voice of the suspect is substituted by the reporting officers' description of 'the suspect' and their use of 'us'. Analogous with Goffman's dissection of speakers' roles, these shifts of footing can be seen as shifts in the alignment of the reporting officers to the texts that they write. For the reporting officers' initial alignment I propose the term 'form-filler' which indicates that they merely activate a set text already programmed in the computer; they then shift to the perspective of 'writer-author' to indicate that it is their own text that they are producing; and finally they become the 'reporter' of the suspect's text, of which the suspect is presented as the 'author'.

Thus, the reporting officers' 'writing roles' mark their alignment to the texts they write and to the professional tasks they perform. As 'form-filler' they follow standard bureaucratic routines that display who are responsible for the document and what kind of document it is; as 'writer-authors' they introduce their current professional commitments and display their adherence to proper procedures; and as 'reporter' they yield the floor to the suspect who is treated as the 'author' of the text to come.

3.2.3 The Contextual Framing of the Suspect's Statement

The suspect's statement is framed further by the texts immediately surrounding it. The two sentences introducing the suspect's statement concern the articulation of the right to silence (the caution) and its acceptance; the two sentences following the suspect's statement mark the completion of the statement:[10]

```
After we informed the suspect that he was not obliged to answer
questions and about what we wished to question him he stated: "

"I understand that you wish to question me and that I am not obliged
to answer questions.
...
...
...
I have nothing further to state."

After the suspect had read through his statement, he stood by it and
signed it.
```

These texts are standard (with slight variations) for all the police reports. As mentioned before, it is a legal requirement that suspects be informed of their right to silence and that this be written down in the police report as having been done. As the law does not require the interrogators to ensure that the caution is understood, the next sentence, the suspect's reported response ('I understand that you wish to question me and that I am not obliged to answer questions') is optional, although it features in most of the police reports in our materials. This is the first time that the suspect figures directly as 'author' of the text of the police report. The sentence is recognisable as a response to the caution, and can be read as the suspect's recognition and confirmation of the voluntariness of his statement. Whereas the right to silence can be accepted passively, the inclusion of this sentence in the police report exhibits what seems to be the suspect's active adoption of a willingness to talk and, by implication, an absence of police pressure.[11]

The quotation marks and the direct reported speech style make the current words appear as literal reproductions of the words spoken in the original context of the police interrogation (Clift and Holt, 2007; Holt, 2000; Matoesian, 1999). However, my materials show that these sentences are reported without equivalent talk in the interrogation; in some cases, suspects are asked if they understand the caution, which they always confirm; but suspects never volunteer expressions of their understanding of their right to silence and of their willingness to talk. Thus, the suspects' reported responses to the caution are routine texts rather than representations of the talk in the interrogation, and create an impression of the suspects' voluntariness and of their acceptance of the circumstances of the interrogations.

[10] Occasionally a police interrogator reads out the report to the suspect. The sentence then reads: 'After I, reporting officer, had read out to the suspect his/her statement, he/she stood by it and signed it.'

[11] The research materials contain no examples of suspects who refuse to speak or to sign the report.

The suspect's final reported sentence ('I have nothing further to state') suggests that he has initiated the completion of his statement. However, although in many interrogations the suspects are asked if they want to say anything else, they never volunteer this sentence. In other words: it is the interrogator who takes the initiative in moving the interrogation towards its completion, not the suspect. The quotation marks close, and then 'writer-authorship' is returned to the police officers.

The completion of the suspect's statement is usually followed by a sentence such as: 'After the suspect had read through his statement, he stood by it and signed it.' This description of the suspect's actions corresponds only partly with the actual events in the interrogation in the sense that suspects usually read their statement after it is printed, and that they usually sign it. Having read the report suspects sometimes mention spelling mistakes or other minor errors. In those cases, the reporting officer corrects the errors and prints out the report again for the suspect to read and sign. The phrase 'he stood by it' accentuates that this is the version that the suspect will endorse and that he will be accountable for from now on. It suggests some interaction, as if it were a reaction to the interrogator's questioning (e.g. 'are you really sure'?). This does not correspond with events in the interrogations. In 'standing by it' and signing the document the suspect is reported to take responsibility for and to accept authorship of his statement so that, from now on, the 'I' of the suspect's reported statement, for all practical purposes, becomes his voice.

In sum, 'the suspect's statement' begins and ends with routine sentences that, although they are presented as produced by the suspect, bear little or no resemblance to the actual talk in the interrogation. These sentences create an impression of the suspects' understanding and acceptance of the conditions of the interrogation. Furthermore, 'the suspect's statement' is introduced and completed by the reporting officers' sentences which frame it as produced voluntarily and according to the appropriate legal requirements.

3.3 The Suspect's Statement

The suspect's statement, i.e. the text in between the quotation marks, differs from the surrounding texts in significant ways. It is a text that may include an account of the suspect's personal circumstances (the 'social interrogation') but its main substance is the suspect's narrative of 'what happened' (the 'fact-related interrogation'). It is also a text that contains the information that may contribute to building a case. In this section I shall examine the understandability of the suspect's statement for readers who have no access to the original interaction in the police interrogating room. I first discuss some of the global differences between the text of the suspect's statement and the original talk.

I then explore the ways in which the interrogators' orientation to future readership becomes visible in the police reports.

3.3.1 Alterations, Additions and Unreported Items

Comparisons between the spoken interaction in police interrogations and the written texts of the police reports have shown a number of substantive and stylistic differences. Jönsson and Linell, who studied the differences between the spoken dialogues in Swedish police interrogations and the written texts of the police reports, proposed that many of these differences are inherent to the transformation of spoken interaction into written reports and, at a more general level, characteristic of differences between speech and writing, or orality and literacy (1991: 435). They found that in the written versions there is a more elaborated and visible narrative structure, there is more emphasis on a legally relevant perspective, there is a movement from vagueness to precision, from incoherence to coherence, and from emotionality to a more neutral tone (see also: Slembrouck, 1992). In an analysis of US materials, Shuy (1998: 98–104) has found similar differences between the original interrogation and the written police reports: details are added, ambiguities in the spoken interaction are solved in the written text, there is an upgrading of the language into a more middle-class version, and a change of sentence type from simple sentences into complex and compound sentences.

Similar differences can be found in our materials. It is noticeable that many words in the suspects' reported statements are more 'legalistic' or more 'literary' than those in the interrogations (e.g. 'My grandpa died two days ago' is reported as: 'My grandfather passed away recently'), that the sentences are more complex, and the narratives more detailed. These kinds of alterations of the original talk could be explained by the 'double recipiency' of the police officers' language: in the interrogation they address the suspect in a colloquial style, and in the report they address future professional readers in language that could be understood as an 'upgrading' of the talk into an idiom more pertinent to its future legal uses. The result is 'a hybrid form of expression, mixing bureaucratic forms with colloquialisms' (Jönsson and Linell, 1991: 430–1).

A comparison of the police reports with the interrogations in our materials shows that only a small part of the interrogations is reported (cf. Malsch et al., 2015). As discussed in Chapter 2, this may be partly a result of the practical constraints of contemporaneous reporting. Another reason is that reporting officers almost inevitably select the items that they consider 'recordable' and appropriate for inclusion in the report (Malsch et al., 2012). The most evident underreported feature of the interrogations is the interaction between the interrogator and the suspect, not only in the monologue-style reports but also although to a lesser extent, in the question–answer and recontextualised monologue-style reports. It has been found that in the Q–A-style reports roughly one in five of the questions asked in the interrogation is reported; in the RM-style reports around one in six of the interrogator actions is written down (De Boer, 2014; see also: Malsch et al., 2015). In spite of the fact that RM-style police reports cover more interrogator actions than the Q–A-style reports, they show a more limited coverage of the talk. This may be due to the 'writer unfriendliness' of this reporting style (see Chapter 2).

Besides questioning the suspect, police officers have a number of practical tasks that are never reported. For example they give suspects coffee or tea and inform them about what they can expect in the further criminal law process. There may also be some social talk that is not reported: police interrogators try to calm down suspects who are anxious or sad, and they sometimes give advice to suspects who seem to have lost control over their lives. In our materials four suspects start crying at some point in the interrogation. One of them is a woman who has brought along her dog, who is also whimpering. The interrogator takes them out on a walk until they have calmed down; at their return the interrogation is continued. In another interrogation the suspect enters the interrogation room with his arm bandaged and in a sling. The interrogator informs him that a doctor is on his way to attend to it. At the end of the encounter there is some more 'social talk'. The suspect tells the interrogator that he recently tried to slash his wrists. The interrogator expresses his concern, advises him to seek help and to start taking responsibility for his life instead of blaming the circumstances. These kind of practical tasks and interpersonal exchanges are generally treated as falling outside the scope of the interrogation proper, and are not written down. Police reports appear to favour topics about 'the facts' rather than about the interpersonal exchanges between the suspect and the police officer.

Readers may become aware of possible unreported interrogator actions when suspects are reported to have produced descriptions that one would not normally volunteer or stories that one would not normally tell. One of the most telling 'absences' in a monologue-style report is the sequence in an interrogation that develops after the interrogator tells the suspect that he does not believe the story she is telling about the theft of a display case from a market stall:

```
(1)
1. Then I bit the lady of the market stall where I bought the brooch in
2. her wrist. I did not bite hard. I bit her because she was pulling at me.
3. I have not told the whole truth, but I shall tell you the truth now.

4. I said that Clive took away the display-case from the market stall.
5. That is not so, for I actually took away the display-case myself
6. from the market stall.
(15, O)
```

Denying suspects do not usually change their position without some inducement from the interrogators. Indeed, a comparison with the talk in the interrogation shows that between lines 2 ('I bit her because she was pulling at me') and 3 ('I have not told the whole truth') there is half an hour of interaction that is not written down, in which the interrogator gradually steers the suspect towards a position that eventually results in a confession (see: Chapter 2; Komter, 2003). Although it can be inferred that the suspect's admission that she has not told the truth (line 3) is responsive to some unreported interrogator actions, the text gives no information about what actions the interrogator took, nor how much effort it took to persuade the suspect to confess. There is only the white line between lines 3 and 4.[12]

Thus, a global comparison of the talk in the interrogations and the text of the police reports shows that items that are usually not included in the report are both the personal and emotional exchanges between the interrogator and the suspect, and some of the more adversarial and investigative actions of the interrogator. This creates an impression of rational and goal-directed relations between the suspects and the interrogators, whereas they are often more personal, more emotional and more contentious.

3.3.2 Correct Procedures

If a police report is to serve as a piece of evidence, it has to contain all the elements of the offence that are required for its adjudication. One of the prerequisites for establishing suspects' guilt and 'punishability' is their knowledge of the illegality or wrongness of what they are accused of (*mens rea*). In Chapter 2 I have shown how interrogators who question the suspect on these points may show an awareness of the 'silliness' of their questions (see also Stokoe and Edwards, 2008). This may result in what can be read as a 'silly answer' or a 'silly expression', especially when a suspect's answer to such a question is reported in the monologue style:

```
(2)
1. I know that it is forbidden to possess or sell an unlawfully
2. obtained passport.
(1, O)
```

It is not very likely that suspects would utter these sentences of their own accord; it is clearly meant for future readers of the report and especially for the judges who have to decide on a legally correct verdict.

[12] I have preserved the original layouts of the police reports.

The next excerpt is from a case where the suspect is accused of having stolen flowers from a flower shop. She was roaming the streets of Amsterdam in the middle of the night; the shop had left a number of flower pots outside, behind a barred gate. The suspect had the feeling that the flowers were imprisoned, and decided to 'liberate' them:

(3)

1. I had the flowers in my arms and walked away.
2. Then I was arrested by the police.
3. The flowers are not my property.
4. I thought at that moment that I was allowed to take them.
5. I felt pity for them. Now I know that it is not allowed.
6. I am willing to pay for the damages.

(5, O)

In this episode it may be inferred that the interrogator elicited the sentence 'the flowers are not my property' (line 3). As mentioned before, interrogators anticipate the reading of the report by the judge, who has to be given sufficient information about all the elements of the crime description of theft in the Criminal Code. The sentence in line 4 seems to have been elicited by the interrogator's questions about the suspect's state of mind at the time of the offence. In this case it is possible that the suspect cannot be held responsible for her acts, because she thought she was allowed to take the flowers (line 4). However, at the moment of the interrogation she appears to be aware of the wrongness of her acts (line 5) and to accept full responsibility, even to the point that she is reported to be willing to pay for the damages. Here the reporting officer anticipates the relevance of her willingness to make amends (line 6) to the prosecutor, who may now conclude the case immediately (somewhat similar to plea-bargaining), obviating a trial.

A comparison with the interrogation shows that every item in this episode has been elicited by the interrogator. As the monologue style transforms responses into first-position actions, the suspect's agreement with the question about paying for the damages is reported as a self-initiated offer (line 6). This overstates the suspect's voluntariness, especially as she added to her agreement to pay for the damages: 'I'll jolly well have to'.

The following excerpt is another example of a monologue-style report, where the suspect, who is accused of having stolen money from registered letters, seems to volunteer legally relevant details:

(4)

1. I have never opened letters, or brought letters to Mick.
2. I have never stolen or embezzled.
3. It is all right if you take a look in my house
4. and search. I understand that I can refuse it.

(18, O)

The suspect's reported denials (lines 1–2) are followed by his permission for his house to be searched (line 3), and by an expression of his understanding that he can refuse this (line 4). Again, it may be inferred that these last two sentences have been pronounced in response to unreported actions of the police detective. In fact, they correspond with the following actions in the interrogation: the interrogator summarised the suspect's denials, asked him if the police could search his house and notified him of his right to refuse it. Later on, acting on the suspect's reported permission, the detectives found sixty-four torn-open envelopes of registered letters in the suspect's house. When the suspect was confronted with this he confessed to the theft.

In the Netherlands, if a suspect gives permission for his house to be searched, the police can do that immediately, while still keeping the suspect in custody. This not only increases the chances that they find something incriminating, it also speeds up matters. Without the suspect's permission the police would have to submit the request to the investigating judge, who would then have to decide on whether there is enough evidence to legitimise a house search. Thus, the report of the suspect's permission to search his house, and of his understanding of his rights, allows the police detective to take a procedural shortcut.

The proactive work of the reporting officers can also be seen in their efforts to display 'proper arrest'. A precondition for making a proper arrest is that the police detective must have a 'reasonable suspicion of guilt' (Code of Criminal Procedure, section 27):

```
(5)
1. During the sales transaction with the latter person I was arrested
2. by two police functionaries in plain clothes, together with the seller.
(2, O)
```

This example shows that the police made a correct arrest because the suspect has been caught in the act: he was seen buying drugs (line 1). Note that the suspect seems to express himself in a literary style that is probably not his own. A comparison with the talk shows that the only contribution of the suspect to this text is his confirmation that he was arrested while he was selling methadone pills. The rest of the text has no equivalent in the original talk.

These examples show that the report is designed to display that the reporting officers know and anticipate the needs of the professionals who will deal with the case in the further criminal law process. The police report is not just a report of 'what happened', but also a specimen of 'good work' (Zimmerman, 1969: 329). This involves the interrogators' adding items that have no equivalent in the talk and their highlighting those items that may be of use for the professionals who will deal with the case. The display of 'proper procedures' contributes to the authoritative status of the documents (Benson and Drew, 1978: 89).

The most pervasive difference between the text and the talk is the transformation of the interaction. In the following sections, more detailed comparisons between the text and the talk will be discussed in conjunction with the writing styles of the police reports.

3.4 The Monologue Style

The monologue style seems to be a fairly general feature of judicial reports in Germany (Scheffer, 1998), the UK (Rock, 2001; Coulthard, 2002), Switzerland,[13] France (González Martínez, 2000) and Belgium (Smets and Ponsaers, 2011; D'hondt, 2014). That this is not just a western phenomenon is shown in an anthropological study among Mexican Indians. During his research among the Tzotzil Indians in Mexico, Haviland asked his respondents to transcribe a tape-recorded multiparty gossip session and a staged conversation. He concluded:

> The process of writing seems to allow a pragmatic restructuring, tending towards an ultimately monologic form, where propositional content takes precedence over the indexical microcosm of the parent interaction, and where interactive richness is pruned in favor of monologic narrative. (1996: 69)

The transformation of the original talk into a monologue-style report changes the sequential basis for the interpretation of the text, as the suspects' reported utterances can no longer be interpreted within their sequential context. That is, when the interrogator's questions are not reported, the suspects' answers, originally uttered in a second position, have become what seems to be a volunteered telling. It has been pointed out that there is an important difference between volunteered stories and invited stories. In volunteered stories the teller controls the production of the story, whereas invited stories are to a certain extent directed at what the recipient wants, and has asked, to hear (Watson, 1990: 275–6). In the monologue-style reports this distinction is blurred (Jönsson and Linell, 1991: 434; see also: Shuy, 1998).

One of the features of 'adjacency pairs' such as question–answer pairs is that, when a question has been produced and an answer is not forthcoming, the answer is seen as 'noticeably absent' (Schegloff and Sacks, 1973). In the monologue-style reports the first pair parts, such as questions or accusations, are absent; they may be 'noticeably absent' when the report contains phrases, sentences or narratives that people would not normally volunteer. In the following sections I shall discuss what inferences about 'missing' interrogator actions may be drawn from the suspect's written statements.

[13] Nadja Capus, personal information.

3.4.1 *Narrative (In)coherence*

When monologue-style reports contain coherent narratives, it may be difficult to infer from the text to what extent the interrogator has helped shape it. An example is an interrogation in a case of shoplifting (Komter, 2002–3):

```
(6)
1.  This afternoon, I think at about three o'clock,
2.  I went to de Bijenkorf in order to steal a T-shirt.
3.  For I only have one shirt left. On the ground floor
4.  I took a T-shirt worth Fl. 15,- from a rack and put it under my coat.
5.  Then I walked out of the store without paying.
6.  Outside I was stopped by two security men. No alarm gates went off.
7.  I said to those security men: "Here, I have this",
8.  and then I gave them the T-shirt.
9.  Then I had to come with them and later I was picked up by the police.
10. The T-shirt was not mine and I had no permission to take it away.
11. I wanted to have it for myself.
12. I have nothing further to ask or to say."
(17, O)
```

The text more or less follows narrative conventions: it is told in the order in which the events originally occurred, it includes introductory information about time, place and circumstances, it contains a narrative that is told in the temporal order of the original events, and it has a recognisable end (Labov and Waletzky, 1967). Although it is likely that the suspect's account has been elicited by an unreported question such as: 'can you tell me what happened this afternoon?', most of it may have been volunteered without any inducement from the interrogator.

However, there are a few sentences that could suggest that there has been some input from the interrogator. The most obvious example is line 10. As a suspect is not likely to volunteer the information that the T-shirt was not his and that he had no permission to take it away (cf. Stokoe and Edwards, 2008), one might infer that this information was entered at the request of the interrogator. The legal professionals who will read this report will understand that the sentence is inserted to achieve legal adequacy by naming all the elements of the crime description in the Criminal Code. The report shows some other signs of interrogator actions. From the denial ('no alarm gates went off', line 6) it may be inferred that it has been uttered in response to a question of the interrogator, as the suspects' accounts are supposed to describe 'what happened' instead of what did not happen (Coulthard, 2002: 30). And, finally, one may wonder whether the suspect would have completed his statement on his own initiative (line 12).

A comparison with the talk in the interrogation shows that the 'fact-related' interrogation starts out with two open questions by the interrogator about 'what happened'. In answer to this the suspect said: 'I went into the store,

I put a T-shirt under my coat, I walked out and I got caught'. All the other information in the suspect's written statement is given at the request of the interrogator, who produces thirty-four additional questions or other actions to elicit this narrative. The text has retained all the elements of the suspect's original narrative, with only slight alterations in phrasing. The suspect's answers to the additional questions have enabled the interrogator to add details about the time of the theft, the reasons for the theft, the location and the cost of the shirt. Moreover, he has added information about the circumstances of the stop and search (lines 6–9), and the legal requirements for identifying the theft (lines 10–11). And, finally, the initiative to end the interrogation was the interrogator's, not the suspect's (Komter, 2001; 2002–3).

The next excerpt is taken from a police interrogation where the suspect is accused of having stolen or embezzled registered letters from the post office where he works, together with his colleague Mick:

```
(7)
1. I wonder why he mentioned my name and not someone else's.
2. I must say that I also gamble a lot.
3. Yesterday I made a telephone call at the Central Station.
4. I got a telephone card. I did not go to the lockers.
5. I went to the book store and bought a magazine.
6. It is right that I also have financial problems.
(18, O)
```

In this part of the report the suspect seems to have produced isolated sentences with little or no apparent connection. This supports the inference that the incoherence of the text is a result of the absence of the reporting of the interrogators' questions. The text contains two other indicators of possible unreported interrogator actions: a denial (line 4) that seems to come 'out of the blue' and a seemingly unsolicited confirmation (line 6).

A comparison with the original talk reveals that almost every item in this excerpt has been told at the instigation of the interrogators, who confronted the suspect with the confession and accusations of his colleague Mick. According to Mick, whose motive for stealing the money was his gambling habit, they hid the stolen envelopes in a locker at Amsterdam Central Station. With this background knowledge it becomes understandable that the unreported questions of the interrogator concerned the suspect's gambling (line 2), his activities at the station (line 3), and his financial situation (line 6); it also becomes understandable that the suspect's reported account of his doings (lines 3–5) and his denial (line 4) are defensive actions in response to the accusatory implications of the unreported question about his activities at the Central Station.

The following reported episode shows the end of the social interrogation, and the introduction to the 'fact-related' part of the report:

```
(8)
1. Sometimes I smoke joints. Formerly I was addicted but now
2. I do not consider myself addicted.

3. I wish to tell you the following about last evening.
4. Yesterday evening I drove in a car of a friend.
5. The car is a white Mercedes.
(7, O)
```

The reporting officer has marked the topic shift between the social and the 'fact-related' interrogation by inserting: 'I wish to tell you the following about last evening' (line 3).

A direct consequence of the absence of interviewer activities in the monologue style is that transitions between conversational activities that are typically organised by the police interrogator, such as 'introducing the fact-related interrogation' or 'changing the topic', now seem to be the managed by the suspect. This not only creates an impression of the suspect's voluntariness, but it also seems to attribute to him some degree of conversational control. A comparison with the interrogation shows that the suspect's reported conversational initiative (line 3) was added by the reporting officer and does not correspond with the talk.

3.4.2 Unsolicited Denials

As mentioned above, when a police report contains a suspect's denial it may be inferred that it has been uttered in response to an unreported question of the interrogator. Moreover, in the police setting the suspect's denials may be taken as responsive to the police officers' accusatory actions (see also excerpt 7, line 4):

```
(9)
1. I got frightened, considering that he might have a fire arm again.
2. We did not swear at one another, we did yell at one another.
3. In this altercation I did not threaten to kill Tim.
4. The witnesses will confirm this if they at least tell the truth.
(11, O)
```

The suspect is reported to have denied two things that may be consequential for an assessment of the case: that he swore and yelled at the alleged victim (line 2) and that he threatened to kill him (line 3). It could be inferred that the suspect would not have uttered these sentences if they had not been elicited by the interrogator. What remains invisible, however, is the amount of effort the interrogator put in to elicit a 'recordable' answer. A comparison with the talk shows that the suspect's denial of the threat to kill Tim (line 3) was not immediately accepted by the interrogator. In the course of this exchange the interrogator wrote down the answer only after the suspect had uttered his denial six times. Thus, the reported denial is a result of the interrogator's unreported question and, because the interrogator's follow-up actions have not been reported, the sentence understates the antagonistic atmosphere of this part of the interrogation. This example also exhibits a feature of police reports discussed above: suspects sometimes seem to use a 'literary' vocabulary. The word 'altercation'[14] (line 3) may appear remarkable, as it is unlikely that suspects would express themselves in this way. In fact, this word has no equivalent in the original talk.

The next excerpt shows how a seemingly unsolicited negation may foreshadow future problems:

```
(10)
1. The knife set, that was kept by the store.
2. I was not asked permission for the return of that set,
3. but I do agree with it.
4. The knife set was not my property and I had no permission to
5. take that away and appropriate it.
(8, O)
```

After the text in the report that the suspect was not asked permission for the return of the knife set (line 2), the suspect's retrospective permission is added (line 3). This could be explained by the legal requirements pertaining to an arrest in this case. It is procedurally efficient when a suspect, who is in possession of stolen goods on his arrest, returns them voluntarily; otherwise it might be necessary for the investigating judge to be called in to confiscate the goods and establish who is the rightful owner of the goods, before they can be returned. Thus, the reporting officer takes a procedural shortcut by obviating the intervention of the investigating judge, and he does a procedural patch-up by repairing something that might cause procedural problems in the further criminal law process. It will come as no surprise that in the interrogation the suspect did not volunteer this information; every item of this text was elicited or proposed by the interrogator.

3.4.3 Details One Would Not Volunteer

A number of suspects are reported to have started their statement by mentioning details about the time and place of the alleged events. In the next excerpt the suspect is reporting something that happened earlier that day:

```
(11)
1. Today, Saturday the 8th of May 1999 at around twenty to six I walked
2. in the Sint Anthoniestraat in Amsterdam.
(5, O)
```

[14] In Dutch: 'twistgesprek'.

As mentioned in Chapter 2 (excerpt 25) these details were elicited to accommodate the requirements of the prosecution officers' tasks of drawing up the indictment. As people normally do not go into such detail when they talk about what they did that day, it can be inferred that these details were told at the interrogator's request.

Other details that suspects regularly seem to have volunteered are descriptions of their accomplices or of other people present at the scene of the crime. In the following excerpt the suspect is reported to have told the interrogator that he met a Moroccan man who gave him a passport and asked him to sell it. The suspect's narrative continues:

(12)

```
1. That Moroccan is around 33-35 years old, typical North African, hair
2. resembling mine, length around 180 cm, presumably right-handed, no
3. moustache or beard, dressed in jeans.
(1, O)
```

As there are many ways in which to describe a person, a selection will be made on the basis of what is the appropriate form for the circumstances at hand (Schegloff, 1996). This type of person description is fairly common in police reports. As this is a typical classification for identification purposes (Kameo and Whalen, 2015) it is unlikely that the suspect would have volunteered this particular description. In fact, each of these items was elicited from the suspect by the interrogator. Details about time and place of the criminal events, and about the looks of the suspect's acquaintances, anticipate the usefulness of this information for the prosecutor's task of drawing up the indictment and for the further investigations by the police into the identification of possible witnesses or accomplices.

3.4.4 Recontextualisation Phrases in Monologue-Style Reports

An awareness of the limitations of the monologue style may be the reporting officers' motivation for inserting their own actions into the police report by way of 'recontextualisation phrases' (Komter, 2006c). The suspect in the following excerpt is a drug addict, who has received a restraining order. He has been arrested because he was spotted in a forbidden area:

(13)

```
1. This afternoon at around 14.00 hrs I was arrested
2. on the Gelderse kade. I was there in order to look for Leo.
3. That is a Surinam friend of mine. For Leo had my house keys.
4. You ask me where I slept the past few days.
5. Well, simply at home with my brother and my mother.
6. You tell me that Leo had my house keys,
```

7. so that I would not be able to enter the house.
8. I told you before that Leo also sleeps at my and
9. my brother' s place.
(13, O)

Although the police report initially reads as if the suspect volunteers the information, it is likely that the interrogator has asked the suspect for his reasons for being in the area. The suspect explains that he was there in order to look for his friend Leo who had his house keys (lines 1–3).This leads the interrogator to go more deeply into the suspect's account, this time recognisably so, by way of two recontextualisation phrases ('you ask me', line 4 and 'you tell me', line 6).

If the interrogator's actions would have been left out of this reported narrative it could have resulted in a monologue-style text such as:

This afternoon at around 14.00 hrs I was arrested on the Gelderse kade. I was there in order to look for Leo. That is a Surinam friend of mine. For Leo had my house keys. The past few days I simply slept at home with my brother and my mother. I told you before that Leo also sleeps at my and my brother's place.

It will be clear that the absence of the interrogator's activities from the police report would result in a text that is difficult to understand; the recontextualisation phrases shown in lines 4 and 6 provide some of the cohesion of the text and the motivation of the suspect's reported talk. Thus, the reporting officer's insertion of part of his own talk in the police report helps the reader's understanding by this display of how the suspect's narrative has come about.

The insertion of a recontextualisation phrase, apart from giving readers a sense of what went on in the interrogation, can also display that the interrogator is 'doing a good job'. The following excerpt is an example:

(14)

1. I haven' t touched anything in this market stall, with the
2. exception of the brooch that I bought.
3. I just looked with my eyes.
4. You tell me that the lady of the market stall has seen
5. that I took a brooch, and gave it to my daughter.
6. I can reply to this that this is not true.
7. I did give a brooch to my daughter, but I put it back later.
8. You repeat once more what the lady of the market stall has seen,
9. and what my statement to that was.
10. You now ask me what I mean with, that it is not true
11. what the woman of the market stall has seen.
12. I mean that I did not give the brooch to my daughter,
13. but that I showed it to her. The woman of the market stall
14. accused me of having taken away the brooch,
15. but I told her that I had not taken away the brooch.

(15, O)

This fragment begins with the suspect's claim that she did not touch anything in the market stall that she did not buy, which is corroborated by her contention that she only looked with her eyes (line 3). The 'you tell me' phrase and the sentence that follows shows that the police interrogator confronts the suspect with an inconsistency between her account and the witness's statement. The suspect denies it, but gives an account that does not appear to support her denial: she accedes that she did touch a brooch but she asserts that she put it back later. In the subsequent recontextualisation phrases ('you repeat once more', line 8; 'you now ask me', line 10) the reporting officer exhibits his continued dissatisfaction with the suspect's answers. These phrases afford an understanding of the text that the 'pure' monologue style cannot; they enable readers to infer that the suspect, under some pressure from the interrogator, provides an erratic and inconsistent account of her activities. This text gives a fair representation of the actions and the antagonistic atmosphere in the interrogation. What the report does not show however, is the effect of the hostile questioning on the suspect, who started to cry and asked for a paper handkerchief.

In sum, the absence of interrogator actions in the monologue-style police reports suggests that the suspect has volunteered the information, whereas most of the texts assigned to the suspect were elicited. Vestiges of unreported interrogator actions may be inferred from texts that contain narrative incoherence, denials that seem to come 'out of the blue' or details one would not volunteer, but the precise nature of the interrogators' original actions remains obscure. As a result, readers cannot tell the difference between what interrogators have wanted to hear and what suspects have wanted to tell. By way of an inclusion of 'recontextualisation phrases' reporting officers put some of their actions on display and make the suspects' reported contributions understandable as responses to prior actions. As recontextualisation phrases can describe hostile interrogator actions they may convey a more adversarial atmosphere of the interrogation, something that the 'pure' monologue style cannot.

3.5 The Question–Answer Style

Whereas the monologue style foregrounds the substance of the suspect's statement, the Q–A style also exhibits some of the interactional conduct of reporting officers and suspects. Questions and answers do not just request and provide information, they also perform a range of actions, dependent on the setting or context within which they are produced. In the police setting, a question may be heard as an accusation, or as leading up to an accusation, and the answer may then be produced and interpreted as a defence (cf. Atkinson and Drew, 1979).

Questions and answers presuppose differential access to an epistemic domain (Stivers and Rossano, 2010): questions may convey what and how much the questioner knows, and what and how much the recipient is likely to know. The act of asking a question invokes the claim that the questioner lacks certain information that the recipient is supposed to know, which makes the question recognisable as a 'request for information' (Heritage, 2012a); questions that are asked from a position of knowledge tend to be recognised as criticisms or challenges (Hayano, 2012: 410). These kind of questions may occur in disaffiliative or confrontational environments (Steensig and Drew, 2008: 9).

The increased adoption of the Q–A style in Dutch police reports is motivated by the idea that it gives a more faithful representation of the suspect's statement than does the monologue style. It enables the readers of the police report to interpret the suspects' utterances in context, that is, as answers responsive to questions, rather than as volunteered statements. This means that also the investigative actions of the interrogator and the degree of cooperation and reasonability of the suspect may become visible in the reports (Clayman, 1990: 97).

In the following sections I shall examine how and to what extent reported questions and answers allow readers to draw inferences about the original conduct of interrogators and suspects. I shall first discuss questions that are recognisable as requests for information; I then look into the effect of the interrogator's knowledge on the type of reported questions and answers; and finally I shall inspect what the interrogator's reported 'next questions' reveal about how the suspect's prior answers have been understood.

3.5.1 *Requests for Information*

In police interrogations the suspect is treated as having first-hand knowledge of 'the facts', whereas police detectives may have some knowledge from other sources, such as witness statements, or reports of prior police investigations. Basically, questions oriented to obtaining information about the alleged criminal events are hearable as 'requests for information'; the suspects are held accountable for providing this information (Heritage, 1984a: 250). In the following I shall discuss what can be inferred about the 'fit' between the interrogators' reported requests for information and the suspects' reported answers, and how this relates to the original talk.

As mentioned before, police interrogators often start the 'fact-related' part of the interrogation by asking the suspect to tell them 'what happened'. The following excerpt is from a case in which the suspect allegedly stole his girlfriend's telephone:[15]

[15] In my collection of police reports questions are introduced as 'Q:' or 'Question:' and answers as 'A:' or 'Answer:' I shall do the same in the excerpts.

(15)

1. Q: Can you tell me in your own words what happened yesterday
2. according to you.
3. A: Yes. I shall tell you what happened.
4. I was in my house together with my girlfriend.
5. I had actually bought a new SIM card for her that day.
6. Because it is a new SIM card, no one else knows her number.
7. Yet I noticed that she was being called several times.
8. But each time she did not answer the phone.
9. I have the feeling that she lies to me actually.
10. She probably does things but does not tell me anything.
11. Together we went on the way to her house. While I was standing in
12. front of her apartment building a man approached on a moped.
((narrative continues, 7 lines))

(15, N)

The reporting officer's reported question is an open question ('tell me . . . what happened') that does not constrain the answer but invites a free narrative, a story about 'what happened'. The suspect's reported answer seems to be in line with the type of question: he is asked for a narrative and he provides one. His reported narrative begins with an introduction: a description of the circumstances that may be relevant for an understanding of the story to come (lines 4–10). After having explained the circumstances that provoked his doubts about his girlfriend's honesty, the suspect proceeds with a description of their activities in the temporal order in which they occurred (lines 11–12). If it were not for the inclusion of the initial question the writing style resembles that of the monologue style, because there is no further reference to the police detective's contributions.

A comparison with the interrogation shows that, apart from the initial question, the interrogator produced twenty-six other actions such as questions, comments or assertions in the course of the episode. The suspect, who is from the Antilles and speaks broken Dutch, gave a rambling and often incomprehensible account of what happened. As a drug addict, he kept yawning and, in the course of the interrogation, he tended to fall asleep in his chair. The interrogator told the suspect not to fall asleep and gave him coffee to keep him awake. His actions were directed at eliciting an account and at making sense of what the suspect told him, especially by means of requests for clarification and confirmation. Thus, the coherence in the suspect's reported answer is an achievement of the interrogator and a result of his questioning.

It can be expected that the passages in the reports with more closed questions and with a higher question density would give more transparent representations of the original interaction. Consider the following excerpt:

(16)
1. Question: Who else visit your uncle' s house?
2. Answer: My friends and my brother.

3. Question: Who are your friends then?
4. Answer: Right to silence.

5. Question: How did you come by those fake drugs?
6. Answer: I made it myself with wheat flour and salt, at home.
7. With that I mean in the kitchen of my uncle' s house.
(7, N)

The questions in this exchange seek specific information, and the answers to the first two questions are direct responses that address the substance of the question. Although the suspect does not answer the second question, his invocation of his right to silence is a 'legitimate' response to the question in this context. The response to the third question (line 6–7) shows that the suspect seems to be 'answering more than the question' (Stivers and Heritage, 2001); he first answers the question ('I made it myself') and then continues with additional information. It cannot be ascertained whether the additional information given in line 6 was volunteered or uttered in answer to further questions. Line 7 may alert the reader to unreported interrogator actions, as people would not normally volunteer an explanation of 'at home'.

Here again, more questions were asked in the interrogation than were reported. A total of nine questions were asked in the course of this exchange and one comment was given. The text of the report suggests that the suspect's invocation of his right to silence (line 4) has been accepted immediately, as the report continues with a next question. In the interrogation however, the interrogator produces an unreported comment on the suspect's invocation of his right to silence. The suspect's reported answer to the third question (lines 6–7) is assembled by combining the responses to four questions asked by the interrogator (see Chapter 2, excerpt 30).

For another example of 'answering more than the question' let us consider a case where the suspect is suspected of dealing in stolen telephones (fencing):

(17)
1. Q: But how did you get the new telephone?
2. A: I bought it on the market in Noord.
3. I sometimes go there on Sundays, then the market is open.
4. The market, also in Beverwijk, is meant for Moroccans,
5. for it is second hand.
(11, N)

The suspect has been arrested with a bag full of telephones; what the interrogator needs to know in cases of fencing is how the suspect acquired the telephones and whether the suspect knew that they were stolen. The suspect not only takes the story further than the question asked for, but his elaborations also portray his doings as 'normal' activities in everyday life. His additions resemble the 'narrative expansions' identified by Galatolo and Drew (2006), that are produced to defend a person against a possible allocation of blame implied in the question. Chapter 2 has shown that suspects often take the opportunity to add defensive turn components such as accounts and justifications in interactional 'slots' that are at first sight 'reserved' for other types of actions (Drew, 1992; Eades, 2000; Galatolo and Drew, 2006; Komter, 2006b). Hence, even though the question and the answer show no perfect fit, it cannot be concluded that fewer questions were reported than were actually asked. In fact, a comparison with the talk in the interrogation shows that most of the suspect's elaborations were volunteered, and that the only intervention of the interrogator has been a request for clarification.

Thus, the assessment of the fit between a reported question and the reported answer depends in part on the kind of reported questions. A reported open question about 'what happened' may be followed by a reported narrative that is hard to distinguish from an account in the monologue style. Whether or to what extent the interrogator helped shape the suspect's account remains invisible. The fit between the reported response to a reported question that projects a concrete and specific answer is easier to assess. However, reported questions that imply blame may be followed by reported answers that cover 'more than the question'. When suspects seem to answer 'more than the question' it is difficult to ascertain from the text whether this is a result of unreported questions or of the suspect's defensive elaborations.

3.5.2 'Knowledgeable' Questions

As mentioned before, the distribution of knowledge has an important impact on the police interrogators' truth-finding efforts (see Chapters 1 and 2). Although the suspect has epistemic priority about 'what happened', the interrogators can bring into play what they assume, conclude or know about the case from other sources. This knowledge can be based on what they have already found out about the case during their prior investigations, or on common knowledge about how people 'normally' commit crimes (Sudnow 1965). The Q–A-style police reports show that the epistemic claims of the interrogators may be asserted and reported with varying degrees of certainty In the following sections I shall discuss the interrogators' increasingly assertive epistemic stances by examining reported questions that suggest that the interrogators may have some knowledge of the case, reported questions that display what they know by 'hearsay', and reported questions that claim or display their own first-hand knowledge of the case.

In the next excerpt the interrogator's knowledge about the case is suggested rather than spelled out:

(18)

1. Q: What do you think of it that you are suspected of street robbery?
2. A: I think it really sucks, because I' m not someone like that.
3. I have my job and I live normally, I have no shortage of money.

4. Q: Did you speak with someone in the street?
5. A: No, I did not speak with anyone in the street.

6. Q: Did you see white people walking around?
7. A: I have only seen dark people, I think they were Africans.

8. Q: Did you see someone from a security agency?
9. A: Not that I know of, no idea, I was drunk and do not walk
10. around looking at people in the street.

(13A, N)

The first request for information introduces the topic and elicits the suspect's stance towards the accusation (line 1). He implicitly professes his innocence by appealing to his character ('I'm not someone like that', line 2) and his lack of motive ('no shortage of money', line 3). At first sight, the next three questions in lines 4, 6 and 8 are also requests for information. These questions follow the same syntactic pattern, starting with: 'Did you . . .'. They do not have any topical relation to the preceding texts in the police report. Although the reported questions have the features of requests for information, they might well be interpreted as requests for verification because they would not make sense if they were not based on some knowledge of the interrogator about the suspect's activities and observations that night. Thus, the assumptions behind the questions are that the suspect might have spoken with someone in the street (line 4), and that he might have seen white people (line 6) or someone from a security agency (line 8). As the interrogator does not spell out the sources of his knowledge, the suspect remains uncertain about how much the interrogator actually knows. It can be inferred then, that the interrogator makes an implicit and strategic use of the knowledge that he has (or seems to have) about the case.

In the more adversarial episodes in the police reports interrogators confront the suspect with discrepancies between what the suspect and the interrogator presumably 'know' about the events. The interrogators may assert their epistemic stance by explicitly naming the sources of their knowledge. This may function to confront the suspects with other people's versions of the events but also to display a 'neutralistic' stance (Clayman and Heritage,

2002: 120). 'Hearsay knowledge' questions typically occur in the more confrontational episodes of the police reports. Consider the following excerpt:

```
(19)
1. Q: If I tell you that witnesses allegedly saw that you
2.    pushed and hit your girlfriend.
3. A: No, that is not possible because they were taking drugs themselves
4.    too and then they walked off at once. So there was nobody there.
(15, N)
```

The question in this excerpt consists of an assertion stating 'witnesses' as the sources of the interrogator's knowledge (line 1). His reference to his source of knowledge allows the interrogator to present himself as only passing on the information that others gave him (Pomerantz, 1984b). In this way he can confront the suspect with accusations without putting himself on display as accusing party. The suspect's reported denial shows his resistance against the accusatory tenor of the question; it also displays his reliance on his epistemic priority: in the last resort, he can claim to know best what has happened. Thus, the interrogator's reported epistemic claim is countered by the suspect's reported reliance on his first-hand knowledge of the case.

It is noticeable that the format of the report is the Q–A style (see Q: and A:, lines 1 and 3), but that the 'question' has the shape of a recontextualisation phrase (line 1). This allows the reporting officer to deal with the limitations of the Q–A style, and to write down an utterance ('if I tell you that . . .') that is recognisable as accusatory. The suspect's response can be seen as defensive, as it contains a denial followed by an account (Atkinson and Drew, 1979). Earlier we saw that when suspects add defensive turn components, it may be difficult to assess whether these were volunteered or elicited (see excerpt 17). A comparison with the talk reported in excerpt (19) shows that the first part of the suspect's account ('they were taking drugs themselves', line 3) was volunteered by the suspect, and that the last two items (line 4) were elicited by the interrogator.

It has been proposed that the possession or lack of knowledge is not a one-dimensional phenomenon, but a 'multidimensional landscape', because people may have different kinds of knowledge about the same things (Sidnell, 2012: 55). Thus, whereas the suspect can claim to have first-hand knowledge of the events, the police detectives may have first-hand knowledge of the evidence that they collected during their investigations (e.g. DNA material, fingerprints, telephone taps). In the next excerpt the police interrogator is reported to have confronted the suspect with the fact that they tapped the suspect's (stolen) telephone, which revealed that the suspect used the telephone before the time that he claimed to have bought it:

(20)
1. Question: We have told you that we have tapped the stolen telephone.
2. So we can see what mobile telephone number it contains at that moment.
3. In this case the mobile number 061537857 was used (your number
4. according to xpol). And this on 21 February 2008 at 01:54 hours.
5. You have stated that you bought the telephone at 12.00.
6. How is that possible?
7. Answer: My card was not in it, that is not possible.
(7, N)

The assertions with which the interrogator introduces his first question are rather elaborate. They are based on knowledge that belongs to the interrogator's epistemic domain, as they refer directly to how the interrogators have conducted their investigations: they have tapped the stolen telephone and they have ascertained its number, its owner and the time when it was used. We see here a clash of two knowledge domains: on the one hand the police interrogator's knowledge derived from the taps that they put on the suspect's phone, and on the other hand the first-hand knowledge of the suspect. The suspect's epistemic priority is exhibited in his reported answer about the location of his SIM card (line 7), suggesting direct access to the relevant facts.

The length of the introduction to the question (lines 1–5) suggests that it is a monologic turn by the interrogator consisting of a series of assertions that serves to confront the suspect with a contradiction between the findings of the police investigation and his stated position. A comparison with the talk in the interrogation shows that, after every component of this introductory information, the interrogator elicited tokens of confirmation or understanding from the suspect. In this way he implicated the suspect in the information so as to suggest that his denial could be seen as self-contradictory. These inferences cannot be drawn from the text of the police report, as the interrogator's elicitations remain unreported.

'Knowledgeable' questions are different from requests for information because, as they express or suggest that the interrogator already has some knowledge of the events, they can be heard as requests for verification or as challenges of the suspect's position. As the Q–A style allows for the reporting of such actions it can convey a sense of the more investigative and adversarial actions of the interrogators.

3.5.3 'Next' Questions

Recipients generally show how they understand the speakers' talk in their next turns (Sacks, Schegloff and Jefferson, 1974). The interrogator's uptake of the suspect's answer in third position may then show whether this answer is accepted or challenged. However, in the Q–A-style reports there is no slot for third-position actions (such as comments or evaluations). As excerpt (16) has shown, the suspect's invocation of his right to silence is followed by a 'next' reported question, which suggests that the interrogator has immediately accepted the suspect's answer. As this remains invisible in the police report, it is difficult to ascertain whether and to what extent the suspects' reported answers were accepted.

In the Q–A-style police reports a 'next turn' after the suspect's reported answer is typically a next question. The following excerpt is an example:

```
(21)
1. Q: What do you think about it that you are suspected
2.    of a robbery at Kleidam.
3. A: I think it is strange, I do not rob people and the fact that
4.    my description corresponds with the perpetrator.[16] I am not violent.

5. Q: Now we are going to talk about last weekend in the town,
6.    what else can you tell me about that?
(12, N)
```

The suspect's reported answer (lines 3–4) is recognisable as a proper response to the question. As in mundane conversations, this would constitute a 'transition relevance point' (Sacks, Schegloff and Jefferson, 1974), giving the first speaker the opportunity to take the floor again. As the reported first question (lines 1–2) is a request for information, the interrogator's reported next question (lines 5–6) conveys that 'enough answer' has been given, at least for the time being. This part of the police report corresponds with the original interaction in the interrogation.

An inspection of my materials shows that denying or 'uncooperative' reported answers may be followed by 'next' questions that pursue the matter further. Let us reconsider excerpt (19) and its continuation:

```
(22)
1. Q: If I tell you that witnesses allegedly saw that you pushed
2.    and hit your girlfriend.
3. A: No, that is not possible because they were taking drugs themselves
4.    too and then they walked off at once. So there was nobody there.

5. Q: Did you hit her?
6. A: No. I did not hit her.

7. Q: Have you ever hit her in the past?
8. A: No. I have never hit her yet.
```

[16] I have translated spelling or syntactical errors with similar errors in English.

9. Q: Have you not threatened her either.
10. A: No. I have not done that either. I have only threatened her
11. by saying: 'I am going away from you. I am going to leave you.'

12. Q: Were you under the influence during the quarrel
13. with your girlfriend in the street.
(15, N)

Initially the interrogator is reported to have formulated the accusation as something that witnesses allegedly saw. The suspect takes this up by accentuating the unreliability of the witnesses' statements ('they were taking drugs', line 3) and their absence from the scene ('they walked off', line 4). This then leads the interrogator to ask the suspect directly about hitting his girlfriend, which the suspect denies. The interrogator pursues the matter with questions about having threatened his girlfriend (line 9) and having been under the influence (line 12). Thus, the police interrogator's reported 'further questioning' conveys that he does not take the suspect's answers at face value. It puts the conduct of the interrogator on display as committed to finding the truth from someone whose (denying) answers need not necessarily be accepted. This is a fair representation of the actual interaction in the interrogation.

Let us now consider the continuation of another fragment discussed earlier (excerpt 20):

(23)
1. Question: We have told you that we have tapped the stolen telephone.
2. So we can see what mobile telephone number it contains at that moment.
3. In this case the mobile number 061537857 was used (your number
4. according to xpol). And this on the 21st of February 2008 at 01.54 hours.
5. You have stated that you bought the telephone at 12.00.
6. How is that possible?
7. Answer: My card was not in it, that is not possible.

8. Question: We have technical proof of it, do you understand?
9. How is that possible?
10. Answer: That is not possible, I tell you, I do not know how it
11. is possible that my number was already in that phone at 01:54.

12. You ask me once more how that is possible.
13. It is not like that, it is not possible. Then you are lying.
(7, N)

We see here a series of three reported questions asking, 'how is that possible?' (lines 6, 9 and 12). The first question is introduced by a detailed account of the available evidence, which shows a pattern that anticipates a potentially hostile sequel: a series of assertions followed by a question (Clayman and Heritage, 2002: 201). The second question is introduced by a conclusion of the first introduction ('we have technical proof', line 8), and the third question is not introduced at all, it stands on itself as a 'you ask me' phrase (line 12).

This example shows that both the interrogator and the suspect claim to know 'the truth' from their own epistemic vantage points: the interrogator has the evidence, the suspect his first-hand experience. They do not seem to make any headway, as both the interrogator and the suspect repeat their positions. However, this episode is informative in that it shows that the interrogator is persistent in confronting the suspect with the evidence, and that he does not give in too easily. It also features the suspect as persistent in his denials in spite of what can be understood as 'solid evidence'. The interrogator and the suspect appear to find themselves trapped in a 'reality disjuncture' (Pollner, 1975) for which the suspect is held accountable: two contradictory versions of the same event cannot both be true. The suspect's final reported utterance 'Then you are lying' (line 13) may then be seen as his solution of this puzzle.

The repetition of the question 'how is that possible' more or less corresponds with the talk in the interrogation. However, the question was not asked three times, as reported, but six. The talk in the interrogation showed two possible reasons for underreporting the adversarial episodes (see Chapter 2): the reporting officer (the interrogation is conducted by two police officers) could not always keep up with the talk between the interrogator and the suspect, and when the atmosphere became tense the reporting officer stopped typing. Thus, even though the report of the interrogator's questions may afford some idea of his 'investigative stance' (Zimmerman, 1969: 331), the degree of adversarialness is underreported.

A comparison with the talk in the interrogation shows that in the course of this exchange the interrogators employed a range of third-position actions displaying that they did not accept the suspects' answers. As these actions remain unreported this also scales down the adversarialness of the original talk. The suspect's last reported sentence ('then you are lying', line 13) seems rather provocative. In reality, the interrogator offered the suspect a way out of their impasse when he ironically concluded that he and his colleague must then have been lying, to which the suspect mumbled an agreement. Thus, the absence in the police report of the interrogator's third-position actions has turned the suspect's original agreement with the interrogator's suggestion that they had been lying into what now appears to be an unsolicited insult.

In sum, Q–A-style reports are not likely to show those actions for which there is no slot in the Q–A format. This is especially noticeable by the absence in the reports of the interrogators' third-position actions, such as comments or evaluations. As a result, Q–A reports may understate the adversarialness of the interrogations.

3.5.4 *Recontextualisation Phrases in Q–A-style Reports*

Excerpt (23) has shown that the last 'question' is formed as a recontextualisation phrase ('you ask me once more how that is possible', line 12). The reason for this style shift may be that the reporting officer felt the need to express some awareness of the fact that the question already has been reported twice. Another reason to include recontextualisation phrases in Q–A-style reports may result from the constraints of a style that does not allow for other actions besides questions and answers (see also excerpt 19):

```
(24)
1.  Question: What exit did you take when you got out at Eendenhof station?
2.  Answer: I took the door on the left. I took the escalator and took the
3.  door on the left. I am sure of that.

4.  You tell me that you have pictures that I took the door on the right.
5.  I tell you, I took the door on the left, I am sure of that,
6.  but if you have proof it may be.

7.  You ask me where I went to first after the exit. I went to the left.
8.  You tell me that I went to the right after I left through the door
9.  on the right. That is on camera. I tell you, I left the metro station
10. on the left. I further invoke my right to silence.

11. Question: Yesterday you signed a waiver ...
(7, N)
```

The first 'you tell me' phrase (line 4) can be read as a motivated rejection of the suspect's prior answer (lines 2–3). This phrase may have been occasioned by the circumstance that comments or assertions do not fit in with the Q–A format of the police report. The reporting officer retains this style in the exchange to come (lines 7–10); the suspect's reported answer to the 'you ask me' phrase (line 7) is followed by a 'you tell me' phrase that introduces another motivated rejection of the suspect's answer (lines 8–9). When the suspect subsequently invokes his right to silence the topic shifts and the Q–A style is resumed (lines 10–11).

The interrogator's confrontation of the suspect with a counter version that is based on prior investigations by the police (the recording of the suspect's movements on CCTV), is reported by way of 'you tell me' phrases. These allow for the reporting of the more antagonistic episodes. However, a comparison with the interrogation shows that a lot of the adversarial actions have not been reported. For example, the suspect's reported invocation of his right to silence is followed by a 'next' reported question (lines 10–11). In reality, the interrogator commented on the possible reasons for the suspect's appeal to his right to silence and challenged him to answer the questions. Only after the suspect invoked his right to silence seven times did the interrogator change the topic and continue with a next question (line 11).

As in the monologue-style reports, recontextualisation phrases may be used to deal with actions other than those which the current reporting style allows for. The phrase 'you tell me' appears to be a solution for the reporting of the otherwise absent third-position utterances of the interrogators. As this phrase is used only occasionally, the full import of the interrogators' third-position actions is difficult to reconstruct from the text.

3.6 The Recontextualised Monologue Style

The recontextualised monologue (RM) style turns the actions of the interrogator (e.g. the asking, the telling) into assertions of those actions by the suspect ('you ask me', 'you tell me'), as if the suspect's reported descriptions of interviewer activities have in fact been those activities in the police interrogation. The RM style is not a uniquely Dutch phenomenon, as it also occurs in Belgium (Smets and Ponsaers, 2011) and in Switzerland.[17] This style differs from the Q–A style in its monologic format, and in that it can comprise more interviewer actions than just asking (usually 'telling'). The RM style differs from both the monologue and the Q–A style in its artificiality and awkwardness, as the suspect is presented as giving voice to both sides of the interaction. Yet in a way RM-style reports are more 'complete' than Q–A-style reports, because they allow for the reporting of more actions such as telling, explaining or showing. In the following sections I shall discuss those phrases that are used most often: 'you ask me' and 'you tell me'.

3.6.1 'You Ask Me' Phrases

The RM style resembles the Q–A style when 'you ask me' phrases are used. These phrases render the suspects' contributions recognisable as answers to the interrogators' questions. Another similarity is that, as only a small portion of the questions asked by the interrogators are reported, it may be difficult to assess whether the suspect has been 'answering more than the question' or whether questions have been left unreported. Excerpt (15) has shown a Q–A-style report that contains an open question about 'what happened', to which the suspect's reported response is a long narrative that is indistinguishable from a monologue-style report. The same can be found in the RM-style reports; the only difference is the grammatical form of the question. The next excerpt is

[17] Nadja Capus, personal communication.

from a police report in which the suspect is asked to explain how he came to be driving a stolen moped:[18]

(25)

1. **You ask me what happened last night.**
2. Last night I walked from Witteveen in the direction of my girlfriend's
3. house, she lives at Diamant. I was going to pick her up at 20.00
4. because we were going to play pool. I was walking there alone.

5. Near the OSC I saw a group of around seven boys whom I know.
6. I know the boys from the street, one of them is called Zachary.
7. I call him Zigi. There were also a couple of mopeds.
8. I asked Zigi if I could borrow his moped for a minute to
9. pick up my girlfriend. I wanted to take her to the pool centre in
10. Drecht. Zigi said that it was fine but that I did have to
11. bring it back quickly.

12. **You ask me how I knew that it was Zigi's moped.**
13. I saw him drive it a couple of times.
14. I don't remember when this was. Last week or something.

15. **You ask me what that moped looked like.**
16. Grey. And for the rest just like a motor scooter.

17. **You ask me about the peculiarities of the moped.**
18. No, not really. Oh yes, the ignition lock had been pulled out.

19. **You ask me how the motor scooter should be started then.**
20. With such a funny iron thing. A kind of rod.

21. **You ask me who started the motor scooter.**
22. It was already on.

23. **You ask me how I know then that the motor scooter**
24. **had to be started with that iron thing.**
25. Zigi gave it to me.
26. He said that I could turn it off with that thing.

(8, N)

The initial 'you ask me' phrase marks the transition from the reported 'social interrogation' to the 'fact-related' part of the report. It may be inferred from the suspect's reported answer that he has been given the opportunity to offer his version of the events without interference from the interrogator, until the next 'you ask me' phrase (line 12). A comparison with the original talk shows that

[18] I have followed the original police report in the bold type writing of the interrogator's reported actions.

initially the interrogator allowed the suspect to tell his version of the events, after which she 'recycled' the telling by asking further questions and writing down the answers as in monologue-style reports (lines 2–11; cf. Van Charldorp, 2014: 14; see also Chapter 2).

The reported exchanges that follow are perhaps easier to reconstruct as they ask for specific items of information about the stolen moped. From the series of questions about the ownership, the looks and the peculiarities of the moped (lines 12, 15 and 17), and about the way to start it (lines 19, 21, 23–4), an impression is given of the accusatory 'direction' of the series of questions (Atkinson and Drew, 1979: 162), suggesting that the suspect could have known that the moped was stolen. On two occasions some unreported interrogator questions may be inferred from the suspect's reported answer: in line 14, where the suspect's reported answer covers more ground than the question asks for, and in line 18, where the suspect appears to suddenly volunteer a change in his position. The other exchanges seem to display question–answer sequences where the suspect immediately answers the questions and the interrogator immediately accepts his answers.

However, a comparison with the talk in the interrogation shows that the interrogator only reported part of her questions and none of her third-position actions. The suspect's reported answers are in fact the result of the interrogator's further probing, her pursuit of answers when she was not satisfied, and her persistence until the suspect eventually affirmed his knowledge of the missing ignition lock (line 18) and of the way to start the moped (line 20). As mentioned before, the small number of reported questions or other actions in RM-style reports may be a result of the 'writer unfriendliness' of this writing style.

3.6.2 'You Ask Me' and 'You Tell Me' Sequences

RM-style reports offer the reporting officers more opportunities for including third-position actions than Q–A-style reports. Most instances of 'you tell me' phrases are recognisable as comments on the preceding answers. The next excerpt shows the continuation of the police report discussed in excerpt (25):

(26)

27. You ask me what happened then
28. Then I went to pick up my girlfriend at her house.
29. She sat down on the back seat and she put the helmet on.
30. On the way to Drecht, in the Koekoekstraat,
31. I was stopped by the police.

32. You tell me that you find that construction of picking up my
33. girlfriend up and bringing her away illogical.

34. Yes but in the meantime I had to babysit my little sister.
35. My cousin and brother were already playing pool and otherwise
36. my girlfriend had to wait at my house and I did not want that.

37. **You ask me if I had a suspicion that the moped was stolen.**
38. No. I also had a moped once where the ignition lock was missing,
39. that is possible, right.

40. **You tell me that you think that I should have known that the moped**
41. **was stolen the moment that I see that the ignition lock is not in it.**
42. I did not know. I just assumed that it was just honest.
(8, N)

The 'you tell me' phrases (lines 32–3 and 40–1) are recognisable as comments on a lack of plausibility of the suspect's reported prior answers (lines 28–31 and 38–9). Apparently, the interrogator does not believe the suspect's description of his activities because they are contrary to common-sense knowledge of what people normally do ('illogical', line 33) and of what people are supposed to know (when a moped has a missing ignition lock, it must have been stolen, lines 40–1).

A comparison with the original talk shows that, in answer to the first question ('what happened then', line 1), the suspect told the interrogator that he picked up his girlfriend and that they were stopped by the police on their way to a café. The other information represented in lines 29–31 was elicited by the interrogator, who asked questions for further elaboration. The interrogator then told the suspect that she did not understand his account. She recapitulated the suspect's version thus far, told him that his activities did not add up, and that the suspect should have known that the moped was stolen when he saw that the ignition lock was missing. The suspect continued to assert that he did not know that the moped was stolen. A discussion followed in which both participants reiterated their positions. This discussion was not reported as the interrogator had stopped typing for about five minutes. It is clear that she did not believe the suspect's account. In this respect the report represents the interrogator's doubts about the suspect's version and the suspect's persistence in denying them. However, the report underrepresents the repetitiveness of the antagonistic exchanges between the suspect and the interrogator.

In sum, the RM style combines features of the monologue and the Q–A style: it has a monologue form and a predominantly Q–A sequential organisation. It is different from the two other reporting styles in that it allows scope for the reporting of more interrogator actions besides asking questions. As it provides for the reporting of the interrogators' third-position actions such as comments or assessments, it can express greater interactional diversity than the Q–A-style reports. Although this reporting style offers some insight into the interrogators' more adversarial actions in the interrogations, this transparency is reduced by the fact that RM-style reports show a relatively smaller number of reported actions than the Q–A-style reports.

3.7 Conclusion

This chapter has shown how the core of the police report, the suspect's statement, is embedded within its textual environments. These environments have been studied by examining the perspectives from which the texts are written and their distance from the core of the police report. The reporting officers relate to the texts they write as 'form-filler', who mechanically reproduce a set text, as 'writer-author', who writes down his or her own text, and as 'reporter', who relays a text attributed to the suspect. These 'writer roles' exhibit their orientation to the bureaucratic requirements of the police report, to their professional responsibilities, and to attributing the 'authorship' of the reported statement to the suspect. The accomplishment of these 'writer roles' provides for the construction of an official document that can serve as a legally adequate piece of evidence.

The reporting officers' 'writer roles' display their alignment to the texts they write. First, the police officers' form-filling role materialises in the anonymous texts that introduce and complete the police report, texts that make the report appear neutral and disinterested, and compatible with the proper bureaucratic and administrative procedures. These texts define the document for what it is and for what it will be used, and identify the organisation and the officers responsible for it. Second, their 'writer-author' role becomes recognisable in the texts that surround the suspect's statement, that are written from their personal professional perspective, and that display their professional identities and tasks. These texts set the stage for the suspect's statement: they introduce the players and the topics, and they exhibit how the rules have been followed. Third, the sentences with which the suspect's reported statement begins and ends frame it as 'authored' by the suspect, and produced voluntarily and in line with the relevant legal requirements. These sentences create an impression of an active suspect, who understands and accepts the conditions of his interrogation, who initiates the conclusion of his statement, and who takes responsibility for its contents. The embedding of the suspect's statement within these bureaucratic and institutional perspectives makes the document recognisable as a valid piece of evidence. The signatures of the participants affirm the authenticity and the accuracy of the document.

The transparency of the suspects' reported statements has been studied by analysing what kind of understandings the written texts afford those who have no access to the original talk in the interrogations. Comparisons of the written texts with the talk in the interrogations have shown the transformations that the suspects' statements have undergone. Substantive differences between the talk in the interrogations and the written reports result from the fact that the reports are summaries in which selections have been made of what the reporting officers consider to be 'relevant' for the case. This creates an impression of rational and goal-directed relations between the suspects and the interrogators, whereas they are often more personal, more emotional and more contentious. More salient differences are the result of the reorganisation of the interaction, related to the writing style used. Each writing style entails specific modifications of the original talk that favour different understandings.

Monologue-style reports foreground the referential meaning of the suspect's statement ('the facts'), disregard the interrogators' contributions, and thus ignore the interactional embedding of the suspect's original talk. The absence of reported interrogator activities may lead to an overestimation of the suspects' cooperation, voluntariness and conversational control, and to an underestimation of the interrogators' investigative and adversarial actions. However, a semblance of voluntariness may also alert the reader to possible unreported interrogator actions, when it concerns items that people ordinarily would not tell or would not produce in a first position.

Q–A-style reports place the suspects' reported utterances within the interactional contexts of answers to questions, and allow for an understanding of the suspects' reported answers as possible 'triggers' of 'next' questions. This writing style enables reporting officers to display the suspects' contributions not just as answers to questions but also as, for example, inadequate or irrational answers to cogent and investigative questions. On the other hand, the selective reporting of questions shows that, as in the monologue-style police reports, the more adversarial episodes are underreported. Another explanation of the underreporting of adversarial episodes is that the Q–A style discourages the reporting of third-position actions such as commenting, asserting and evaluating.

In RM-style reports more actions are reported than just questioning and answering. As RM-style reports can accommodate actions such as commenting or telling, it offers more scope for reporting the more adversarial moments in the interrogations. This does not mean that this writing style gives a more 'accurate' representation of what was said in the interrogations than the monologue and the Q–A styles, as it disregards the syntactic and sequential structure of 'normal' talk and writing. Moreover, probably because of its 'writer unfriendliness', RM-style police reports show an even lower rate of reporting the original questions than the Q–A-style reports, and thus a greater degree of 'monologisation'.

Differences between monologue, Q–A and RM-style police reports are differences of degree as well as of kind. In monologue-style reports there is no reporting of interrogator actions, but these can be reconstructed to some extent by assessing what kind of utterances are usually produced in a first, second or third position, and by comparing the written texts with how people usually tell stories. In both the Q–A and the RM-style reports the relatively small number of the interrogator's questions or other actions in the interrogation that have survived the reporting process blurs the differences with monologue-style reports. This 'monologisation' of the Q–A, and especially of the RM-style police reports, obscures the transparency gained by the reporting of interrogator actions.

4 The Trial

Documents in Action

4.1 Introduction

The police report is now part of a case file that contains not only the suspect's reported statements but also a number of other reports of case-related activities drawn up in earlier stages of the criminal law process by the officials involved in the case. The suspect's reported statement is embedded in a collection of other documents that complete the case file (see Chapter 1, Figure 2), that together serve as evidence for adjudicating the case. This allows the legal professionals in court (judges, prosecutors and defence lawyers) to read the reports as parts of a whole. They can juxtapose suspects' statements and those of witnesses, or compare suspects' statements to the police with those made to the investigating judge or to the judge in court (cf. Lynch, 2015). Moreover, as the case file is assumed to have been drawn up through correct procedures, it achieves the authoritative status of an official collection of legal documents (cf. Benson and Drew, 1978).

Although the case file is readable as 'the same' for every reader, it is meant to accommodate the needs of different professional users and can therefore embody different courses of action (Harper, 1998: 4; Smith, 2001: 175). As judges are legally required to read aloud or summarise in court those passages from the case file that they may need for their verdict in order to ratify them as legal evidence (Code of Criminal Procedure, section 301.4), they are responsible for the great majority of references to the case file in court. The judges' main tasks in court are to organise the court session, and to carry out an examination of the evidence as a disinterested search for the truth; by contrast, the interested parties (prosecutor and defence lawyer) argue the positions of the prosecution or the defence in order to persuade the court of their points of view.

When there is doubt about whether something is true or not, people routinely attend to the sources of their knowledge (Pomerantz, 1984b: 609). This not only holds for 'ordinary' conversation but also for institutional interaction, especially for interaction organised around dispute (Hanks, 2012: 169–70). Courtrooms are places where interaction typically revolves around finding out 'what happened' from a variety of versions based on different knowledge domains (Stivers et al., 2011: 8). In court, the judge's questioning rests on the suspect's alleged first-hand knowledge of 'what happened'; for the legal professionals the 'second-hand' information in the case file is their main source of knowledge.[1]

The use of documents as resources for questioning witnesses has been described as the 'documentary method of interrogation' (Lynch and Bogen, 1996: 214). As a procedure for going back over prior testimony, the judge's references to the case file may be used as 'stepping stones' in their questioning of the suspect (Komter, 2002: 177–8), including soliciting confirmation and elaboration of the reported statements (Dupret et al., 2015b: 17; Lynch and Bogen, 1996: 225). Moreover, the case file provides judges with opportunities for challenging the suspects' answers by confronting them with counter versions (cf. Dupret et al., 2015b: 17; Galatolo, 2015: 141–2; Komter, 1998: 17, 46; Komter, 2002: 180; Lynch and Bogen, 1996: 225; Scheffer et al., 2010: 178, n. 29; Van der Houwen, 2013).

The aim of this chapter is to examine the impact of the case file on the activities of the participants in court. I shall first discuss how the case file informs and exhibits the tasks of the professionals in court. I then examine how judges and suspects display what they know, how they know it, and what they are able or willing to tell about it. I finally investigate how the judges' references to the case file affects their interaction with the suspects.

4.2 Professional Reading

Judges, prosecutors and defence lawyers read and refer to the case file in different circumstances and for different ends: in the privacy of their office when preparing for the trial, as well as in the public space of the courtroom. The prominent role of the case file in court is evident, not only as a central source of information around which the events in the courtroom are organised, but also as material presence, as a physical object that is leafed through, pointed at, read from, etc., by the judges, prosecutors and defence lawyers (Komter, 1998; cf. Lynch and Bogen, 1996: 201–35). The ways in which they invoke the case file in court show how their 'professional reading' attends to their distinctive professional tasks and interests (cf. Goodwin, 1994: 606).

4.2.1 The Judge

Part of judges' tasks in court is to organise the court session (Komter, 1998; Licoppe, 2014: 86; Maryns, 2013: 108).[2] The presiding judge acts as 'chair-person' who opens and closes the session, distributes turns at talk, sees to i

[1] The documents in the case file are referred to as 'de auditu' (i.e. 'hearsay') testimony.

[2] Other displays of the judges' 'professional reading' of the case file will be studied further in the section on 'documents in interaction'.

that correct procedures are being followed, and so on (cf. Pomerantz and Denvir, 2007: 31–2). The 'agenda' of the activities in the courtroom is prescribed by law and thus always the same. However, the actual performance of the judges' organising tasks is managed in interaction, subject to local contingencies (cf. Depperman et al., 2010).

Judges frequently refer to the case file to initiate their questioning of the suspect (Komter, 1998). These references serve to mark the transition from the prior courtroom business – the prosecutor's presentation of the indictment – to the judge's current business of questioning of the suspect:

(1)

1. J: Well I have of course been reading it again last weekend right,
2. S: hm hm,
3. J: so I do remember exactly what you have stated,
4. but I want to give you the opportunity here in court right,
5. to just tell me once more in short what happened according to you.
6. S: Yes but then I have to think back about it all and so on
7. it's been so long ago for me=
8. J: =°Yes. yes.°
9. S: actually.
10. J: °Yes okay°.
11. Well perhaps that I uh will just tell you
12. what kind of statements there are right,
13. and then I start with the report of the complaint,
14. S: Hm hm.
15. J: and then I will occasionally ask you a question, and then uh
16. and then uh perhaps you will remember your things again, (2)
17. and uh (2) yes let's start with uh the report of the complaint.

(2, N)

The judge introduces the questioning of the suspect by inviting him to tell his version of the events (lines 4–5). The suspect's implicit claim of non-recall (lines 6–7) results in a course of action different from what the judge initially proposed. When the suspect does not come forward with an answer, the judge tells the suspect how the case file will support the activities to come. First he indicates that he will tell the suspect what kinds of statements the case file contains (lines 11–12), then he announces the order in which he is planning to proceed (line 13), next he announces how he will engage the suspect in interaction (line 15), and finally he mentions a possible result of these upcoming actions: they may jog the suspect's memory (line 16). Thus, the judge turns to the case file as an alternative to what he originally planned. He indicates what he will deal with first and how he will do that. In this way, he organises not only the events to come but also the suspect's listening and prospective participation.

The explicitness with which the judge outlines these activities, his planning of these activities, and the role of the case file in accomplishing them is a general feature of the judges' organising activities. It is comparable with the explicit ways in which physicians accomplish activity transitions in their interactions with patients, in order to reduce patient uncertainty and secure cooperation (Robinson and Stivers, 2001: 256). As the recipiency of the judges' talk in court also includes the other legal professionals and 'the public', these actions have the additional effect of creating an impression of transparency.

Excerpt (1) has shown how the judge's references to the case file at the beginning of the examinations in court structure the activities to come. These kind of organising activities are also found in the course of the questioning, especially around topic shifts. In the next excerpt the judge has been discussing the suspect's written statement:

(2)

1. J: Those u::hm yes then those are <u>your</u> statements, (1)
2. ((leafs through file))
3. then (2) I shall just put to you (2) what (3)
4. the victim concerned has stated. (3)
5. That was (2) Elberta Bouwstra.
6. She stated and that is a statement that (1)
7. I shall go over with you in some detail, (1)
8. so that we can just see what happened according to <u>her</u> statement.

(27, O)

The judge summarises the documents she has just been discussing ('<u>your</u> statements', line 1) as occasion for moving towards completion of this phase. This is then the link to the next topic, the discussion of the victim's statement (lines 3–4). As she is leafing through the case file, the judge first indicates which of the written statements she is going to put to the suspect, she then mentions the name of the victim (line 5) and specifies how she is going to deal with her statement ('go over . . . in some detail', line 7). In this way she shows her preparation and her competence in selecting those passages from the case file that are relevant for managing the business at hand.

The distinction between 'I shall just put to you' (line 3) and 'I shall go over with you' (line 7) draws attention to the participation formats of what is to come. The suspect is first expected to attend to what the judge will 'put to' him, and then to participate in what she will be 'going over' with him. The judge finally highlights the lack of correspondence between the suspect's and the victim's version of the events by emphasising '<u>her</u>' (line 8). Thus, she prospectively organises the listening and participation of the suspect by explicating what she is doing, what she is going to do, and how she will be doing that.

The next excerpt shows how the judge manages the transition from questioning the suspect to the next stage in the trial, the prosecutor's closing statement. The excerpt starts after the judge has completed a round of 'any questions' addressed to the two other judges, the defence lawyer and the prosecutor:

(3)

1. J: No more questions.
2. Is there anybody who still wants something to be read aloud,
3. then it is to be understood that I have read aloud everything
4. and then the floor is for the prosecutor.
5. P: Thank you madam.

(4, O)

The judge's conclusion (line 1) and question (line 2) summarise what actions the prior phase of the trial has accommodated: asking questions of the suspect and reading aloud statements from the case file. To accomplish the transition to the next phase the judge offers the professionals a final opportunity for asking questions or for having something read aloud from the case file, before yielding the floor to the prosecutor. During these transitional moments the judge displays her orientation towards sharing with the other professional actors in the courtroom responsibility for the completeness of past activities. In these transitional environments judges often assert that, when there are no requests for something to be read aloud, 'it is to be understood that I have read aloud everything' (line 3). This secures the right of the judge to ratify 'everything' in the case file as evidence for her verdict, including those items not read aloud.

What judges have in common with prosecutors and defence lawyers in their attempts to make sense of 'the facts', is their orientation to the consistency or inconsistency of the information in the case file. Excerpt (4) is from a case of robbery (see: Komter, 2013). The suspect, a drug addict, is accused of having stolen money from a woman during a drug deal. The presiding judge starts the questioning of the suspect as follows:

(4)

1. J: Uhm Mr Rutten,
2. the court has come across in the case file
3. of this case that has been documented, uhm (2)
4. stories and statements that (1) don't always coincide.
5. Your own stories too are rather inconsistent.
6. You remember that.
7. I think it is best,
8. before going over the documents with you,
9. that you yourself just tell us once more
10. what according to you happened then.
11. You know what it is about, from the indictment.
12. S: It happened exactly as I told the invasti- investigating judge.
13. (2)
14. J: Yes,
15. S: As for the rest I have nothing to add.

(12, O)

After a general introduction about the kind of information the court has come across ('stories and statements', line 4) and the problems they contain ('don't always coincide', line 4), the judge specifies a problem: the suspect's inconsistent stories (line 5). The judge concludes by mentioning the suspect's memory of his inconsistent stories (line 6). This conclusion is presented as undisputed, and treats the suspect as fully aware of the inconsistent positions he took in the interrogations with the police and the investigating judge.

Up to this point the judge has been describing his problems with the case file, problems that now turn out to be a resource for organising the interaction. First the suspect is given the opportunity to clear up his own inconsistencies, then they will discuss the documents (lines 8–10). The judge's announcement of what is to come does not just set the agenda, it also implicitly instructs the suspect on how to understand these activities and on how to act within the relevancies mentioned by him. His lexical choice of 'going over the documents with you' (line 8) suggests a kind of co-reading that will include other witnesses' versions of the case. It displays the judge's prospective listening: he will attend to the suspect's version in the light of the other versions available in the case file. By using the phrase 'according to you' with the emphasis on 'you' (line 10) the judge does not ask to be told what happened but what the suspect's current version of it is, after having suggested that he knows that there are more.

A noticeable feature of the judge's observations of the suspect's inconsistencies is the cautiousness in which he expresses them. In line 4 he mentions 'stories and statements that *don't always* coincide', and in line 5 he says: 'Your own stories too are *rather* inconsistent'. This can be attributed to the effect of the 'dilemma of conflict and cooperation': judges tend to mitigate the accusatory implications of their talk to avoid generating the suspect's defensiveness, while retaining their orientation to the accusations as expressed in the indictment (Komter, 1998).

4.2.2 The Parties

Whereas judges are required to be impartial, the institutional orientation of prosecutors and defence lawyers is to persuade rather than to observe and examine. Another difference is that prosecutors and defence lawyers present their points of view in monologic talk addressed to, but generally not responded to by the judge. These monologues are often presented with the aid of written notes or documents, which are sometimes read aloud.

The following two excerpts are fragments from the prosecutor's and the defence lawyer's closing statements in an attempted murder case. The suspect, Zaoli, is accused of having attempted to kill Etuli, who has been shot and is now confined to a wheelchair. The prosecutor has just mentioned the conclusion of two forensic experts that the abrasion found on the suspect's left thumb might well be a result of an inexperienced shooter's use of a pistol. He continues:

(5)

1. P: But then also the statement of Etuli becomes relevant again at this moment.
2. I point out to you three very short passages.
3. Page 29. I saw that he held the pistol with both hands.
4. Page 32, the shooter held the pistol with two hands.
5. And notably page 110,
6. I saw that Meklor Zaoli, held a pistol in his right hand.
7. I also saw that he closed his left hand around his right hand.
8. Subsequently he fired.
9. So the statement of Etuli seamlessly fits in with
10. the conclusions of the two experts mentioned,
11. and make those conclusions thereby more than merely plausible.
12. In my opinion the conclusion can be drawn that the hand,
13. that the wound, on Zaoli's left that is the supporting hand,
14. is a result of the use of a pistol.

(18, O)

The prosecutor refers to the relevance of a particular document (line 1), which projects his upcoming talk as an illustration of the forensic experts' conclusion (line 10) (Sneijder, 2014: 473). He introduces his arguments as 'I point out . . .' (line 2), thereby highlighting the judge's task as fact finder, and making his (the prosecutor's) actions understandable as 'assisting' the judge to find the truth (cf. D'hondt, 2014: 75).

Having identified the document that he will invoke and having specified the actions he will perform, the prosecutor does not use quotatives (e.g. 'he says') to introduce his quotations, but merely mentions the page numbers on which to find them (lines 3–5). His naming of the page numbers and his reading aloud quotations display his orientation to the authenticity of his sources of knowledge and to the verifiability of 'the facts'. The emphasis on 'saw' (line 3) conveys the epistemic force of the witness's first-hand knowledge of the events; the emphasis on 'both' suggests a consistency with the conclusion of the forensic experts mentioned before. The quotations are followed by the prosecutor's evaluation and conclusion (lines 9–14). He uses the qualifier 'seamlessly' (line 9) to accentuate the correspondence between Etuli's statement and that of the expert witnesses, and draws the 'more than merely plausible' conclusion (line 11) that the suspect must have been the shooter (lines 12–14).

In his closing argument that follows the prosecutor's, the defence lawyer also quotes the victim's statement:

(6)
1. D: What struck me in that second statement Mr president,
2. and I'm sorry to say that I haven't heard Mr prosecutor mention it,
3. on uhm (2) in this statement on page 33 of the case file,
4. Mr uh Etuli says I have seen Mr Zaoli drive,
5. on the twenty-first of March, in a red Nissan.
6. Whereas, when I consider the statement made by uh
7. the man from the car rental, he says on the twenty-second of March
8. Mr Zaoli, or (Meklor) Zaoli, has picked up a red car here.
9. Again I point out a contradiction, in the statement of Mr Etuli.
10. Mr Etuli has seen something, that he could not have seen.
11. ((4 lines omitted))
15. That cannot have happened, conclusion he states something,
16. that objectively speaking, cannot have been observed, simply because it-
17. that that car then was not in the neighbourhood of Mr Zaoli
(18, O)

The defence lawyer begins his argument by introducing the document he is going to deal with ('that second statement', line 1). He frames his talk as referring to something noticeable ('what struck me', line 1), which makes his observation that the prosecutor did not mention that second statement (line 2) hearable as holding the prosecutor accountable for a careless or deliberate oversight. After this he mentions the page number of the documents he will be quoting as introduction to his quotations (line 3) and quotes the passages relevant for his argument (lines 4–8). He places special emphasis on the date mentioned in the statement of the man from the car rental (line 7) so as to highlight the contrast with Etuli's statement (line 5). As in the previous excerpt, the defence lawyer describes his actions as 'I point out'. A difference is that the prosecutor uses the verb to introduce his quotations (excerpt 5, line 2), whereas the defence lawyer uses it to introduce his conclusion (line 9). As this conclusion is meant to undermine the testimony of Mr Etuli (lines 10–17) the judge is here not only addressed as fact-finder, but also as decision-maker.

The defence lawyer's line of reasoning is similar to the prosecutor's. They both introduce their arguments by naming the documents and page numbers of the statements to be quoted. These page numbers are referred to as evidence of the authenticity of the statements and are offered for co-reading and verification (Lynch and Bogen, 1996: 231). They both read aloud selected parts of the witnesses' statements and impose their own interpretations on their quotations. They both refer to the victim's statements in relation to the statements of others, but they select different 'quotables' to argue different points of view. The prosecutor argues for the credibility of the victim on the basis of the consistency of his statement with that of forensic experts; the defence lawyer's quotations seek to undermine the credibility of the victim on the basis of an inconsistency of his statement with that of a witness. The source of these conclusions is the common knowledge that is shared by the participants in the courtroom (cf. Garfinkel, 1967c: 78). The prosecutor appeals to the idea that forensic experts know how to interpret the facts, and that a consistency between statements contributes to the plausibility of those statements; the defence lawyer refers to the assumption that two contradictory statements cannot both be true (see: Pollner, 1987).

4.3 The Distribution of Knowledge

Roughly speaking, three domains of knowledge are invoked in court: the suspects' alleged first-hand knowledge of the events, the professionals' second-hand knowledge from the case file, and the common-sense knowledge about the world that the participants share (cf. Komter, 1995, 1998). This is not to say that the invocation of these domains of knowledge in the courtroom is self-evident. In the following sections I shall examine how judges and suspects express their access to these epistemic domains and how they negotiate their epistemic stance.

4.3.1 Epistemic Domains and Access

The terms 'first-hand' and 'second-hand' knowledge designate the nature of, and access to, the suspects' and the judges' domains of knowledge. The following fragment illustrates how a judge explicates his sources of knowledge to a suspect, in response to the suspect's reluctance to talk:

(7)

1. J: Yes look we weren't there so we have to go on
2. what we read here and what you tell us.
3. S: Yes.

(2, N)

'We weren't there' (line 1) displays the judge's recognition of the priority of the suspect's first-hand knowledge of what happened, and highlights his epistemic right to ask questions.[3]

What we read here reflects the judge's current epistemic position based on the documents in the case file; and 'what you tell us' describes the judge's access to 'what happened' through his current questioning of the suspect. These epistemic domains have a location: 'there' at the scene of the crime,

[3] In fact, if the judge had been 'there', for example as witness to the facts, he would not have been able to use that knowledge for adjudicating the case.

'here' in the case file and 'what you tell us' in court. In drawing attention to these epistemic domains the judge anticipates and informs the questioning to come. It shows that the suspect is held accountable for his first-hand knowledge of the events (Stivers et al., 2011: 17) in that the judge has the right to ask questions and the suspect has the knowledge to answer them.

Excerpt (1) has shown how the judge invokes the case file as introduction to the activities to come. Let us consider it again to examine its use as a source of knowledge:

(8)

1. J: Well I have of course been reading it again last weekend right,
2. S: hm hm,
3. J: so I do remember exactly what you have stated,
4. but I want to give you the opportunity here in court right,
5. to just tell me once more in short what happened according to you.
6. S: Yes but then I have to think back about it all and so on
7. it's been so long ago for me=
8. J: =°Yes. yes.°
9. S: actually.
10. J: °Yes okay°.
11. Well perhaps that I uh will just tell you
12. what kind of statements there are right,
13. and then I start with the report of the complaint,

(2, N)

The judge starts questioning the suspect by referring to the fact that he has reread the case file the weekend before the trial. The judge's invitation to tell him 'once more' what happened (line 5) shows his recognition of the fact that suspects tell their stories many times in the course of the criminal process (Eades, 2008b). His addition to tell him what happened 'according to you' (line 5) highlights the fact that what the suspect is asked to tell is only one version. The judge juxtaposes 'what you have stated' (line 3) and 'what happened according to you' (line 5), thereby drawing attention to the two epistemic domains in play: the case file and the criminal events.

He accentuates his knowledge by claiming exact memory of the suspect's written statement (line 3), which underlines his epistemic status as 'knowing recipient' and his actions as 'verifying' what is already held to be known. This puts the suspect's prospective narrative at risk, as it allows the judge to compare the information from the case file with the suspect's current talk, and thus to discover inconsistencies or contradictions. The suspect replies that the events took place a long time ago (lines 6–7). Although he does not spell it out, the implication is that he cannot answer the question as he does not remember what happened. The events that the suspect has been asked to talk about have passed and, because they can only be retrieved by memory, they are 'forgettable'.

The judge then turns to the case file and announces that he will start with the report of the complaint (lines 11–13). In spite of the fact that it contains second-hand information, the case file affords the judge 'first-hand' accessibility; it is an object lying on the table in front of the judge, available for immediate consultation and reference. Thus, the judge's epistemic domain ('what kind of statements there are', line 12) is brought into play when the suspect claims insufficient access to his.

The judge's talk resembles that in another trial discussed in excerpt (4). Let us reconsider this fragment:

(9)
1. J: Uhm Mr Rutten,
2. the court has come across in the case file
3. of this case that has been documented, uhm (2)
4. stories and statements that (1) don't always coincide.
5. Your own stories too are rather inconsistent.
6. You remember that.
7. I think it is best,
8. before going over the documents with you,
9. that you yourself just tell us once more
10. what according to you happened then.
11. You know what it is about, from the indictment.
12. S: It happened exactly as I told the invasti– investigating judge.
13. (2)
14. J: Yes,
15. S: As for the rest I have nothing to add.
(12, O)

The similarities between these two cases reside in the judges' displays of their knowledge of the case, their placement of these displays as preceding their invitations of the suspect's talk, and their attentiveness to the fact that what the suspect is invited to tell is only one version ('according to you', excerpt 8, line 5; excerpt 9, line 10). Another similarity is that the suspect's memory is called upon, only this time his memory concerns his previous 'stories' instead of 'what happened' (lines 5–6). 'You know what it is about, from the indictment' (line 11) resonates with 'you remember that' (line 6) in that the judge does not so much appeal to the suspect's memory and knowledge of 'what happened', but rather to his knowledge of his prior statements and of the accusations as formulated in the indictment.

These actions draw the suspect into the epistemic domain of the professionals who deal with the case, which prospectively organises the way in which the suspect is to tell his story: as a legally relevant one, relating to the charges as written down in the indictment. The suspect's response (line 12) displays that he understood the judge's 'instructions' about how to answer his question: he does not tell directly what happened, but he refers the judge to what he told the investigating judge as reported in the case file.

4.3.2 *Epistemic Status and Stance*

A distinction has been made between epistemic status and epistemic stance. Epistemic status is based on participants' access to an epistemic domain, and is conceived as a somewhat enduring feature of human relationships, whereas epistemic stance concerns the moment-by-moment expression of these relationships (Heritage, 2012a: 6). The relation between epistemic status and epistemic stance is shown by the positions that participants display towards the knowledge that they have or are assumed to have.

Judges often start their questioning of the suspect by establishing what suspects are willing or able to tell about events, in relation to what they have stated in earlier phases of the process as written down in the case file. This may serve to verify the suspect's stance and thus to create a body of knowledge on which everyone can agree (Komter, 1998: 12–13). The following excerpt is an example:

(10)
1. J: Is it correct what you have stated to the police then,
2. and do you stick with that?
3. S: Sure.
4. J: Yes. Yes.
5. ((4 seconds, he looks in the case file))
6. You said uh that you (1) went inside <u>first</u>
((continues by summarising the police report))
(17, O)

The judge asks two questions, the first addressing the truth of the suspect's statement (line 1) and the second the suspect's stance in court (line 2); the suspect's 'sure' answers both questions simultaneously. As the suspect has confessed to the police, and as confessions are considered to be more credible than denials (Goffman, 1970: 111), the judge can here assume a correspondence between the truth and the suspect's stance.

In those cases where the case file contains contradictory statements by suspects, judges may ask them to explain and to indicate which of their earlier statements in the case file is true. For example, a suspect in a murder trial is accused of having assisted her current boyfriend in the murder of her former boyfriend. The case file reveals that she made conflicting statements to the police and to the investigating judge about whether or not she knew that her boyfriend had a gun. The judge confronts her with these inconsistencies, to which the suspect replies that she was confused and felt pressured by the police interrogators. The judge responds:

(11)

1. J: My question then is always, is that an obstacle to telling the truth.
2. S: Well I have finally- I have uh told the truth to the investigating judge.
3. J: Yes, but that is then a truth,
4. that is rather different from the truth that you told before.
5. For you told the police I'm going to tell you the truth now.
6. After that you've altered your statement a few times more,
7. but well finally we did have something which gives one the impression
8. that that could be the truth,
9. but your statement to the investigating judge is again totally different.
10. And then you slowly but surely begin to wonder what to believe right?

(22, O)

The judge's response shows that he has heard this explanation before and that he is not convinced by it (line 1). The suspect's utterance 'I have told the truth to the investigating judge' (line 2) implies that she admits that she did not tell the truth in her previous statements to the police. This is what the judge then focuses on in his reply. In spite of the fact that she told the police 'I am going to tell you the truth now', she has altered her statement a few times more (line 6). As it is common knowledge that there can only be one version of 'the truth' (Pollner, 1987) and that liars present their stories as correct (cf. Sacks 1995, part I: 255), the suspect's claim to have told the truth to the investigating judge does not convince the judge (lines 3–10). Thus, in spite of the fact that the case file does not give direct access to the events, it does give the judge the warrant to gloss and assess its contents (cf. Glenn and LeBaron, 2011: 5).

The interaction continues as follows:

(12)

11. S: Yes I stick with the last.
12. What I've told the investigating judge.
13. J: You stick with the last.

(22, O)

While the judge's problem is that he does not know what to believe, the suspect's problem is that she cannot tell him what to believe. Instead, she tells him what her position in the criminal process is. The suspect's expression of her current stance 'I stick with the last' obviates further discussion, and bypasses questions of truth and falsehood (Komter, 2002).

Later on in the trial the judge reminds the suspect of her statements to the police about her observations of her boyfriend's firearm, statements that she withdrew later when she was questioned by the investigating judge:

(13)
1. J: Do you know that, that you told the police twice
2. that the gentleman uh had a firearm?
3. The first time you just said it
4. he had a firearm and I saw it, it was in his inside pocket,
5. and the second time you said that uh
6. yes about that firearm that had already been discussed
7. there was no point in pursuing it further.
8. S: No I cannot remember it.
9. J: You cannot remember it well it is true,
10. the one statement is written on page 85,
11. and the other on the C-report on page 44.
((continues by summarising the police report))
(22, O)

The judge asks the suspect about her knowledge of her two statements to the police (lines 1–2), after which he quotes these statements (lines 4 and 6). Her response 'I cannot remember it' (line 8) may refer both to the events themselves and to her telling the police about them. The problem of the suspect's lack of memory appears to be cleared up by the judge's pointing at the undisputed existence of the suspect's earlier statements. The judge's reference to the page numbers (lines 10–11) on which the information is to be found highlights the authority and authenticity of his source of knowledge. The page numbers, in combination with the direct quotes (lines 4 and 6), are proffered as undeniable evidence of what the suspect has told the police. The truth that the judge points out (line 9) is the truth of the case file rather than that of the events described in it. So the judge's page identifications, as the material expressions of his epistemic domain, allow him to trump the suspect's position of non-recall.

As the case file contains more information than just the suspect's statement, the suspect's version may be contrasted with those of others, which may undermine the effects of the suspect's epistemic priority. In the next excerpt from a robbery case, the judge has just been reading aloud from the statements of the suspect's two accomplices, who accused the suspect of having assaulted the victim. The suspect responds:

(14)
1. S: Those stories they- just aren't- just aren't right.
2. That they- that they tell.
3. J: Just aren't right.
4. S: Well if you read it through carefully well then you'll see it yourself.
5. J: Well I've read it through carefully right,
6. I merely put to you what these witnesses are stating.
(25, O)

The suspect claims epistemic priority by first denying the truth of the testimonies of the two witnesses (lines 1–2), after which he buttresses his claims by appealing to the information in the case file (line 4). In response, the judge explicates what he has been doing ('I merely put to you', line 6).[4] The expression 'I put to you' is often used by judges, especially in the environment of conflicting statements; it suggests that the judge is not judging or assessing, but only passing on information of others. When people 'merely report' other sources they avoid taking positions on their own behalf (Pomerantz, 1984b: 624; see also Galatolo, 2007: 219). Thus, by highlighting the 'second-handness' of his knowledge the judge avoids giving the impression of siding with the witnesses' testimonies.

4.4 Documents in Interaction

The judges' two main tasks during their examinations of the evidence are to ratify the evidence (i.e. read aloud those passages from the case file that they may base their verdict on) and to question the suspect (and witnesses, if any). Although these are different activities they are difficult to separate because any invocation of the case file may serve simultaneously as ratification of the evidence and as resource for questioning the suspect.

I shall first examine how the sequential position of the judges' references to the case file informs the actions they perform. Then I explore the interactional effects of the judges' references to the case file and the conversational resources that suspects may draw on to participate in interaction. And finally I investigate how judges may use multiple resources to mobilise the suspects' responses.

4.4.1 Action Sequences

As judges refer to the case file in interaction with suspects, these references inevitably become enmeshed in the judges' actions. A sense of what these actions are can be inferred from, among other things, their sequential placement (Levinson, 2012: 104). Let us consider the following excerpt:

(15)

1. J: Mr Pol and Mr Baan, those policemen, they arrived there
2. and on September 28th around twenty to ten, (1)
3. they saw a male person who held a small- a small child (then),
4. picked it up and lifted it outside through the open window.
5. Subsequently we saw the child who was held by his arms,
6. squirming outside the window.
7. We heard the child cry, we saw that the child made movements

[4] In Dutch: 'voorhouden', which means literally: 'to hold before someone'.

8. apparently in order to get inside again.
9. Could that be [correct?
10. S: [That's a lie. A big lie.=
11. J: =Yes.
12. He said no police, fuck off or I'll throw the child down.
13. We saw that he made throwing and swinging movements with the child.
14. ((continues reading aloud 40 lines, ending in: 'is that correct?'))
(O: 4)

The judge is quoting a statement of two police detectives who witnessed the suspect while he held a small child outside a window (lines 1–8). She then asks the suspect whether he agrees with this version of the events, which he vociferously disputes (lines 9–10). The suspect's indignant response is acknowledged by the judge (lines 10–11) but, instead of going into it, she continues by reading aloud the witnesses' statement about the suspect's threat to throw the child out of the window (lines 12–14).

In this episode the judge produces the quote[5] in a first position, and follows it with a request for confirmation (line 9). The demonstrative pronoun 'that' (line 9) refers to the passage just read aloud, which retrospectively exhibits that the reading aloud has been a preface to the request for confirmation. After the suspect's response the excerpt continues with a similar episode of reading aloud followed by a similar request for confirmation. The judge's disregard of the suspect's defensiveness and her continued reading aloud from the case file suggests that her larger projects are to ratify the evidence and to verify the suspect's stance, which she does by reading aloud lengthy passages from witness statements, interjected by requests for confirmation or verification. Her primary orientation to the case file also allows her to virtually ignore the suspect's protestations, and thus to avoid getting drawn into a discussion.

The next excerpt is from a case in which the suspect is accused of having robbed a hotel, together with his companion (Van Lommel). The judge summarises the initial events of the robbery and continues:

(16)

1. J: You said to the police
((6 lines omitted))
7. that when you came into the lobby of the hotel,
8. that you saw Van Lommel standing before two boys,
9. and that you saw that he had a pistol in his hands,
10. and was aiming it at those two boys.
11. Is that right?

[5] I use the term 'quote' here to cover all types of references to the case file.

12. S: ((nods))
13. J: And what happened then? (4)
14. S: He pressed a gun into my hands, (2)
15. and then yes I tied those people up. (1)
(16, O)

The judge reads aloud from the suspect's statement (lines 1–10) which is again constructed as a preface to the request for confirmation (line 11). Then, after the suspect's confirmation, the judge proceeds with a request for elaboration (lines 12–13).

The excerpt initially shows the same organisation as excerpt (15) but it has a different continuation. In both excerpts the quotes are followed by requests for confirmation. The difference is that in excerpt (15) the suspect contradicts the information read aloud, whereas in excerpt (16) he confirms it. The suspect's confirmation leads to the judge's inviting the suspect to continue by telling the story from that point on ('And what happened then?', line 13).

The exchange following this question shows how the judge's listening relies on the information in the case file:

(17)
14. S: He pressed a gun into my hands, (2)
15. and then yes I tied those people up. (1)
16. J: He pressed a gun into your hands?=
17. S: =Yes,
((4 lines omitted))
21. J: You uh told the police, when the police asked you
22. if you did not take the gun from uh Van Lommel,
23. or got it from him,
24. that you took the gun from him. (1)
25. And that is then something different what you stated then,
26. from what you're stating now. (5)
27. How is that?
28. S: I tell the truth now.
((10 lines omitted))
38. J: Right you're saying now in any case
39. that he pressed that gun into your hand,
40. S: Right.
41. J: And what happened then?
(16, O)

After the judge's surprised response to the suspect's answer (lines 14–16) she refers to the suspect's statement in the case file and observes a change in his position: now he says that his companion pressed the gun into his hands (line 14), whereas he told the police that he took the gun from his companion (lines 21–4). The judge holds the suspect accountable for this inconsistency and invites him to explain it (line 27). What follows resonates with their earlier exchange (lines 11–13) where the judge asks for the suspect's confirmation of what has been established thus far (lines 38–9), and invites him to continue telling the story from there (line 41).

The questions 'And what happened then?' (lines 13 and 41) are not 'open' questions as their design suggests but, as shown by the judge's response in lines 16 and 21–6, they can also be taken as 'verification questions', the answers to which are judged for their congruence with the written statements in the case file. As the judge already knows what the suspect has stated earlier, she monitors the suspect's talk for its correspondence with the information in the case file. In this way a collaborative telling is constructed, where the judge goes over part of the suspect's statement, verifies the suspect's position towards the information told thus far, and uses that as occasion to invite him to continue his narrative.

In contrast with the excerpts (15) and (16), the quote (lines 21–4) occurs in a third position and is recognisable as responsive to the suspect's prior talk. Quotes in a third position may exhibit the speaker's assessment or understanding of something problematic in prior actions (cf. Drew, 2006: 74–9; Frers, 2009). In court these third-position quotes are produced when the suspect's answer is 'contradictable' or inadequate, and may serve to confront the suspect with counter versions.

4.4.2 Quotes and Participation

It has been observed that there are variations in the 'tightness' of the sequential organisation of initial actions and their responses. Some actions require a specific next action from the recipient (e.g. an initial greeting is routinely followed by a return greeting), whereas other actions are more loosely organised and leave more scope for alternative responses (Clayman and Heritage, 2002: 22–3; Stivers and Rossano, 2010). My materials show that, instead of requiring or inviting a response, the judges' practices of reading aloud statements from the case file may actually discourage response. I shall here discuss those features of the judges' quoting from the case file that discourage suspects' responses, and the interactional resources suspects draw on to respond in these circumstances.

To some extent the format of the judges' references to the case file is specified by law: those passages on which judges base their verdict should be read aloud (Code of Criminal Procedure, section 301.1). In addition, the law says that reading aloud can be substituted by summarising (Code of Criminal Procedure, section 301.3). However, the law does not specify how these injunctions are to be realised in interaction with suspects or witnesses. In a study of Belgian trials D'hondt has observed that the attorneys refer to the documents by summarising, indirectly quoting or literally 'animating' them (2014: 78). In Dutch courtrooms similar 'production formats' (Goffman, 1981 can be seen in the ways judges design their references to the case file: they literally quote the texts of the case file, summarise the texts of the case file in their own words, and paraphrase the texts of the case file as 'enactments' of the events (cf. Holt, 2007; Sandlund, 2014). The design of these 'quotes' and the actions they perform may mobilise the relevance of the suspect's responses (Stivers and Rossano, 2010).

My materials show that during the judges' reading aloud suspects usually do not respond until they are asked a question (see excerpts 15 and 16). This interactional passivity of the suspect may be a result of the design of the judges' quotes, because judges who are visibly occupied with reading aloud texts from the case file display their commitment to producing an extended turn at talk, which discourages the suspect's participation (Licoppe, 2014: 86–8, 92).

In the following excerpt the judge starts questioning a suspect who is accused of having robbed three women of their handbags:

(18)

1. J: On the 19th of June you were questioned by the investigating judge, (1)
2. do you stick with the statement that you made then, or was it ( )
3. S: Yes.
4. J: Well there uh (2) you confess to the first count,
5. you say on April the 3rd I robbed a woman of her handbag,
6. I did that by taking the bag from a basket, (1)
7. yes there still is (1) a question whether you <u>also</u> took the basket, (1)
8. I dispute that I (4) have (1) pushed and kicked that woman
9. I am sure that lady did not fall down.
10. Yes and then I shall go over that with you right now,
11. there is a report of a complaint (1) of Mrs Dorst, (3)
12. and she has a story that is slightly different from <u>yours</u>,
13. you're talking about that uh bag,
14. and perhaps that you took it from that basket,
15. but she says I rode my bicycle there.
16. ((continues reading aloud witness statement))
17. (31, O)

The judge starts the examinations by verifying the suspect's stance (see excerpt 10). The fact that the suspect confirms his confession (line 3) does not obviate the judge's subsequent reading it aloud because of the legal requirements of ratifying the evidence. That is, after the judge has verified that the suspect has confessed she now makes explicit what the suspect has confessed to, so that she can use it for her verdict (lines 5–6). The judge adds an expression of doubt about the credibility of part of the suspect's version of the events (line 7), after which she reads this part aloud (lines 8–9). She continues by indicating what will be her next action (going over the report of the complaint, lines 10–11), mentions the gist of its contents ('slightly different from yours', line 12) and specifies a point of difference between the suspect's version (lines 13–14) and that of the complainant (line 15). In the passage that the judge subsequently reads aloud (see line 16) the complainant is reported to have said that the suspect pushed and kicked her while she was riding her bicycle, that as a result of this she fell down, after which the suspect took away her bicycle basket containing her handbag. The suspect keeps silent during the judge's reading aloud until he is eventually invited to respond.

In the episode represented in excerpt (18) the judge's direct quotes from the case file (lines 5–6, 8–9, 15) are embedded in her observations and announcements (line 4, 7, 10, 11–12), which means that she alternates between speaking *to* the suspect with the pronouns 'you' and 'yours' and speaking *as* the suspect by way of the pronoun 'I'. This shows how she is continually shifting 'footing' (Goffman, 1981) as she divides her attention between the suspect and the documents. However, the frequency of the judge's shifts of footing does not mean that she is continually 'changing hats' (Goffman, 1981: 145), but rather that she is involved in a configuration of alignments with the suspect that may be relevant simultaneously.

Her reading aloud resembles direct reported speech as it preserves its original deictics and retains the original personal pronouns and tenses (D'Hondt, 2014: 71). As in direct reported speech, quotations tend to be introduced by a verbum dicendi or 'quotative' such as 'you say' (line 5) or 'she says' (line 15). It has been noted that, although direct reported speech claims to reproduce the original talk, it is unlikely that it is accurate because it is selective and taken out of context, and because verbatim recall is not usually possible (Clift and Holt, 2007: 6; Galatolo, 2015: 140; Holt, 2000: 432). In this respect, conversational quoting differs from quoting from written materials in the courtroom, as it can be assumed that the judges' quotations are accurate representations of the written texts in the case file.

There is another difference between directly quoting what was said on an earlier occasion and quoting from a police report: it is not the talk in the police interrogation but the talk reported by the police that is quoted, resulting in what could be called 'reported reported speech' or 'quoting once removed'. An indication that the judge quotes the police report rather than 'the suspect's own words' verbatim, is the occurrence of two reported denials by the suspect (lines 8 and 9). It is likely that the suspect did not volunteer these sentences but that they are constructed as a combination of the police detective's questions and the suspect's answers (see Chapters 2 and 3). However, the judge typically treats the suspect as the 'author' of his reported talk (Komter, 2002, 2013; Maryns, 2013: 120).

The design of judges' reading aloud and their visible preoccupation with the documents show their dual orientation to the suspect and the documents. They address the suspects with 'you' but do not invite their response. The suspects are potential participants in interaction but they do not participate. Although the judges' primary orientation to ratifying the evidence discourages the suspects' participation, there may be circumstances conducive to suspect responses. The next excerpt is an example:

(19)

1. J: You told the police that uh ((5 seconds leafing through pages))
2. °let's look where it's written°, (4)
3. that you uh (3) had seen that mr Van Lommel
4. uh for the first time the day before in a disco,
5. the next day so Sunday the 19th of September 1989 I met him again,
6. then I asked him if he felt like taking a ride with me,
7. and then you were in uh your mother's car,
8. S: Right. (2)
9. J: and at a certain moment it was Monday then,
10. Van Lommel uh asked me if I'd drive to the Iris hotel in Utrecht. (1)
11. And he then told you exactly how you had to drive, (1)
12. and at his request you parked the car behind the hotel in such a cul-de-sac,
13. in such a way that you could drive off immediately. (1)
14. You said to the police when I had parked my car,
15. I heard from my accomplice what was going to happen.
16. He did not tell me much. I do not remember what.
17. But I could assume that something was going to happen,
18. that was not acceptable.

(16, O)

The judge starts this episode by introducing a quote in the indirect reported speech style (line 1), interrupting her sentence while she leafs through the documents, looking for the passage that she wants to read aloud to the suspect (line 2). After this interlude she remains with the indirect reported speech style of the sentence she broke off (lines 3–4). She then switches to the direct reported speech style (lines 5–6), which she follows by a remark about the suspect's means of transport, addressing him directly in her own voice (line 7). This receives a confirmative response of the suspect (line 8).

As in excerpt (18) we see that the judge designs her references to the case file in three different formats, between which she continually switches: direct reported speech (lines 5–6, 9–10, 14–18), indirect reported speech (lines1–4) and summaries or observations (lines 7, 11–13). These formats embody the judge's footing, i.e. her alignment to the texts she utters. By shifting footing the judge does not terminate a prior alignment but holds it in abeyance to be re-engaged at any subsequent moment (Goffman, 1981: 155). This reflects the multiplicity of her tasks: she selects those items from the case file that need to be ratified as evidence, she goes over some of the events by summarising them, and literally quotes those texts that are important for ratifying as evidence.

The shifts of footing allow her to read aloud the relevant parts of the evidence without losing contact with the suspect.

The suspect's response (line 8) shows that he is still 'with' the judge, although he does not provide any substantive contributions. Two features of the judge's prior talk may have driven the suspect's response. In the first place the judge has shifted footing from quoting from the case file to directly addressing the suspect (line 7); and second the topic of her talk lies within the suspect's epistemic domain, which makes the judge's prior talk hearable as a request for confirmation (Labov and Fanshel, 1977: 100) or verification (Goodwin, 1981: 156).

On the other hand, there is another moment in this episode where the same circumstances apply, and that does not generate a response (line 11). Moreover, the suspect's confirmation has little interactional effect, as the judge continues reading aloud the suspect's reported narrative (lines 9–10). It could then be suggested that in these circumstances a response is optional, as it is not expressly invited and its absence is not treated as problematic (cf. Stivers and Rosano, 2010). Goffman has observed how people can be involved in an 'open state of talk', where participants have the right but not the obligation to talk (1981: 134–5). Those episodes of interaction in the courtroom when the judges are oriented mainly to the case file could then be described as 'half-open states of talk', where the judge does the talking and the suspect may or may not participate.

The judge's dual orientation to the documents and the suspect may result in interactional ambiguities. The following excerpt is from a case where the suspect (Berlage) is accused of having tried to run over with his car the social workers employed in a 'methadone bus'.[6] The judge is reading aloud a witness statement of Henk Schipper, one of the social workers (the number 211 refers to the house number of their office, Annemieke and Jan Willem are two colleagues):

(20)

1. J: The statement of Henk Schipper,
2. they're all people of uh 211, (1)
3. page seventeen,
4. ((17 seconds of rustling of papers))
5. well he was in that bus,
6. and that is then the background,
7. I'll just skip the problem inside, (2)
8. and uhm Jan Willem crossed the road,
9. for he had gone outside with him,
10. and Annemieke already was outside,
((44 lines omitted))

[6] A bus that stopped at regular hours at some fixed places in the larger cities in the Netherlands in order to dispense methadone to drug addicts. These services have been dismantled gradually over the past decade.

54.   If Annemieke had not jumped between those two parked cars
55.   she would certainly have been run over
56.   by the car in which Berlage drove at her.
57.   Then Berlage drove on on the pavement past the chemist's.
58.   Made a strange turn with his car too. (1)
59.   I was profoundly shocked. (1)
60.   By the way, u::h it appears from the statements
61.   of the people of 211 that afterwards they were
62.   actually sitting together more or less dejected
63.   like well we're used to something,
64.   but if it happens like that, then uh
65.   we don't really know how we must go on.
66.   (2)
67. S: Well yes it was not my intention that they would uh yes (1)
68.   that it would get so serious. (1)
69. J: But I haven't finished yet for then we have here
70.   Jeanne, who has already been mentioned, Jeanne Poulon,
71.   ((8 seconds of paper rustling))
72.   I heard that right close to us a car drove off at full speed
        ((continues by reading aloud this witness statement, 20 pp.))

(14, O)

We see here a number of actions already discussed: the judge displays in various ways how he organises this part of the questioning: he names the statement that he is about to deal with (line 1) and the page number in the case file on which it is to be found (line 3). The judge's identification of the page number, although addressed to the suspect, is directed at the professional participants in the trial, who are now in a position to check and verify the judge's reading (line 4). The judge then gives some 'background' (lines 5–6), provides an account of what he is doing (line 7), after which he reads aloud a long passage from the witness Henk Schipper's statement (lines 8–59). The duration and the monologic format of his reading aloud attests to his primary orientation to ratifying the evidence.

His parenthetical 'by the way' (line 60) marks a shift of footing, as he announces that his talk to come is based on the social workers' statements (lines 60–1). He addresses the suspect and 'enacts' (Holt, 2007) how the social workers might have described their feelings after the incidents (lines 63–5). The judge introduces the enactment with the quotative 'like' (line 63). This suggests that the quotation is not meant to represent the social workers' actual talk but what they might have said under these circumstances (cf. Holt, 2007: 51; Lamerichs and Te Molder, 2009; Sandlund, 2014: 647). Prosodic features of the judge's talk, such as the emphasis on something (line 63) and on that (line 64), show the judge's interpretation of the gist of what the social workers must have felt (Holt, 2007: 57), as if he gives a 'live performance' of their feelings of dejection. After a two-second pause this is taken up by the suspect as an opportunity to respond (lines 66–7).

As in excerpt (19), the suspect's response occurs after the judge's shift of footing. The judge moves from reading aloud to addressing the suspect, and introduces an illustration of the social workers' feelings. In contrast with excerpt (19), what the judge says does not lie within the suspect's epistemic domain, but it does have other features that encourage or provide an opportunity for a response on the part of the suspect. The judge's enactment operates simultaneously as an illustration and as an assessment of the events (Sandlund, 2014: 662). It has been observed that assessments may invite but not require a response, as they are often responded to but they put no pressure on the recipient to do so (Stivers and Rossano, 2010). The occurrence of the suspect's response at this moment in the talk can be explained further by the kind of action the enactment performs. The judge's expression of the social workers' feelings of dejection implicitly blames the suspect for being responsible for these feelings. Moreover, the judge's two-second pause following the enactment opens the floor for the suspect's defensive response, in which he denies that it was his intention to cause any harm (lines 67–8).

However, the judge rejects this response as not in line with his planning ('I haven't finished yet', line 69; cf. Licoppe, 2014: 91) thereby affirming the character of his prior talk as an 'aside' and the purpose of his upcoming talk as reading aloud from the case file again. Thus, the interactional ambiguity visible in the moments following the judge's 'aside' can be attributed to two conflicting orientations: the suspect's orientation to making use of the opportunity to give a defensive account, and the judge's orientation to continuing his reading aloud of witness statements.

The next excerpt from a case of child abuse shows a more argumentative example of this ambiguity:

(21)

1. J: You took him by his right arm again,
2. and with your free left hand you opened the door and put him outside
3. then he landed on his feet,
4. S: I've just pulled him outside like this.
5. J: then you shut the door,
6. at <u>that</u> moment I realised that I'd gone too <u>far</u>,
7. you let him in again,
8. and the moment that I had hold of him
9. Mineke tried to pull him out of my hands.
10. S: No, he walked in himself after that.
11. J: This is <u>your</u> statement,
12. S: Yes,

13. J: as long as you know that.
14. S: I uh know that.
15. J: (You know that)
16. Later I saw the bruises on Mark then I became frightened
17. I realised afterwards I have handled him too roughly,
18. ((continues reading aloud the suspect's statement))
(11, O)

Throughout this episode the judge is occupied with summarising (lines 1–3, 5) and reading aloud (lines 6, 8, 16–17) the text of the suspect's statement from the police report. Although, as mentioned before, these activities project an extended turn at talk and discourage the suspect's contributions, the suspect volunteers a clarification ('I've just pulled him outside like this', line 4) and a denial ('no, he walked in himself after that', line 10). The judge does not attend to the suspect's clarification (lines 4–5), and she explicitly rebuts the suspect's denial by reminding him of the fact that she is reading aloud his own statement (lines 11, 13), before resuming her reading aloud (lines 16–17). The judge's orientation to the documents and her disregard of and her dismissive response to the suspect's contributions discourage the suspect's further participation.

What appears to prompt the suspect's interventions is first the distribution of knowledge. The suspect designs his first contribution (line 4) as a correction or elaboration of the judge's prior talk, and his second (line 10) as a denial, by virtue of his first-hand knowledge of the events (Goodwin, 1981: 156). Second, the suspect's objections can be an effect of the potentially harmful tenor of the judge's text. 'He landed on his feet' (line 3) and 'Mineke tried to pull him out of my hands' (line 9) suggest a struggle, which the suspect's contributions are designed to mitigate and contest. However, the judge's response (lines 11 and 13) invalidates the suspect's interventions.

Instead of getting drawn into a discussion the judge makes use of the availability of the case file to foreground her orientation to the documents. Thus, what kind of action the judge's references to the case file perform is negotiable (Levinson, 2012: 104): what is expressed by the suspect as a defence (lines 4 and 10) is rejected by the judge's observation of the suspect's 'authorship' of his statement (lines 11 and 13). The judge's continued orientation to the documents operates both to avoid discussion and to retain the initiative.

The following excerpt from a robbery case shows how the suspect expresses his disagreement with a witness statement (Doorn is the suspect, Kalari and Rutten are witnesses):

(22)

1. J: Then I saw, and that's Kalari again,
2.   that she was grabbed by Doorn and Rutten.=
3. S: =That's not possible (I went) around the corner.
4.   How can I then I mean can we at the same time ( )
5.   those two initially wanted to rob her.
6.   [I swear they initially wanted to rob her
7. J: [Oh
8. S: and then he testifies against me.
9.   While I wanted to help her.
10.   It's too ridiculous for words. (1)
11. J: And Kalari says I have been able to secure her handbag.
12.   But you say it is quite [different
13. S: [No, they-
14.   That's sure quite different yes.
15. J: Hm Hm, (2)
16.   Well Rutten . . . uh he says
17.   ((continues going over the next witness statement))

(13, O)

The judge reads aloud a sentence from a witness statement (lines 1–2), in response to which the suspect vigorously protests (lines 3–10). The suspect's protestations rest on his first-hand knowledge of the events, and are triggered by the incriminating nature of the witness's statement. In his efforts to neutralise the accusation and bolster his claim of innocence the suspect's responses show a range of defensive actions (cf. Atkinson and Drew, 1979): denial (line 3), account (lines 3–4), counter-accusation (lines 5–6), expression of his own moral virtue (line 9) and indignation about the wrongness of the accusation (lines 8–10). The judge allows the suspect to express his disagreement and indignation, after which he returns to the case file and continues his reading aloud (line 11), which is followed by a summary of the suspect's stance (line 12). After the suspect's confirmation the judge turns his attention to the case file again and reads aloud the statement of the next witness, while the suspect does not respond until the judge completes his reading aloud and asks a question.

As in excerpt (21) the incriminating nature of the text read aloud by the judge mobilises the suspect's broadly negative responses. The judge neutralises these responses by negotiating the nature of the interaction. The suspect treats the reading aloud as an accusation, which is then redefined by the judge as verification and affirmation of the suspect's stance (lines 11–12). In doing this, the judge treats the suspect's statement as 'a version' that can be compared with those of others. As in excerpt (21) the judge's continued orientation to the documents allows him to avoid discussion and retain the initiative.

4.4.3 Multiple Resources for Managing Participation

As we have seen, the response-discouraging effects of judges' reading aloud may be overruled by features of talk that may generate response, such as the judge's shift of footing, the suspect's epistemic priority and the incriminating nature of the judge's talk. The excerpts (19)–(22) show how judges dismiss, ignore or acknowledge these uninvited responses as part of their continued orientation to the documents. In this section I examine how judges may use a number of interactional resources to engage the suspect in interaction. The video recordings of the 'new' materials afford additional insights into the effects of the judges' gaze direction on the suspect's participation.

The next example is from a case where the suspect is accused of fencing[7] because he was in possession of a stolen motorcycle. The excerpt starts when the judge summarises the charges that have just been presented by the prosecutor:[8]

(23)

1. J: ▼. . . you had uh uh yes uh let's say a motorcycle at your disposal
2. while you uh knew that it was uh obtained by theft.
3. ▲ What do you want to say about that today, are those charges correct?
4. S: Uh yes.
5. J: Yes? ▼
6. For the police has uh seen you right,
7. that was on uh Tuesday uh February the 5th,
8. S: Right.
9. J: then you were riding there in the evening at 25 to 11,
10. without a ▲ helmet ▼ on a yes (motorcycle or) moped,
11. uh but then you're riding without a helmet
12. and then ▲ you're ▼ stopped by the police officers,
13. and then the officers uh see that the ignition lock has been forced open.
14. And then you say to the uh officers
15. yes you have to start that moped with a screwdriver.
16. (2) ▲ (1)
17. That's how it happened right?=
18. S: =Yes.
19. J: ▼ Well and then uh the police finds out that uh
20. that the moped, that that turns out to be a motorcycle,
21. that had been uh ▲ reported stolen. ▼ =
22. S: =Hm.
23. J: And it also appears that Mr. uh Kwant,
24. there is a ▲ report ▼ of his complaint uh in the case file,
25. he says that his motorcycle that he ha – had locked ▲ in a parking lot ▼ in Diemen,

[7] Offence of buying or selling stolen goods.

[8] (▲ and ▼ are the symbols for upward and downward movements of the judge's gaze direction; see Chapter 1 and Transcription Conventions.)

26. that it has been stolen between Friday the 25th of January
27. and Saturday the 26th of January.
28. ((continues by going over the witness statement))
(1, N)

Having checked whether the suspect agrees with the charges (lines 3–5, the judge looks down at the document and begins summarising the police report (lines 6–13). The judge then produces a direct quote of the suspect's reported talk (line 15), introduced by the quotative 'you say' (line 14). The judge's quote serves to elicit the suspect's confirmation and to verify his stance (line 17). After the suspect's confirmation the judge continues summarising and reading aloud statements from the police (lines 19–21) and from the owner of the moped (lines 23–8).

Most of the time in this episode the judge looks down at the documents, but she often shifts her gaze direction from the documents to the suspect and back. These shifts in gaze direction occur in three interactional environments, with different effects on the suspect's response. First, there are a number of brief moments of the judge's looking up in the middle of an utterance (line 10, 12, 24 and 25). As these moments are very short and have no interactional effects they can be explained as a way of maintaining and affirming contact with the suspect (Licoppe, 2014: 90).

Second, the judge produces similar upward and downward shifts in gaze direction in the course of the completion of a turn-constructional unit (line 21). This generates an acknowledgement token (line 22) that displays that the suspect is attentive to the judge's talk. This has no further effects on the interaction as the judge continues reading aloud from the case file. Thus, the judge's upward and downward gaze movements just before the end of turn completion embodies a 'weak' response-encouraging environment in line with a 'half-open state of talk' in which the judge does the talking and the suspect has the right but not the obligation to respond.

Third, there are two moments when an upward gaze movement before a question is followed by a downward gaze movement after the answer (lines 3–6 and 16–19). Here the upward gaze movement accompanies the questions and helps involve the suspect in the interaction (cf. Glenn and LeBaron, 2011; Licoppe, 2014; Rossano, 2012; Stivers and Rossano, 2010). The downward gaze movement accompanies the judge's return to the reading aloud from the documents. These two episodes are alike in that their question–answer structure, accompanied by upward and downward gaze direction, serves as a way of obligating the suspect to answer; they are different in that the judge's upward eye movement introducing the second question–answer sequence occurs in the course of a three-second pause (line 16).

In order to understand the origin and meaning of this pause let us inspect the episode immediately prior to it:

(24)
6. J: For the police has uh seen you right,
7. that was on uh Tuesday uh February the fifth,
8. S: Right.
9. J: then you were riding there in the evening at 25 to 11,
10. without a ▲ helmet ▼ on a yes (motorcycle or) moped,
11. uh but then you're riding without a helmet
12. and then ▲ you're ▼ stopped by the police officers,
13. and then the officers uh see that the ignition lock has been forced open.
14. And then you say to the uh officers
15. yes you have to start that moped with a screwdriver.
16. (2) ▲ (1)
17. That's how it happened right?=
18. S: =Yes.

The judge's quote starts with mentioning her source of knowledge ('the police', line 6), followed by an enumeration of a succession of events linked together by 'then', 'but then', 'and then' (lines 9–14), which culminates in a direct quote from the suspect's statement to the police (line 15). This is a central and incriminating piece of evidence because it conveys that, as the suspect knew that the motorcycle had to be started with a screwdriver, he must also have known that it was stolen (the legal prerequisite for establishing his punishability).

The interactional forces at work here could be accounted for by the simultaneous operation of response-encouraging and response-discouraging circumstances. First, as the excerpts (19), (21) and (22) have shown, the judge's shift of footing between her summary of the events and her direct quote (lines 14–15), her emphasis on 'you' (line 14) and the recognisable turn completion followed by a two-second pause might encourage the suspect's response. Second, the incriminating nature of the quote of the suspect's reported talk may both discourage and encourage a response: when it is taken as an accusation it may encourage response but, as it concerns 'the suspect's own words', it tends to discourage response (see excerpt 21). Finally, the judge's visible orientation to the case file projects an extended turn at talk that discourages the suspect's response. Thus, when the judge offers an opportunity for turn transition (line 16) the suspect's non-response could be an after-effect of his role of passive recipiency thus far or a result of his reluctance to confirm an incriminating piece of information.

In the following excerpt we can see the combined effects of the judge's gaze direction and the occurrence of pauses. The suspect is accused of having tried to rob a boy, together with two friends. The suspect denies having used a knife to threaten the boy, asserting that he was only holding the knife in his hands and that he did not mean any harm. The judge inquires further:

(25)

1. J: But not to threaten him.
2. S: No. (1)
3. J: Why did you do it then?
4. S: °(I don't know)°
5. J: ▼ I have – in your statement to the police right, on page 22, (3)
6. (there) your statement starts, (1) of the case file, (1)
7. and uh you say
8. I took the knife and was waving it about
9. in order to impress Melinho. (1)
10. It was clear that Melinho wanted to go away. (2)
11. I however, stayed in front of the door to prevent that. (3)
12. He could not get away because I held my foot against the door,
13. when he wanted to ▲ open the door.
14. (3)
15. That is what you say to the police.
16. (4)
17. ▼ And at the police station then it looks as if you say like
18. well yes I wanted to ▲ impress him, with that knife.
19. He wanted to get away, but that was not allowed.
20. ((puts his hand under his chin and keeps looking at S for 3 seconds))
21. S: °No I didn't do anything with that knife.°
22. J: You didn't do anything with that knife.

(2, N)

In response to the judge's questions (lines 1 and 3) the suspect first denies that he wanted to threaten the boy and his next answer is so quiet that it can hardly be understood (lines 2 and 4). At this moment the judge turns to the case file and introduces what he is about to do: he names the kind of statement he is going to read aloud and mentions the page on which it is written (line 5). After this introduction he reads aloud the suspect's statement to the police (lines 8–13). In that statement the suspect is reported to have specified how he wielded the knife ('waving it about', line 8) and why (to impress Melinho in order to prevent him from leaving, lines 9–11). The judge then summarises the statement in such a way as to make it recognisably at odds with what the suspect has just said (lines 17–19).

Again, the combination of the judge's shifts in gaze direction, pauses and other actions performed by his reading aloud sheds light on the response-encouraging and -discouraging features of the judge's talk. The judge looks down at the case file when he introduces his quotes from the case file (line 5). In the course of his reading aloud it becomes clear that the quote reflects back on the 'inadequacy' of the suspect's preceding answer and that it challenges the suspect's current position. Just before the end of a turn-constructional unit the judge looks up again, completes his turn and leaves a three-second pause (lines 13–14). This shift in gaze direction can be taken as a visual prompt for the suspect to take the floor (Glenn and LeBaron, 2011: 9), which is underlined by the three-second pause that follows.

When the suspect does not respond the judge shifts footing and produces a 'coda' (Labov and Waletzky, 1967) which returns the talk to the present moment ('that's what you say to the police', line 15). He leaves a four-second pause and keeps looking at the suspect, who still does not respond. The judge then directs his gaze at the documents for a short while (lines 17–18), as if he is 'pointing' to his source of knowledge (cf. Frers, 2009: 290; Glenn and LeBaron, 2011: 16). He does not read aloud any longer, but produces an enactment of the suspect's written statement in the course of which he looks up at the suspect again (lines 17–19). When he is finished he puts his hand under his chin and leaves a three-second pause. This finally occasions the suspect's – almost whispered – response, in which he maintains his earlier position in the interrogation ('I didn't do anything with the knife', line 21), contrary to his written statement to the police.

As in excerpt (24), the suspect's reluctance to respond may result from the response-discouraging after-effects of the judge's orientation to the documents and from the self-incriminating nature of the suspect's quoted statement to the police. Hence, the judge has to do more work to mobilise the suspect's participation. He starts out with looking up from the documents just before turn completion and leaving a pause; he then produces an utterance that underlines the completion of his prior turn and leaves another, longer pause; he finally produces an enactment of what he just read aloud, after which he puts his hand under his chin, demonstrating that he is waiting for an answer. It is only then that the suspect responds. Thus, although the judge avoids asking a question to induce the suspect to respond he puts increasingly more pressure on the suspect by employing multiple resources for inviting response (Stivers and Rossano, 2010: 9).

4.5 Conclusion

The case file is a versatile object for the legal professionals in the courtroom. It serves as a support for their preparation of the trial, as an aid for the management of their professional performance in court, and as their main source of knowledge about the case. Their references to the documents show how they are handling the case, how they have read and understood the case file and how they guide the attention of others to its salient features.

Although the professionals have access to the same case file, their selection of items to bring up and the ways in which they quote them are distinctly different. Judges invoke the case file for organising the court session, for ratifying the evidence, and for questioning the suspect. Their references to the case file may serve to exhibit procedural correctness and transparency, to guide suspects' listening and participation, and to maintain an appearance of neutrality. Prosecutors and defence lawyers select those items for quotation that support their institutional positions. These references serve for presenting a version of the events to the judge that, although they are packaged as 'assisting' the judge's truth-finding, are aimed at convincing as much as informing the judge. The 'professional reading' of the case file by the professionals in the courtroom both exhibits and performs their different institutional tasks and interests.

Much of what goes on in the courtroom centres around what the participants know, how they know it, how certain they are about it, and what they are willing to tell about it. Suspects may have first-hand knowledge of the facts but they may not be willing to tell it. On the other hand, their privileged access to 'what happened' gives them the right to confirm, amend or contradict statements of others. The professionals in court have second-hand knowledge of the events and incidents in question, but the repository of this knowledge, the case file in front of them, has 'first-hand' accessibility. This enables judges to turn to the case file when the suspect claims non-recall or gives an inadequate answer. To a certain degree the 'second-handness' of the information in the case file is its strength; it offers judges the opportunity to claim that they are merely passing on what others have said, which allows them to confront suspects with competing statements without aligning themselves with those statements.

The case file has a significant impact on the interaction between judges and suspects. The sequential position of the judges' quotes from the case file helps to understand the actions they perform. Generally speaking, the judges' references to the case file come in two sequential formats: in a first position as introduction to further questioning, and in a third position, as responsive to the suspects' answers. The judges' references to the case file in a first position provide the materials for making requests for confirmation, clarification or elaboration; the judges' references to the case file in a third position may serve to retrospectively designate the suspects' answers as inadequate or faulty and to confront suspects with counter versions.

The judges' two main tasks during their interaction with the suspect, ratifying the evidence and questioning the suspect, are embodied in their dual orientation to the suspect and the documents. In general, the judges' invocations of the case file for ratifying the evidence do not require or encourage the suspects' participation, whereas their references to the case file for questioning the suspect clearly do. However, the simultaneous relevance of these two tasks may result in interactional ambiguities. This makes the judges' reading aloud vulnerable to 'dialogisation', exhibited by the suspects' production of uninvited – and perhaps unwanted – responses. In those cases the judges' continued orientation to the case file is a resource for avoiding discussion and retaining the initiative.

On the other hand, the response-discouraging effects of the judges' reading aloud may hamper the suspects' participation when it is invited or required. Because of the interplay of response-discouraging and response-encouraging circumstances judges may have to make a greater effort to mobilise suspects' responses. They may have to use a greater variety of actions for pursuing answers, with increasing pressure on reluctant or reticent suspects to respond. Thus, the 'tightness' of the sequential organisation of initial actions and their responses does not only depend on the response-mobilising actions themselves, but also on their embedding in a response-encouraging or response-discouraging environment.

5 The Career of a Suspect's Statement

5.1 Introduction

The aim of this chapter is to trace a suspect's statement through successive stages of the criminal law process in one criminal case. The case discussed here is a simple case, with a more or less confessing suspect. It concerns events that started when a group of adolescents were standing in front of a supermarket. According to Dan, the alleged victim, about seven boys were standing around him; they closed in on him and one of the boys, 16-year-old Elmer, took €5 and keys from his coat pocket. The next day Dan's father went to Elmer's house, threatened to rip off his hand, and got the money back. In spite of this Dan pressed charges; he accused Elmer and his friend Jairo (also 16 years old), who were then picked up by the police. Some two months after the police interrogation Elmer and Jairo appeared in juvenile court, where they stood trial for a series of five street robberies that they allegedly committed together. As the charges against Jairo for the case analysed here were eventually dropped, Elmer stood trial alone for the sixth count on the indictment, the theft of €5.

I start with a step-by-step examination of the construction of the report of the police interrogation. I then consider the complete text of Elmer's statement and inspect its transparency for readers unacquainted with the original interaction in the interrogation, by exploring what understandings the text affords and by comparing the text with the original talk. I finally investigate the ways in which the judge refers to the police report in the course of his questioning activities in court.[1]

5.2 The Construction of the Police Report

The police interrogation is conducted by two police officers, a man (P^1) and a woman (P^2). The man asks (most of) the questions and the woman types up the police report as they go along. The standard bureaucratic and institutional

[1] I refer to the suspect as 'Elmer' and to the professionals in the case by their institutional identities, to highlight the fact that Elmer acts as an individual on his own behalf, whereas the professionals operate on behalf of the institution they are part of.

features of the police report of our case have already been discussed in Chapter 3. Here I shall examine the construction of the text of the police report between quotation marks, as this represents the text that is attributed to Elmer (see Appendix A). As it is a relatively short interrogation most of the talk will be presented and some episodes will be summarised. The focus will be on the coordination of the talk, the typing and the text. The interconnections between the talk, the typing and the text will be visualised in the transcripts by shading the moments of overlap of the talk and the typing, and by juxtaposing the talk and the text in two columns, so that the same line indicates the approximate simultaneousness of the talk and the (writing of the) text (see Chapter 1).

Chapter 2 has shown that the differential pace of the talk and the typing especially affects interrogations with two police officers, as the interrogating officer usually does not wait for the reporting officer to complete the typing before asking the next question. In our case the division of labour between the two police officers is immediately demonstrated at the start of the interrogation. The interrogator delivers the caution and tells Elmer what the interrogation will be about, while the reporting officer starts typing. These introductory exchanges are reported as:

You tell me that you wish to question me about a robbery of 5 Euros on the 7th of February at Bloemhof in Liemen. Tha[2] complainant is called Dan.

The police interrogator then starts the interrogation proper as follows (the shading signifies overlapping talk and typing, see Chapter 2 and Transcription Conventions, at the beginning of the book):

(1)

1.	P^1:	Can you yourself tell what happened,	
2.		that e- that afternoon, that evening?	
3.	S:	No.	
4.	P^1:	No? (3)	**You ask me**
5.		According to Dan uh you were with uh	**if I want**
6.		(1) a number of other boys	**to tell**
7.		amongst whom Jairo, (1)	**something**
8.		shopping centre Bloemhof in Liemen. (2)	**about it.**
9.		There uh there was a boy, (1)	**No I do**
10.		he was addressed first by Jairo, (2)	**not want**
11.		and uh (1) then uh (1) at a certain moment	**that.**

P^1's initial invitation 'can you … tell what happened' is flatly refused by Elmer (lines 1–3). P^1's response, the repetition of Elmer's 'no' pronounced with a questioning intonation, is followed by a three-second pause (line 4).

2 I have translated spelling mistakes with similar spelling mistakes.

Because a minimal 'no' answer can be heard as inadequate (Clayman, 2001: 413) the pause is understandable as the interrogator's offer to Elmer of an opportunity to elaborate on his answer. Instead, Elmer appears to put his right to silence into practice by keeping silent (line 4), after which P^1 starts summarising the report of the complaint. In sum, these first moments of the interrogation are characterised by Elmer's refusal to talk and by the interrogator's subsequent provision of the information from his own source, the report of the complaint.

The use of documents in the criminal law process may start as soon as there are any. The case is launched by Dan's filing a complaint, which will be the first report in a series; the police report under construction is the third (see Chapter 3; Appendix A). The report of the complaint is now used by the police officer to confront Elmer with the complainant's statement. This reflects the distribution of knowledge in a setting where Elmer has privileged access to 'the facts' but also has a right to disregard his concomitant speaking rights and responsibilities, and where the police interrogator has access to documents that were drawn up earlier.

From the beginning of the interrogation the reporting officer has been busy typing. As the typing is continuous, it is difficult to ascertain at what moment she starts typing up the interrogator's first question. It can be assumed that, when P^1 invites Elmer to tell him what happened (line 1) she is still writing down the introductory sentences of the police report. As she will type up the question–answer sequence of lines 1–3 after its production, the report of those actions, written in the recontextualised monologue style, will be drawn up in approximate overlap with lines 4–11.[3]

In order to trace the relation between the talk, the text and the typing I present part of this passage once more, together with its continuation:[4]

(2)

4.	P^1:	No? (3)	**You ask me**
5.		According to Dan uh you were with uh	**if I want**
6.		(1) a number of other boys	**to tell**
7.		amongst whom Jairo, (1)	**something**
8.		shopping centre Bloemhof in Liemen. (2)	**about it.**
9.		There uh there was a boy, (1)	**No I do**

[3] I refer to the text by way of bold type line numbers, to distinguish it from references to the talk represented in the same line.

[4] The reporting officer stops typing after line 45 (see excerpt 3). She resumes her typing some moments after P^1 asks a next question (see excerpt 4, lines 53–61). A comparison of the talk and the text suggests that the text about the talk between lines 1 and 37 is written down in overlap with the talk between lines 4 and 45, which allowed me to establish approximately what was typed when.

10.	he was addressed first by Jairo, (2)	**not want**
11.	and uh (1) then uh (1) at a certain moment	**that.**
12.	they go outside, then they are closed in,	**You read**
13.	Jairo addressed that boy, (1) and uh (1.5)	**to me**
14.	then uh (1) then you want of him uh (2)	**from**
15.	or you want, you	**the report**
16.	put your hand in his coat pocket. (1)	**of the**
17.	U::h and then five Euros are taken	**complaint**
18.	from it and his keys. (2) Jairo-	**that the**
19.	and he has just now confirmed that	**complainant**
20.	once more he then told you like	**is being**
21.	give the money back for it is not funny,	**closed**
22.	that did not happen, then the father	**in by**
23.	of that boy came to your door, and then	**a group,**
24.	you gave him those five Euros back. (1)	**that I**
25.	That's right isn't it?	**had my**
26. S:	°Yes°.	**hand**
27. P[1]:	°Okay°. (8)	**in his pocket.**

In response to Elmer's refusal to answer the question P[1] summarises the report of the complaint (lines 5–24), after which he invites Elmer's response with a tag-question that projects a confirmation (line 25). Elmer's soft-spoken agreement (line 26) is then hearable as passive acceptance of the information just given. This passage shows the convenience for the interrogator of the availability of the earlier report, as it provides the opportunity for dealing with Elmer's refusal to talk by moving from the initial actions of 'requesting information' to 'requesting verification'.

Elmer's confirmation appears somewhat to contradict his earlier unwillingness to talk (excerpt 1, line 3); it may be explained not only by the fact that the tag question projects a confirmation, but also by the circumstance that the information summarised by P[1] lies within Elmer's epistemic domain, and can be heard as a request for confirmation (Labov and Fanshel, 1977: 100). After Elmer's confirmation P[1] produces an okay-receipt which is followed by an eight-second pause (line 27) that conveys his acceptance of the answer, provides a pause to facilitate the typing and anticipates a transition to the next question–answer sequence.

As shown in excerpt (1), the reporting officer writes down the first question–answer sequence (lines 1–3) in the course of P[1]'s summary of the report of the complaint (lines **4–11**). After she has completed this sequence she writes down P[1]'s recontextualised next action (**'you read to me from the report of the complaint'**, lines **12–17**), still in overlap with P[1]'s summary. The differential pace of the talk and the writing, and the 'writer unfriendliness' of the recontextualised monologue style may explain how the written text lags behind and why only a small selection from P[1]'s talk (**'closed in'**, lines 12 and **21–2**;

'group', lines 6 and **23**; **'hand in his pocket'**, lines 16 and **26–7**) is written down.[5] The eight-second pause left by P^1 after the information from the report of the complaint (line 27) is not sufficient for the completion of the reporting of the talk thus far.

The interrogator's next questions show that his summary of the report of the complaint includes a number of topics that are now available for further elaboration:

(3)

28.	P^1:	Question to you is, (0.5)	**Took 5 Euros**
29.		who were you with there.	**from**
30.	S:	°When.°	**that**
31.	P^1:	That afternoon. You were there,	**and that**
32.		Jairo was there, who else was there.	**his father**
33.	S:	°Number of boys°.	**fetched**
34.	P^1:	Number of boys.	**the money**
35.	S:	°Yes°.	**back a day**
36.	P^1:	And what are those boys called.	**later**
37.	S:	I'm not going to tell.	**That is**
38.	P^1:	You're not going to tell. (1)	**right.**
39.		That's okay, not forbidden. (2)	**You ask me**
40.		But Jairo does tell it.	**with whom**
41.	S:	Yes then- why do you ask me	**I was**
42.		when you already know it from him.	**that day**
43.	P^1:	To ver- to verify and to confirm,	**I do not**
44.		that you tell the same as Jairo.	**want**
45.		For the judge will also ask it of course. (4)	**to tell that.**
46.		And if it then deviates, (1) then wi- then that	
47.		judge will say yes but this isn't right.	
48.		But well your choice right, you're the suspect right,	
49.		So you can have that choice. (2)	

P^1 asks for clarification of the first item summarised from the report of the complaint: the 'number of other boys' that accompanied Elmer (excerpt 2, line 6). Elmer's first response ('when', line 30) delays or avoids answering the question, which leads to P's specification of the question (lines 31–2). In response to this prompt Elmer produces a non-committal answer ('a number of boys', line 33) that almost repeats the words that P^1 has used earlier (line 6). P^1 then asks for concrete details, which Elmer refuses to give (lines 36–7). The interrogator explicitly accepts Elmer's invocation of his right to silence (line 39), but he also sets it off against the more cooperative conduct of Elmer's friend Jairo (line 40).

This induces Elmer to question the relevance of the question on the grounds that people are not supposed to ask for information they already have. P^1

[5] Differences between the talk and the text will be considered more fully in the next section.

explains that it is not the information he is after but an opportunity for its verification and confirmation (line 43). He supports this position by reference to the judge's future actions and assessment (lines 45–7). His explanation and his appeal to the judge's authority convey that there are 'good' reasons for asking questions about facts that are already known; by adding the evidential 'of course' (line 45) he implies that Elmer is supposed to know that (Haviland, 1987: 349); this, in retrospect, contests the 'askability' of Elmer's question (Stivers, 2011).

Although P^1 emphasises that the invocation to the right to silence is okay (lines 39 and 48–9), it appears to be a mixed blessing as he also suggests that inferences about Elmer's position of reticence will inevitably be drawn by the judge. As mentioned in Chapter 3, police interrogators frequently ask suspects to give them the names or descriptions of their companions. This anticipates future uses of the police report, not so much for the benefit of the other professionals in the criminal law process, but rather for their own ongoing investigations.

After the four-second pause (line 45) the reporting officer stops typing for the first time in this interrogation. In retrospect, this makes it likely that she has now finished writing down her version of the prior question–answer sequence (lines **39–45**), and that she has decided not to report the subsequent talk. This selectivity appears to be induced here not only by the practical circumstances of the constraints of time as in her earlier reporting tasks, but also by her assessment of the relevance of the talk for future readers of the report.

The completion of the interrogator's warnings about the possible negative effects of Elmer's refusal to answer (lines 48–9) leads him to ask a further question:

(4)

50.	P^1:	Right what happens then uh Elmer. (1)	
51.	S:	°When°.	
52.	P^1:	There. With that boy. How <u>is</u> that.	
53.		Is it right, did Jairo address that boy?	
54.	S:	Yes he addressed him.	
55.	P^1:	Okay,	
56.		(4)	**You ask me if**
57.		did that bo-	**it is right**
58.		Did you close in on that boy with all of	**that Jairo**
59.		you, or stood around him,	**Addressed**
60.	S:	We stood in front of the supermarket.	**that boy.**
61.	P^1:	In front of the supermarket. (2)	**Yes that**

P^1 invites Elmer to continue the narrative in the temporal order in which the events occurred (Sacks, 1978: 252); but, as Elmer once more responds with a return question that delays his answer ('when', line 51) P^1 substitutes his open question for a more specific request for verification (line 53; see excerpt 2, line 13). He displays his acceptance of Elmer's answer with an 'okay' receipt, followed by a four-second pause (lines 55–6).

The reporting officer, who has been listening to the talk for a while without typing it up (lines 46–55), chooses this moment to resume her typing. She does not write down P's original question (line 50) but she waits for Elmer's answer and P^1's response, and then writes down the question that produced a recordable answer (lines 53–4). Apparently, the recordability of Elmer's answer, followed by P^1's expression of acceptance (lines 54–5) affects her selection of the questions to write down.

After the four-second pause (line 56) P^1 embarks on the next topic that verifies another item summarised from the report of the complaint: Dan's statement that he had been closed in on by a group of boys. Part of this passage is presented here again, together with its continuation:

(5)

55.	P^1:	Okay,	
56.		(4)	**You ask me if**
57.		did that bo-	**it is right**
58.		Did you close in on that boy with all of	**that Jairo**
59.		you, or stood around him,	**addressed**
60.	S:	We stood in front of the supermarket.	**that boy.**
61.	P^1:	In front of the supermarket. (2)	**Yes that**
62.		Did you have your hand in his coat pocket,	**is right.**
63.	S:	°yes.°	**You ask**
64.	P^1:	°yes.°	**me**
65.		Did [you take five-	
66.	P^2:	[What did he say?	
67.	P^1:	[Yes coat pocket	
68.	S:	[Yes.	
69.	P^1:	Did you take five Euros and keys from it?	
70.	S:	°Saw no keys.°	**if we closed**
71.	P^1:	No key- but did you take five Euros	**in on that boy.**
72.		from [his pocket,	**Yes that is right.**
73.	S:	[°yes°	

P^1's question (lines 58–59) offers two options, the first of which is more accusatory than the second ('closed in on that boy' as against 'stood around him'). Elmer responds to the second part and repeats a word contained in the question ('stood', lines 59 and 60), which underlines the part of the question that he is answering and displays his answer as a proper response to that part (Clayman, 2001: 410). His answer neither confirms nor denies the question but broadens the description of where they were standing ('in front of the supermarket' instead of 'around him', (lines 59–60), thereby defusing the potentially harmful elements of the question. P^1 accepts the answer with a repeat receipt followed by a two-second pause (line 61).

As we have seen, the reporting officer starts typing up the previous question–answer sequence about Jairo (excerpt 4, lines 53–4) in the four-second pause following P^1's 'okay' receipt (line 56). To understand the extent of the reporting officer's time constraints I have compared the length of the talk with the length of the typing. The reported text covering the question–answer sequence can be typed in around fifteen seconds. Fifteen seconds of talk from the start of the typing (line 56) last to the end of P^1's next question (line 62). So the reporting officer is likely to have typed up the exchange about Jairo's addressing the boy in overlap with the talk represented in lines 56–62. Shortly after that she stops the typing for a moment to ask for clarification of current talk (lines 65–9), after which she continues the typing.

Again, the episode shows the complexity of the reporting officer's task: she has to divide her attention between what she remembers and writes down of prior talk, what she is hearing now of the current talk, and what she will select of that in preparation of her next entries in the police report. When she initiates repair (line 66) she has to keep her other commitments in abeyance until the resumption of her typing (line 70). Her typing lags behind in that her current writing covers a question–answer sequence already concluded (lines 53–4) while it overlaps two following question–answer sequences (lines 58–60 and 62–3).

The effects of her multitasking can be seen in her rendition of the next question–answer sequence (lines 58–60). She types up only the first, more harmful part of the question ('did you close in', line 58), disregarding the second part of the question ('stood around him', line 59) that is answered by Elmer. She does not attend to P^1's repeat receipt and the two-second pause that follows it (line 61), but she fashions Elmer's answer so as to be consistent with the text already on the screen and with her current police report style (**'yes that is right'**, line **72**).

Let us now take up the talk from P^1's next question and inspect its continuation:

(6)

62. P^1: Did you have your hand in his coat pocket,	**is right.**
63. S: °yes.°	**You ask**
64. P^1: °yes.°	**me**
65. Did [you take five-	
66. P^2: [What did he say?	
67. P^1: [Yes coat pocket	
68. S: [Yes.	
69. P^1: Did you take five Euros and keys from it?	
70. S: °Saw no keys.°	**if we closed**
71. P^1: No key- but did you take five <u>Euros</u>	**in on that boy.**
72. from [his pocket,	**Yes that is right.**
73. S: [°yes°	
74. P^1: °Okay°, (2)	**You ask me if it is rigt**
75. has- have they also said that you	**that I had my**
76. must give that money back?	**hand in his**

77.		Is that right?	**coat pocket**
78.	S:	No.	
79.	P^1:	Not. (0.5)	**and thook**
80.	P^1:	Why did you take it away,	**5 Euros.**
81.		can you explain that.	**Yes that is right.**
82.	S:	No I cannot explain.	**I saw no keys.**
83.	P^1:	°Cannot explain° (0.5)	**I took 5 Euros.**

P^1 continues with the verification of the elements summarised in the report of the complaint. He asks a number of yes/no questions about the events, starting with 'did you . . .' (lines 62, 69, 71; see also excerpt 5, line 58). As these questions formulate the terms of the required answer, they restrict Elmer's scope for saying things in his own terms (Edwards, 2008; Raymond, 2006). Elmer confesses to the theft of €5 from the boy's coat pocket (line 73) but denies the questions about the keys (line 70) and about the return of the money (line 78).

That P^2 has to deal with the constraints of time is shown in the lapse of time between the talk and the reporting of it and in her selection of reported items. She reports a recontextualised version of the initial question (lines 62 and **74–7**), an elided version of P^1's second question (line 69, 71–2 and **79–80**), Elmer's expressions of confirmation (lines 63, 73 and **81**) and his answer 'saw no keys' (lines 70 and **82**).

Thus far, the talk has focused on the verification of the information already known from the report of the complaint. Now P embarks on the new topic of Elmer's motives:

(7)

80.	P^1:	Why did you take it away,	**5 Euros.**
81.		can you explain that.	**Yes that is right.**
82.	S:	No I cannot explain.	**I saw no keys.**
83.	P^1:	°Cannot explain° (0.5)	**I took 5 Euros.**
84.		When did that father come to your door.	**You ask me why I did it.**
85.	S:	The next day.	**I cannot say.**
		((35 lines not given))	

Elmer responds negatively to the question about his motives (line 82), after which P^1 displays an acceptance of the answer by producing a repeat receipt (line 83) and by broaching a new topic (line 84). This exchange about the visit of Dan's father (35 lines not shown here), is reported as:

(8)

You ask me when that complainant's father came to visit me.
The next day. My cousin was also present. That father said a number of things.
He also threatened me. He was going to rip off my hand.
I told him that he should do that. I do not know that boy.
That Dan has heard where I live in the neighbourhood.

This text is based on a series of questions, answers and other actions concerning the circumstances of Elmer's return of the €5 to the complainant's father. During this episode there is continuous typing. After its conclusion the interrogator returns to the topic of Elmer's motives while the reporting officer is still typing:

(9)

Transcript	Report
120. P^1: Do you know why you did it?	**That Dan has**
121. S: What.	**heard where**
122. P^1: Take those five Euros.	**I live in the**
123. S: I don't know what I [( )	**neighbourhood.**
124. P^1: [showing off?	
125. S: No but uh he did get those 5 Euros back he-	
126. I don't know why he files a complaint	
127. when you've got it back.	
128. (1)	**I do not**
129. P^1: Yes,	**Understand**
130. (6)	**why someone files**
131. P^1: Would that boy have been <u>scared</u> of you,	**a complaint**
132. you think, or not.	**when you already**
133. S: (°I don't know°) (5)	**got your 5 Euros back**

In the course of Elmer's noncommittal response (line 123) P^1 offers a candidate answer ('showing off?', line 124) that is rejected by Elmer, who chooses to bring up the outcome of the events ('he did get those 5 Euros back') rather than explain his motives. P^1 shows his orientation to P^2's typing by not immediately continuing with a next question and by offering an acknowledgement token followed by a six-second pause (lines 128–30). P^1 then makes another suggestion that might help explain Elmer's actions, which once more gets a noncommittal answer (lines 131–3) .

In contrast with the series of yes/no questions asked before, in the exchanges about Elmer's motives the distribution of knowledge is different: this time P does not know the answers as Elmer is supposed to have privileged access to what has motivated him. However, when Elmer claims he cannot answer the question P takes recourse to a source of knowledge that he can assume they share; his suggestions are based on his common-sense knowledge about the conduct of adolescents (lines 124 and 131).

Excerpt (9) shows two periods of typing. It is likely that during the talk transcribed in lines 120–4 the reporting officer finishes writing down the last utterances of the prior talk about the visit of Dan's father. She then stops the typing, listens to Elmer's answer (lines 125–7) and types it up (lines **128–33**). The talk in overlap with her typing is not written down.

After this exchange there is a five-second pause (line 133), after which the reporting officer stops the typing, turns to Elmer and says:

(10)
134. P^2:I don't quite understand that you say like
135. well as he got it back why would he file a complaint.
136. It's surely a matter of (0.5)
137. in the first place that you take it away from him.
138. S: Yes but he did get it back yes.
139. P^2:But if his [father hadn't gone- come to your door,
140. S: [’t was already- ’t was already
141. P^2:then it surely would not have got back.
142. S: Yes it would.
143. P^2:How then?
144. S: For we were going to give it back ourselves
145. for we were going out anyway.
146. P^1:O:h

This episode retrospectively shows P^2's understanding of the text she is typing. As she is writing down Elmer's answer (lines 125–7, excerpt 9) she notices an inconsistency between Elmer's interpretation of the events and her own perspective on the case. She stops typing and asks for clarification of Elmer's incomprehension of Dan's filing a complaint. Her assumption is that Elmer returned the money under the pressure of Dan's father's threats rather than of his own volition (lines 139, 141), which would imply that he meant to keep the money. This is contradicted by Elmer's assertion that he had planned to give the money back later (lines 144–5).

At this point the other police officer produces an 'oh' response (line 146) that acknowledges the information given by Elmer as 'new' (Heritage, 1984b), after which he resumes his role as interrogating officer:

(11)
146. P^1:O:h
147. S: I was going to meet him anyway
148. at the community centre. (0.5) So
149. P^1:Oh so you had- before the father came to the door,
150. you yourselves had planned
151. or you had already planned
152. S: We [were going to give it back.
153. P^1: [I am going to give it back.
154. S: Yes we were going to give it back [anyway.
155. P^1: [Hmmm.

156. (7)	**We were going to**
157. So this this this actually has been	**give it**
158. like pestering.	**back**
159. S: Yes it was just fooling around.	**at the**
160. P^1:Fooling around. Yes. Yes.	**community**
161. For that boy has never done	**centre.**
162. anything to you right, or has he.	**We did**
163. S: No. (1)	**give**
164. P^1:No I can imagine if they- that boy is	**it back,**

165.	being a pain in the ass	**didn't we?**
166.	that you at a certain moment (say) well	**It was**
167.	we'll just teach him a lesson, (2)	**foolishness.**
168.	but that is apparently not the case.	**We were going**
169.	(8)	**to give it back.**

In the course of P^1's formulation of Elmer's position (lines 149–50, 153; Heritage and Watson, 1979) Elmer states and confirms his intention to return the money (lines 152 and 154). This is acknowledged by P^1, who leaves a seven-second pause to facilitate the typing, and then continues with another formulation ('So this ... like pestering', lines 157–8). This conclusion could be taken as an observation or as an assessment of Elmer's actions; Elmer's response initially confirms P^1's formulation but he follows this with a more harmless alternative ('yes ... fooling around', line 159), downplaying the potentially negative connotations of 'pestering'. This enables him to agree with P while at the same time mitigating his actions (cf. Drew, 1992).

P^1 acknowledges this answer with a repeat receipt (line 160), followed by a suggestion that the boy had not provoked Elmer (lines 161–2). Elmer confirms this, after which P gives an example that could explain Elmer's conduct ('a pain in the ass', 'teach him a lesson', lines 165–6). Elmer's silence leads P to accept the fact that Elmer will not expand on his motives any further (line 168). This conclusion and the subsequent eight-second pause make relevant a transition to a next topic.

An examination of the sequential placement of the typing onset (line 156) shows that the reporting officer starts the typing after Elmer's answer to her question is acknowledged and verified by P^1 (lines 146–55). The text she writes occurs in overlap with P^1s further questioning. Most of this talk is not reported. Elmer's answer, marked by P^1s repeat receipt ('fooling around') and two acknowledgement tokens (lines 159–60), is reported as **'It was foolishness',** lines **166–7**).

After the eight-second pause (line 169) P embarks on a new topic:

(12)

170. P^1:	But, it is perhaps- just for your information,	
171.	(1) according to the Dutch crime-	
172.	criminal code this <u>this</u> event is classified	**You explain**
173.	as a <u>street</u> robbery.	**to me that**
	((P. explains Elmer's legal position))	**it is still**
	((30 lines not given))	**a street robbery.**

The interrogator's reference to the Dutch Criminal Code follows his and Elmer's negotiations about the interpretation of Elmer's actions (see excerpt 11: 'pestering', 'fooling around', 'teach him a lesson'). It conveys that whatever the description of Elmer's actions, according to the law it is a criminal offence. The interrogator continues by explaining some of the legal technicalities and the possible consequences of this for Elmer's future (30 lines not given here). This episode is not reported.

After this exposé about Elmer's position in this criminal case there is a five-second pause followed by an 'okay' receipt by P¹. This is where P², who has stopped typing for some time, comes in to ask once more about Elmer's companions:

(13)
203. P²: Don't you want to tell who you were with?
204. S: °No.° (2)
((16 lines not given))

In the talk that follows P² tries to persuade Elmer to be more specific about his companions than he was before. Elmer repeats the position he took earlier, invoking the rule that people should not ask for information already known. P²'s response deviates from what the other interrogating officer asserted before about Jairo's cooperation with the police (excerpt 3, line 40), as she concedes that Jairo did not tell all the names of the other boys. Elmer continues being cautious as he only gives numbers ('perhaps two or three') not names, and as he describes the other boys as only casual acquaintances. This is reported as:

(14)
You ask me who the other boys were with whom I was.
Jairo and two or three others. I am not going to give names.
There were some other people that I know from the street,
they were with us, but we did not hang out with them.

When it is clear that Elmer will not give any more details about his companions, the interrogating officer stops talking and there follows a forty-five-second pause, during which the reporting officer finishes her typing. She then turns to P and asks:

(15)
220. P²: Did you- are we done,
221. P¹: Yes. This is fine.
222. (8) **I have nothing further to state."**

After this exchange P² writes down the final sentence of Elmer's statement and closes the quotation marks. As mentioned in Chapter 3, this sentence is a routine element of the police report rather than an accurate description of the suspects' talk.

This is followed by a period in which P² edits the text with P¹'s assistance:

(16)
223. (10)
224. P²: °It's this one.°
225. ((58 seconds of editing))
226. ((90 seconds of intermittent editing and quiet exchanges between P and P²))

The final moments of the encounter are spent on editing the text. The two police officers work on the report together; they are both oriented to the text on the screen, and their quiet exchanges suggest that they take the presence of Elmer into account but exclude him from current business, until the moment of the completion of the document, when it is printed and signed by Elmer and the two police officers.

5.2.1 Summary

The division of labour between the two police officers affect the 'typeability' of the talk in the interrogation. Although the interrogating officer does sometimes take the reporting officer's task into account, the typing typically lags behind the talk. Moreover, the time-consuming recontextualised monologue style intensifies the pressures of time on the reporting officer. The reporting officer has to type up prior talk without enough time to write down everything, while listening to current talk for future 'recordables'. This means that she must summarise the talk and make a selection of the items to be reported on the basis of their 'recordability'. A consequence is that parts of the talk are misheard or overlooked.

Another constraint on the construction of the text originates from the requirements of creating a coherent text. The text on the screen may affect what comes next so that, for example, the reported answers are made to be compatible with the questions already written down. By the same token, the reporting officer may listen for possible appropriate continuations of her text-under-construction and select those items that are consistent with the emerging narrative on the screen.

At times the reporting officer actively participates in the interrogation. She interrupts the talk for a moment when she has not heard something and when she notices an incongruity in Elmer's narrative that needs clarification, and she repeats a question dealt with some time earlier because it has not yet been answered satisfactorily. Thus, the division of labour between the interrogating and the reporting officer is not strict, as both officers take into account some of the tasks of the other. This also comes to the fore at the final moments of the encounter, when both officers work on the text and review the report together.

5.3 The Transparency of the Police Report

In this section I shall inspect Elmer's statement in its textual environment (cf. Clayman, 1990: 83) and examine its transparency by comparing it with the original talk. Two aspects of transparency will be dealt with here: of substance and of interaction. Substantive transparency relates to the degree of completeness of the information that readers of the police report are offered about the topics discussed in the interrogation. Interactional transparency refers to the degree of insight that readers are offered into the original sequential environment of Elmer's talk. I shall first present the text in its entirety and offer a global examination of its substance and composition. I then consider the reported interactional organisation of Elmer's statement in more detail and go over each paragraph of the text separately, in comparison with the talk.

5.3.1 The Text

As we have seen in its introductory texts, the police report gives no information about a division of labour between the two police officers (see Chapter 3 and Appendix A). It is not clear who asked the questions and who did the writing, which makes the report indistinguishable from the reports of 'solo' interrogations, as can be seen in the complete text of Elmer's statement:[6]

(17)

1. "I understand that you wish to hear me and that I am not obliged to answer questions.

2. You tell me that you wish to question me about a robbery of 5 Euros
3. on the 7th of February at Bloemhof in Liemen. Tha complainant is called Dan.
4. You ask me if I want to tell something about that.
5. No I do not want that.

6. You read to me from the report of the complaint that the complainant is being
7. closed in by a group, that I had my hand in his pocket. Took 5 Euros from that
8. and that his father fetched the money back a day later.
9. That is right.

10. You ask me with whom I was that day.
11. I do not want to tell that.

12. You ask me if it is right that Jairo addressed that boy.
13. Yes that is right.

14. You ask me if we closed in on that boy.
15. Yes that is right.

16. You ask me if it is rigt that I had my hand in his coat pocket and thook 5 Euros.
17. Yes that is right. I saw no keys. I took 5 Euros.

18. You ask me why I did it.
19. I cannot say.
20. I do not understand why someone files a complaint
21. when you already got your 5 Euros back.
22. It was foolishness. We were going to give it back.

23. You ask me when that complainant's father came to visit me.
24. The next day. My cousin was also present. That father said a number of things.

[6] For the original layout, see Appendix A. The numbering of the lines is my addition.

25. He also threatened me. He was going to rip off my hand.
26. I told him that he should do that.
27. I do not know that boy. That Dan has heard where I live in the neighbourhood.
28. We were going to give it back at the community centre.
29. We did give it back, didn't we?

30. You explain to me that it is still a street robbery.
31. It was foolishness. I don't understand that.

32. You ask me who the other boys were with whom I was.
33. Jairo and two or three others. I am not going to give names.
34. There were some other people that I know from the street,
35. they were with us, but we did not hang out with them.

36. I have nothing further to state."

The report is written in the recontextualised monologue style, which is meant to give the reader some insight into the interactional environment in which Elmer's statement has been elicited. The text suggests that eight questions have been asked (lines **4**, **10**, **12**, **14**, **16**, **18**, **23** and **32**) and that three other actions have been performed by the interrogator: telling, reading and explaining (lines **2**, **6** and **30**).

A global understanding of the interactional organisation of the interrogation can be inferred from the composition of Elmer's reported statement. It is subdivided into a number of paragraphs, each beginning with a reported action of the interrogator (mostly 'you ask me') followed by Elmer's reported response. It highlights the participants' conversational positions: the interrogator is in a first position doing the asking, telling, reading and explaining, to which Elmer's actions are responsive. It is only Elmer's final reported sentence (**'I have nothing further to state'**, line **36**) that seems to have been produced without any inducement of the interrogator.

As the reported talk is understandable by reference to its surrounding texts (Clayman, 1990), it can be noticed that in the question–answer sequences reported in lines **16–17**, **18–22** and **23–9** Elmer seems to be progressively answering more than the question. It can also be observed that these answers contain unsolicited denials (lines **17** and **27**) and that they show narrative incoherence (lines **24** and **27**). Consequently, it may be inferred that at least some follow-up questions or other interrogator actions have not been reported.

Although the interrogator's actions are recognisable as 'first position' actions, they can also be considered in relation to prior reported talk. Thus, the '**you read to me**' sentence (line **6**) can be understood as the interrogator's response to Elmer's unwillingness to talk; and the '**you explain to me**' phrase (line **30**) is understandable as responsive to Elmer's defensive utterances in lines **28–9**. The other reported questions or actions involve a shift to a new item or topic, which means that they can be read as acceptance of the prior answers.

For a reader who has no access to the underlying interaction, the text of the police report shows a fairly cooperative suspect who confesses to most of the charges, but who does not want to name his companions (lines **5** and **33**). Besides, he does not see his actions as a street robbery but as an act of 'foolishness' because he claims that he never intended to keep the money (lines **22**, **28** and **31**). The main 'message' of the police report is that the contested issue is not so much 'what happened' but rather how to interpret it.

5.3.2 The Text and the Talk

In this section I present the consecutive paragraphs of the text to examine what understandings these texts afford. I then juxtapose the talk and the text in order to examine their differences and similarities. The text and the talk do not always run parallel, because at the end of the interrogation the two police officers review and edit the text. As a result, the text does not always follow the talk, and some passages are moved or added.

The report begins with Elmer's reported expression of understanding and acceptance as a response to the interrogator's delivery of the caution (see Chapter 3):

(18)
1. **"I understand that you wish to hear me and that I am not obliged to answer questions.**

At this moment in the interrogation the recording device had not yet been switched on, so the text cannot be compared with the talk. However, as mentioned before, suspects' initial expressions of understanding and acceptance have little or no correspondence with the actual talk in the interrogation.

The text that follows introduces the topic of the interrogation and states the events (the robbery of €5), their location, the date and the name of the complainant (lines **2–3**):

(19)
2. **You tell me that you wish to question me about a robbery of 5 Euros**
3. **on the 7th of February at Bloemhof in Liemen. Tha complainant is called Dan.**
4. **You ask me if I want to tell something about that.**
5. **No I do not want that.**

In spite of the artificiality of Elmer's recontextualised reported talk, the original interaction can be reconstructed so that the sentence introduced by the 'you tell me' phrase (line **2**) can be understood as representing the interrogator's introduction of the substance of the interrogation, followed by a 'you ask me' phrase (line **4**) that invites Elmer to tell his story; the 'you tell me phrase can then be read as the introduction to the question formulated in the 'you ask me' phrase. Elmer, who has just been told that he is not obliged to answer questions, appears to invoke his right to silence (line **5**).

The lines **4–5** are based on the following interchange:[7]

(19a)

1.	P^1: Can you yourself tell what happened,	**You ask me if I want to tell**
2.	that e- that afternoon, that evening?	**something about it.**
3.	S: No.	**No I do not want that.**
4.	P^1: No? (3)	

There is a clear correspondence between the text and the original talk (lines 1–3). What obviously differs is the recontextualised monologue style of the report, in which Elmer seems to give voice both to the interrogator's and to his own talk. The text and the talk also differ in that Elmer's curt refusal to talk is reported as a full sentence (line **3**), and P^1's implicit invitation to elaborate (line 4) is not reported. The comparison of lines 1–4 with the reported text shows a decontextualisation and a recontextualisation of the talk. The decontextualisation entails a loss of interactional detail; the recontextualisation concerns the transformation of conversational talk into a sentence that follows the conventions of written texts, in a specific police-report writing style.

The lines that follow are understandable as P^1's acceptance of and response to Elmer's unwillingness to talk:

(20)

6. You read to me from the report of the complaint that the complainant is being
7. closed in by a group, that I had my hand in his pocket. Took 5 Euros from that
8. and that his father fetched the money back a day later.
9. That is right.

Instead of Elmer it is now the interrogator who presents a version of what happened, naming the report of the complainant's statement as his source. The fact that Elmer is reported as volunteering his agreement with this (line **9**) seems to be inconsistent with his earlier appeal to his right to silence.

The text is based on the following episode:

(20a)

4.	P^1: No? (3)	
5.	According to Dan uh you were with uh (1)	**You read to me from the report**
6.	a number of other boys	**of the complaint**
7.	amongst whom Jairo, (1)	
8.	shopping centre Bloemhof in Liemen. (2)	
9.	There uh there was a boy, (1)	

[7] In the excerpts in this section I shall not consider the moments at which the texts are typed but, for purposes of comparison, I shall present the text of the report in the same lines as its corresponding talk.

10.	he was addressed first by Jairo, (2)	
11.	and uh (1) then uh (1) at a certain moment	**that the complainant is being**
12.	they go outside, then they are closed in,	**closed in by a group,**
13.	Jairo addressed that boy, (1) and uh (1.5)	
14.	then uh (1) then you want of him uh (2)	
15.	or you want, you	
16.	put your hand in his coat pocket. (1)	**that I had my hand in his pocket.**
17.	U::h and then five Euros are taken	**Took 5 Euros from that**
18.	from it and his keys. (2) Jairo-	
19.	and he has just now confirmed that	
20.	once more he then told you like	
21.	give the money back for it is not funny,	
22.	that did not happen, then the father	**and that his father**
23.	of that boy came to your door, and then	
24.	you gave him those five Euros back. (1)	**fetched the money back**
		a day later.
25.	That's right isn't it?	
26.	S: °Yes°.	**That is right.**
27.	P^1: °Okay°. (8)	

A comparison with the original talk shows that the text in the report is only part of what P^1 originally summed up. The reporting officer does not report the talk in lines 5–11, 13–15, 18–21, 23, which means that the information about the presence and actions of Elmer's friend Jairo and the alleged theft of Dan's keys is not reported.

Apart from the loss of information as a result of the selection of reported items, there are other differences between the text and the talk. It is noticeable that the reporting officer writes down an item (**'a day later'** line **24**) that, as it has no equivalence in the talk thus far, may have been added later (cf. excerpts 7 and 25 a, line 85). Second, the interrogator's tag question 'That's right isn't it?' and Elmer's quiet agreement (lines 25–6) are, as in monologue-style reports, transformed into what seems to be Elmer's volunteered confirmation (**'That is right'**, line **26**). This creates the impression of a more pronounced change of position – from an invocation of his right to silence to a voluntary agreement with the alleged victim's version – than can be heard in the original talk.

The following paragraph concerns the question about the identification of the boys present at the scene, boys who may have been involved in the incident besides Elmer and Jairo:

(21)

10. You ask me with whom I was that day.
11. I do not want to tell that.

This seems a straightforward question–answer exchange that creates the impression that Elmer's response is given straight away without any further inducement of the interrogator. The original talk is more complex than that:

(21a)

28. P^1: Question to you is, (0.5)	**You ask me**
29. who where you with there.	**with whom I was that day.**
30. S: °When.°	
31. P^1: That afternoon. You were there,	
32. Jairo was there, who else was there.	
33. S: °Number of boys°.	
34. P^1: Number of boys.	
35. S: °Yes°.	
36. P^1: And what are those boys called.	
37. S: I'm not going to tell.	**I do not want to tell that.**
38. P^1: You're not going to tell. (1)	
39. That's okay, not forbidden. (2)	
40. But Jairo does tell it.	
41. S: Yes then- why do you ask me	
42. when you already know it from him.	
43. P^1: To ver- to verify and to confirm,	
44. that you tell the same as Jairo.	
45. For the judge will also ask it of course. (4)	
46. And if it then deviates, (1) then wi- then that	
47. judge will say yes but this isn't right.	
48. But well your choice right, you're Elmer right,	
49. So you can have that choice. (2)	

A comparison of the text with the talk shows that the reporting officer has only reported the original question (line 29) and Elmer's refusal to answer it (line 37). Elmer's initial evasiveness and reluctance to be specific (lines 30 and 33) and P's pursuit of an answer (lines 31–2 and 36) remain unreported, as do the subsequent negotiations about their respective epistemic responsibilities (lines 40–4; cf. Stivers et al., 2011), P^1's invocation of the judge's future actions, and his assertions about the consequences of not mentioning the names of the other boys (lines 45–7). Although the main elements of the exchange have been preserved, the reader gets no insight into the interrogator's efforts to persuade Elmer to disclose the names of the other boys present, nor into Elmer's continued resistance. One of the reasons for the reporting officer's selectiveness is, as we have seen in excerpt (3), the fact that for most of the time she is still reporting previous exchanges.

The absence in the police report of P^1's response to Elmer's refusal to name his companions (lines 38–49) creates the impression that the interrogator has immediately accepted Elmer's refusal to talk, as the next reported question (line **12**) follows Elmer's reported answer:

(22)

12. You ask me if it is right that Jairo addressed that boy.
13. Yes that is right.

The construction of the sentence (**'you ask me if it is right'**) suggests that P^1 is verifying information of which he already has some knowledge. Because P^1's initial information about Jairo's actions (excerpt 20a, lines 7–10; 13) has not been reported, this sentence is not recognisable as the question for verification that it originally was.

An inspection of the talk in the interrogation shows that originally P^1 asked a different question:

(22a)

50. P^1: Right what happens then uh Elmer. (1)	
51. S: °When°.	
52. P^1: There. With that boy. How is that.	**You ask me if**
53. Is it right, did Jairo address that boy?	**it is right that Jairo addressed that boy.**
54. S: Yes he addressed him.	**Yes that is right.**
55. P^1: Okay,	
56. (4)	

As in excerpt (21), the text of the police report gives a representation of a selection of the talk, but it does not give insight into the interactional organisation of Elmer's reluctance to answer P^1's initial question, nor into P^1's subsequent specification of the question and pursuit of an answer. The text written down represents lines 53–4, but the wording of Elmer's reported answer has been altered so as to create a correspondence with the reported question (**'you ask me if it is right ... Yes that is right'**).

The report continues with another question–answer sequence based on the information from the report of the complaint:

(23)

14. You ask me if we closed in on that boy.
15. Yes that is right.

Again this text reads as a straightforward question–answer sequence. The reported question–answer sequence will be understood as Elmer's confession to one element of the charges. What the reader does not know is that the reported question represents only the first half of the original question, and that P offered an alternative, less harmful version that was mitigated even further in Elmer's response:

(23a)

57. P^1: did that bo-	
58. Did you close that boy in with all of	**You ask me if we closed in on that boy.**
59. you, or stood around him,	
60. S: We stood in front of the supermarket.	**Yes that is right.**
61. P^1: In front of the supermarket. (2)	

As I observed in the previous section, during this part of the interrogation the reporting officer is still in the process of typing up the prior exchange as reported in excerpt (22), which may have made her fail to notice the second part of the question (line 59), P^1's repeat of Elmer's response and the subsequent pause (line 61). As a result, Elmer's 'we stood in front of the supermarket' is reported as **'yes that's right'** (line 60), transforming Elmer's noncommittal reply into an admission.

As before, the text continues with the next items as summarised from the report of the complaint, in a style that is recognisable as 'verifying':

(24)

16. You ask me if it is rigt that I had my hand in his coat pocket and thook 5 Euros.
17. Yes that is right. I saw no keys. I took 5 Euros.

The text differs from the previous paragraphs in that Elmer's answer **'Yes that is right'** (line **17**) is followed by two items that he seems to have volunteered: a denial (**'I saw no keys'**) and a repetition of something that he already seems to have confirmed (**'I took 5 euros'**, lines **16** and **17**). Together with the text given in excerpt (23), these four lines (lines **14–17**) comprise Elmer's confession to the acts he has been accused of (with the exception of the alleged theft of the keys).

The fact that Elmer appears to answer 'more than the question' and to produce an unsolicited denial may alert the reader to the possibility that more questions may have been asked than have been reported. This can in fact be seen in the corresponding talk:

(24a)

62. P^1: Did you have your hand in	**You ask me if it is rigt that I had**
63. his coat pocket,	**my hand in his coat pocket**
64. S: °yes.°	
65. P^1: °yes.° Did [you take five-	
66. P^2: [What did he say?	
67. P^1: [Yes coat pocket	
68. S: [Yes.	
69. P^1: Did you take 5 Euros and keys from it?	**and took 5 Euros.**
	Yes that is right.
70. S: °Saw no keys.	**I saw no keys.**
71. P^1: No key- but did you take	
72. 5 <u>Euros</u> from [his pocket,	
73. S: [°yes°	
	I took 5 Euros.
74. P^1: Okay, (2)	
75. has- have they also said that you	
76. must give that money back?	
77. Is that right?	
78. S: No.	
79. P^1: Not. (0.5)	

The reporting officer reports one question (line **62–3**, **69**) whereas four questions were asked (lines 62–3, 65/69, 71–2, 75–7). Three of these questions (lines 62–3, 69/71, 71–2) are combined and reformulated as one (lines **62–3**, **69**) and one question–answer sequence is not reported (lines 75–9).

Although it does not correspond with the wording of the interrogator's questions, the reporting officer makes the reported question recognisable as a verification question (**'You ask me if it is rigt'**, line **62**), and designs the reported answers ('yes', lines 64 and 73) so as to correspond with this construction (**'Yes that is right'**; see also excerpt 22a). The item about the theft of the keys (line 69) is not reported but the – denying – answer is (line **70**), which makes this part of Elmer's reported response appear volunteered and defensive. Elmer's reported reiteration that he took €5 has no equivalent in the talk; because of its sequential position in the text after **'I saw no keys'** (line **70**) it can be read as support of his defensive position, as suspects often bolster the credibility of their denials by adducing – partial – confessions (Komter, 1998: 24–6).

The reduction of reported questions shows a monologisation of the talk and creates an impression of a suspect more forthcoming and talkative than Elmer. What Elmer actually said in the reported episode is °yes.° (line 64), Yes (line 68), °Saw no keys.° (line 70), and °yes.° (line 73), which is reported as: **'Yes that is right. I saw no keys. I took 5 Euros'** (line **17**). Thus, these differences between the talk and the text show a decontextualisation in terms of a loss of interactional detail, and an emphasis on Elmer's confession that recontextualises the talk to accommodate future uses of the police report.

After Elmer's reported confession to the theft of €5 the text shifts perspective in that it is no longer 'the facts' that are discussed but Elmer's motives:

(25)
18. You ask me why I did it.
19. I cannot say.
20. I do not understand why someone files a complaint
21. when you already got your 5 Euros back.
22. It was foolishness. We were going to give it back.

The lines **18–19** are a rendition of the talk below:

(25a)

80.	P[1]: Why did you take it away,	**You ask me why I did it.**
81.	can you explain that.	
82.	S: No I cannot explain.	**I cannot say.**
83.	P[1]: °Cannot explain.°	
84.	When did that father come to your door.	
85.	S: The next day.	
	((35 lines not given. P[1] and Elmer discuss the return of the money))	

Although the reporting officer's portrayal of the question–answer sequence is different from the original, it captures the gist of the exchange.

The text of the report follows the talk until '**I cannot say**' (line **82**). Then the interrogator broaches a new topic about the visit of Dan's father to Elmer's house (line 84), but the report continues with some more lines that appear to be in response to the question about Elmer's motives (excerpt 25, lines **20–2**). These lines are traceable as answers to questions that have not yet been asked (see excerpts 27a and 28a).

This new topic is reported as:

(26)
23. You ask me when that complainant's father came to visit me.
24. The next day. My cousin was also present. That father said a number of things.
25. He also threatened me. He was going to rip off my hand.
26. I told him that he should do that. I do not know that boy.
27. That Dan has heard where I live in the neighbourhood.

The text initially shows a correspondence between what the question asks for and what Elmer answers ('the next day', line **24**); the continuation of his reported answer is unrelated to the gist of the 'you ask me' question. The text resembles a monologue-style report in that Elmer seems to answer much more than the question; it contains an unsolicited denial, details that one would not volunteer and incoherent bits of information, which suggests that the reporting officer has reported fewer questions than were actually asked. Thus, it may be inferred that the text of Elmer's answer was constructed with some – unreported – inducement from the interrogator, although it cannot be determined what was said in response to what.

Actually, the lines 84–5 (excerpt 25a) correspond with line **23** and the first three words of line **24**. The rest of the text is a result of Elmer's responses to thirteen unreported actions of the interrogator, aimed at eliciting information about the events around Dan's father's retrieval of the €5 (35 lines not given here). This monologisation of the text conceals the input of the interrogator and thus overstates the voluntariness of Elmer's contributions.

In the talk following this episode the interrogator returns to the question about Elmer's motives, the reported answers to which are added to the earlier paragraph about the same topic (see excerpt 25):

(27)
18. You ask me why I did it.
19. I cannot say.
20. I do not understand why someone files a complaint
21. when you already got your 5 Euros back.
22. It was foolishness. We were going to give it back.

The lines **20–2** are not direct answers to the reported question about Elmer's motives; they make an impression of unsolicited defensiveness, which may suggest that additional questions have been asked that have not been reported.

The lines **20** and **21** are based on the following talk (line **22** does not correspond with the talk thus far):

(27a)

120. P¹: Do you know why you did it?	
121. S: What.	
122. P¹: Take those five Euros.	
123. S: I don't know what I [( )	
124. P¹: [showing off?	
125. S: No but uh he did get those 5 Euros back he-	
126. I don't know why he files a complaint	**I do not understand why someone files a complaint**
127. when you've got it back.	**when you already got your 5 Euros back.**
128. (1)	
129. P¹: Yes,	
130. (6)	
131. P¹: Would that boy have been <u>scared</u> of you,	
132. you think, or not.	
133. S: (°I don't know°)	
134. P²: I don't quite understand that you say like	
135. well as he got it back why would he file a complaint.	

It now becomes clear that the reporting officer has decided to add the answers to the second question about Elmer's motives (line 120) to the paragraph reported earlier (excerpt 25, lines **18–19**). What cannot be inferred from the text is that P¹'s second question about Elmer's motives (line 120) exhibits his effort to pursue a response after Elmer's initial refusal to answer (excerpt 25a, line 82).

Elmer's guarded response to P¹'s question (line 123) gives rise to some interaction, of which only Elmer's response (lines 125–7) is reported but not P¹'s subsequent actions. The talk reported as lines **20–1** (lines 126–7) has been uttered as response to P¹'s unreported suggestion 'showing off' (line 124). Thus, the circumstance that readers are offered no insight into P¹'s efforts to elicit a response nor into Elmer's resistance to P¹'s candidate answers creates the impression of an overly defensive suspect.

What follows are the reporting officer's request for clarification and her expression of doubt about the voluntariness of Elmer's return of the money to Dan's father. The report of this (lines **28–9**) is added to a prior paragraph of the report (see excerpt **26**):

(28)

23. You ask me when that complainant's father came to visit me.
24. The next day. My cousin was also present. That father said a number of things.
25. He also threatened me. He was going to rip off my hand.
26. I told him that he should do that. I do not know that boy.
27. That Dan has heard where I live in the neighbourhood.

28. We were going to give it back at the community centre.
29. We did give it back, didn't we?

As mentioned before, the incoherence of the monologic text may alert readers that the talk could have contained more interrogator actions than are reported. It cannot be inferred from the text of the report that the talk represented in lines **28** and **29** has been elicited by the interrogators' questions about Elmer's (lack of) voluntariness of his return of the money:

(28a)

134.	P^2:	I don't quite understand that you say like	
135.		well as he got it back why would he file a complaint.	
136.		It's surely a matter of (0.5)	
137.		in the first place that you take it away from him.	
138.	S:	Yes but he did get it back yes.	
139.	P^2:	But if his [father hadn't gone- come to your door,	
140.	S:	[’t was already- ’t was already	
141.	P^2:	then it surely would not have got back.	
142.	S:	Yes it would.	
143.	P^2:	How then?	
144.	S:	For we were going to give it back ourselves	**We were going to give it back**
145.		for we were going out anyway.	
146.	P^1:	O:h	
147.	S:	I was going to meet him anyway	
148.		at the community centre. (0.5) So	**at the community centre.**
149.	P^1:	Oh so- before the father came to the door,	
150.		you yourselves had planned	
151.		or you had already planned	
			We did give it back, didn't we?
152.	S:	We [were going to give it back.	**We were going to give it back.**
153.	P^1:	[I am going to give it back.	
154.	S:	Yes we were going to give it back [anyway.	
155.	P^1:	[Hmmm.	
156.		(7)	
157.	P^1:	So this this this actually has been	
158.		like pestering.	
159.	S:	Yes it was just fooling around.	**It was foolishness**
160.	P^1:	Fooling around. Yes. Yes.	
161.		For that boy has never done	
162.		anything to you right, or has he.	
163.	S:	No. (1)	
164.	P^1:	No I can imagine if they- that boy is	
165.		being a pain in the ass	
166.		that you at a certain moment (say) well	
167.		we'll just teach him a lesson, (2)	
168.		but that is apparently not the case.	
169.		(8)	

We see here a monologic text created by the fact that none of the interrogators' actions are reported. Apart from this loss of reported interaction, the text of the first sentence more or less copies parts of the talk (lines 144 and 148). The second sentence (**'We did give it back, didn't we?'**) is added on the initiative of the reporting officer; it is a transformation of Elmer's talk, the rhetorical structure of which suggests that he is being argumentative or defensive. The repetition of '**we were going to give it back**' (lines **144** and **152**) may reflect Elmer's talk (lines 144, 152, 154), but without the reports of the interrogators' actions that elicited these sentences suggest repetitiveness or volunteered insistence on Elmer's part.

Elmer's explanation of his conduct as 'fooling around' (line 159) is the source of the entry in the report '**it was foolishness**'. As a result of the absence of the reporting of the interrogator's actions the sentence is not recognisable as Elmer's attempt to downgrade P's formulation of Elmer's motive ('pestering', line 158). The interrogator's further suggestions of possible alternative motives are not reported. Again, the lack of visibility of the interrogator's actions keeps this sentence 'hanging in the air' and makes it difficult to interpret from its context of surrounding text.

The character of these reported sentences as 'answers without their questions' may have induced the reporting officer to add the first two sentences (lines 144 and 148) to the paragraph beginning with the question about the visit of Dan's father (excerpt 28, lines **28–9**), and the two sentences that follow (lines 152 and 159 in reverse order) to the reported question about Elmer's motives (excerpt 27, line **22**). An effect of this is that some of Elmer's answers are reported as responsive to questions different from the original, which creates an impression of defensiveness.

Because of its placement as the next entry in the report the following paragraph may be understood as the interrogator's response to Elmer's reported defensiveness (excerpt 28, lines **28–9**):

(29)

30. You explain to me that it is still a street robbery.
31. It was foolishness. I don't understand that.

These two lines show a sequence in which the interrogator defines Elmer's actions as a 'street robbery', against which Elmer offers a counter definition ('foolishness') followed by an expression of incomprehension. These lines suggest that, whereas Elmer agrees with 'the facts', he disagrees with the interpretation of these facts.

This text is based on the following talk:

(29a)

170.	P[1]: But, it is perhaps- just for your information,	
171.	(1) according to the Dutch crime –	**You explain to me**
172.	criminal code this this event is classified	**that it is still**
173.	as a street robbery.	**a street robbery.**
		It was foolishness.
		I don't understand that.

((30 lines not given. P. explains Elmer's legal position))

The placement of these sentences creates the impression that Elmer's earlier reported description of his actions (**'foolishness**', excerpt 25, line **22**) is now uttered once more as a defensive response to the interrogator's interpretation of the events as a street robbery (line **31**). However, Elmer's only responses to the interrogator's explanations about the legal definition of his acts are some acknowledgement tokens. Although line **31** does not represent the original talk, excerpt (29) highlights the two contradictory positions of the participants: for the police interrogator it is a street robbery, for Elmer it is 'foolishness'. Again, line **31** may have been added during the reporting officer's editing activities at the end of the interrogation.

The final question–answer sequence covers a topic already dealt with, about the identity of the other boys present (cf. lines **10–11**):

(30)
32. You ask me who the other boys were with whom I was.
33. Jairo and two or three others. I am not going to give names.
34. There were some other people that I know from the street,
35. they were with us, but we did not hang out with them.

The suspect maintains his earlier position of not giving the names of his companions (line **33**; cf. excerpt 21, line **11**), but this time he seems to be more forthcoming about how he came to know these boys and what relationship he has with them.

This paragraph of the police report is a summary of Elmer's responses to twelve unreported questions and other efforts of the two police officers to make Elmer disclose the identities of the other boys. The fact that this question is not only asked but also reported twice exhibits that the interrogators have not accepted Elmer's initial refusal to answer; the monologic style of Elmer's reported answer conceals the interrogators' efforts to draw it out of him.

The last sentence in the report is routine (see Chapter 3):

(31)

36. I have nothing further to state."

The suspect's reported final sentence suggests that he took the initiative in ending the police interrogation. In reality, the interrogation is concluded as follows:

(31a)
220. P^2: Did you- are we done,
221. P^1: Yes. This is fine.
222. (8) **I have nothing further to state."**
223. (10)
224. P^2: °It's this one.°
225. ((58 seconds of editing))
226. ((90 seconds of intermittent editing and quiet exchanges between P^1 and P^2))

This last sentence bears no resemblance to the original talk, as the police officers' decision to end the interrogation is made without consulting Elmer.

5.3.3 *Summary*

The composition of the text of Elmer's statement in the police report shows that Elmer's reported contributions are, with the exception of the last sentence, responsive to the interrogator's first-position actions. But, although the recontextualised monologue style shows some of the interrogator's contributions, many of the questions and actions of the interrogator remain unreported. This monologisation of the text obscures the interrogator's contributions, overstates Elmer's voluntariness, and understates the interrogator's more adversarial actions. As a result, the police report offers little insight into the tension between the reticence and evasiveness of Elmer and the investigativeness of the two police officers.

A comparison of the text with the talk reveals that a number of sentences have been moved around and that some sentences have been added. It can be assumed that these entries are a result of the reporting officer's editing in the course of or at the end of the interrogation. The effect of this is that some of Elmer's answers are reported as responses to questions different from the ones originally asked, that some utterances of Elmer have been incorrectly reported as responses, and that some sentences have been added without corresponding utterances in the talk. The final adjustments to the police report made in the editing stage can be understood as the streamlining of the report and as highlighting those elements that are assumed to be of use to the professionals in the further criminal law process, viz. that Elmer confesses to 'the facts' but that he contests the interpretation of those facts.

5.4 Invoking the Case File in Court

When Elmer and Jairo appear in court the case file contains all the relevant documents for adjudicating the five offences of street robbery for which they now stand trial.[8] Elmer and Jairo are accused of having stolen telephones, an iPod, a wallet with money, a bicycle, a public transport card and keys. They are also accused of having used violence such as hitting, kicking and punching their victims, even when they were already in possession of the stolen items. In one case Elmer is accused of having hit a man with a baseball bat because he

[8] In juvenile cases, after the judges' examination of 'the facts', more time is usually spent on 'the person', as punishment is directed at rehabilitation and redress rather than at retribution. So the case file also contains the reports of a child protection officer, a juvenile probation officer and a psychologist.

resisted the assault, which resulted in a broken cheek-bone. The documents containing evidence of these other offences create a new context for understanding the current case, the theft of €5.

In the following sections I shall show how the text of the case file is recontextualised and incorporated into the judge's management of courtroom business.[9] I shall first outline the importance and affordances of the case file as source of knowledge for the judge and as basis for his questioning. I then examine the design of the judge's references to the police report, the actions they perform and their embedding in the sequential organisation of the talk.

5.4.1 Epistemic Domains

After the prosecutor's presentation of the indictment the judge begins the examinations by asking Elmer's opinion about the accusation:

(32)
1. J: ((looks at S)) What do you think of that accusation.
2. S: Uh yes what do I think of that accusation
3. but he himself also knew that [it was a joke
4. J: [Can you try and speak up a little?
5. S: He himself also knew that it was a joke and he got it back.
6. We were just fooling around.
7. J: Yes.
8. S: It is not so that we have stolen it.
9. J: Yes.
10. So you say it is right that I've done that ▼ and you've also-
11. on page 20 ▲ in the case file you also say right, that you did it.
12. But you said like
13. yea::h, it was not a robbery it was just foolishness.
14. S: °Yes°

In response to the judge's question Elmer reiterates what he also told the police: the boy got his money back and they were just fooling around (lines 5–6), after which he concludes that they have not stolen it (line 8). Both the sequential position and the substance of his response show its defensiveness: it is uttered as response to the accusation, and it contains a mitigation ('just fooling around', line 6) and a denial ('it is not so that we have stolen it', line 8).

The judge's response displays how the police report, highlighting Elmer's confession to the theft, has shaped the way he now listens. The beginning of his response (line 10, 'so you say') seems to indicate that he is going to quote or summarise Elmer's prior talk. However, the substance of his subsequent quote ('it is right that I have done that', line 10) is in contradiction with

[9] As the prosecutor and the defence lawyer do not directly refer to the police report of this case I shall only discuss the judge's references to the police report during his questioning of Elmer.

Elmer's prior utterance ('it is not so that we have stolen it', line 8). The judge's reference to the case file (line 11) then serves as evidence of the consistency of Elmer's position, and as support for his conclusion that Elmer's talk thus far amounts to a confession.

In these first moments of the questioning stage of the trial the judge's actions show how important the case file is as his primary source of knowledge. His first question (line 1) appears to yield epistemic priority to Elmer, who is given the opportunity to express his views on the case (lines 2–6). Yet this is overruled by the judge's reliance on the information in the case file. He supports the authenticity of his quotation of Elmer's confession by indicating the page number of the case file (line 11): 'on page 20 in the case file' is presented as concrete proof that Elmer said he did it, irrespective of what Elmer just told him. This is highlighted by the changes in the judge's gaze direction. Just before he refers to the case file he looks down at it (line 10) and when he starts summarising its contents he looks up again (line 11). He appears to be 'pointing' with his gaze direction at the relevant page of the case file as if to indicate that this is the location of his source of knowledge (Glenn and LeBaron, 2011: 16).

Lines 10–13 show how the judge summarises the two perspectives on the case as highlighted in the police report: Elmer's confession to 'the facts' and his disagreement with their legal interpretation as a robbery. The judge confirms the correspondence of the information in the case file with what Elmer just said in slightly different wording: 'it is not so that we have stolen it' (line 8) now becomes 'it was not a robbery' (line 13) and 'fooling around' (line 6) becomes 'foolishness' (line 13, the term used in the police report).

The judge's questioning is distinctly different from the questioning during Elmer's interrogation by the police. In the police interrogating room the general issue is what Elmer *did*; in the courtroom this is also relevant, but an additional – and perhaps more important – focus is on what he *said he did* to the police (or at least on what he is reported to have said to the police).

That the judge monitors Elmer's prior talk as verification and corroboration of the information in the case file is also evidenced in the next episode:

(33)
15. J: Well he got it back, I read that too,
16. U::hm but yes he apparently did not think it was foolishness
17. for he did file a complaint.
18. (5)
19. J: Right?
20. S: Yes. You could see it like that.

The judge confirms that 'he got it back' (line 15), repeating what Elmer has just said (line 5). However, he offers it as something that he has read instead of learned from Elmer a few moments earlier. This underlines the differences between their sources of knowledge; in spite of Elmer's first-hand knowledge of the case, the judge's reference to the written documents in front of him exhibits his preparation of the trial and his reliance on the authority of the document.

Whereas Elmer mentioned 'he got it back' in support of his description of his actions as 'a joke' and as 'fooling around' (lines 3 and 6), the judge now disputes that interpretation on account of the fact that Dan filed a complaint (line 17). His use of the modal adverb 'apparently' (line 16) suggests that this conclusion is not based on his direct knowledge of the state of mind of the complainant but on common-sense inferences that he draws from the particulars of the situation. The idea is that people go to the police to file a complaint for a good reason, not to report an act of 'foolishness'. This shows another type of recontextualisation of the 'suspect's statement': its inclusion in the case file has made it understandable by reference to the other documents, which gives the judge an opportunity to confront Elmer with the existence of counter versions.

After the judge draws this conclusion he leaves a five-second pause, providing an opportunity for Elmer to respond (line 18). When Elmer does not do so, the judge utters a prompt (line 19) after which Elmer expresses his agreement ('Yes', line 20). However, he adds 'you could see it like that'. This signifies in the first place that Elmer too has drawn his inferences on the basis of common-sense knowledge about why people file a complaint. Yet he shows his epistemic independence through an uncertainty marker ('you could see it like that', line 20) different from the judge's 'apparently' (line 16). Moreover, because this uncertainty marker is uttered as a response it also reflects back on the position taken by the judge. The judge's conclusion can then be viewed as just one way of looking at it. In this sense 'Yes. You could see it like that' can be taken both as a confirmation and as a challenge of the judge's conclusion. It allows Elmer to agree with the judge without contradicting his own prior position that the complainant knew that it was a joke (line 5).

In response the judge concedes that there is another way of looking at it:

(34)
21. J: Yes (2)▼ u:::hm (2)▲
22. and perhaps it may be that his <u>fa</u>ther wanted him to do that
23. that's <u>al</u>so possible, I don't know,
24. but there <u>is</u> a report of a complaint and and uh
25. but you say like yes it was not the intention to to steal that.
26. But at a certain moment you did give it back
27. but that was not straight away right,
28. S: No no no

The judge now reflects on alternative interpretations of Dan's actions ('perhaps ... his father wanted him to do that'), but he then juxtaposes the speculative nature of this line of reasoning (expressed by the uncertainty markers 'perhaps it may be', line 22) against the certainty of the existence of the report of the complaint (expressed by the emphasis on 'is', line 24). As he argued before (excerpt 33, lines 16–17), the judge takes the existence of the report of the complaint as evidence of the seriousness of the offence.

The judge proceeds with a reference to Elmer's claimed intention to return the money (line 25) followed first by an assertion that seems to bolster this claim 'you did give it back' (line 26) and then by a circumstance that could undermine it ('not straight away'), followed by the tag ending 'right', that projects a confirmation (lines 27–8). On the assumption that a person's intentions are expressed in his conduct, the view that Elmer did not intend to steal the money can then be challenged by the fact that he did not give it back straight away:

(35)
29. J: But if it was foolishness why didn't you give it back straight away.
30. S: °Because we would go out again later on°.
31. J: Because?
32. S: We would go out again later on.
33. J: Ah. (2)

Again, the judge assesses the plausibility of Elmer's assertions on the basis of his common-sense knowledge about what constitutes a 'normal' joke, implying that the unserious nature of 'foolishness' requires an immediate return of the money.

Elmer's reply is somewhat cryptic. Earlier he has explained to the police that he was planning to return the money when they met Dan at the community centre later on (excerpt 11). As he gives only half of this explanation it may seem strange that the judge does not ask for clarification. On the other hand, as this information is given in the police report of Elmer's statement (excerpt 28, line **28**) the judge may deem it unnecessary to pursue the matter further.

These first moments of the trial display what epistemic domains are in play: Elmer's first-hand knowledge and the judge's second-hand knowledge of the events, and their common-sense knowledge about why people lodge a complaint and about what constitutes a 'normal' joke. These epistemic domains are invoked not only to find and establish the truth, but also to assess the logic of Elmer's accounts and his behaviour.

5.4.2 Documents in Interaction

For a discussion of the design and actions of the judge's quotations of the case file, let us consider the beginning of the judge's questioning again:

(36)

1. J: ((looks at S)) What do you think of that accusation.
2. S: Uh yes what do I think of that accusation
3. but he himself also knew that [it was a joke
4. J: [Can you try and speak up a little?
5. S: He himself also knew that it was a joke and he got it back.
6. We were just fooling around.
7. J: Yes.
8. S: It is not so that we have stolen it.
9. J: Yes.
10. So you say it is right that I've done that ▼ and you've also-
11. on page 20 ▲ in the case file you also say right, that you did it.
12. But you said like
13. yea::h, it was not a robbery it was just foolishness.
14. S: Yes°
15. J: Well he got it back, I read that too,
16. U::hm but yes he apparently did not think it was foolishness
17. for he did file a complaint.
18. (5)
19. J: Right?
20. S: Yes. You could see it like that.
21. J: Yes (2)▼ u:::hm (2)▲
22. and perhaps it may be that his father wanted him to do that
23. that's also possible, I don't know,
24. but there is a report of a complaint and and uh
25. but you say like yes it was not the intention to to steal that.
26. But at a certain moment you did give it back
27. but that was not straight away right,
28. S: No no no

During this episode the judge quotes Elmer four times (lines 10, 11, 12–13 and 25). The quotes are all introduced by a quotative, or 'verbum dicendi' (line 10: 'so you say', line 11: 'you also say', lines 12 and 25: 'but you said/say like'), but their form and content differ.

The first quote ('So you say it is right that I have done that', line 10) is formulated as direct reported speech, as is indicated by the judge's use of the personal pronoun 'I'. What appears to be a direct quote is in fact the judge's transformation of Elmer's prior talk ('It is not so that we have stolen it') into a 'police-report-style' confession: 'it is right that I have done that' (line 10). This 'quote' is followed and supported by another quote, in indirect reported speech ('that you did it', line 11), supplemented with the identification of the location of the source of the information (line 11: 'page 20 in the case file'). So, whatever the (lack of) authenticity of the two quotes (lines 10 and 11), their claim that Elmer has confessed is substantiated by concrete proof of what Elmer has said according to his statement in the case file.

The third quote (line 13) represents the judge's version of Elmer's attempts to neutralise the wrongness of his actions. The juxtaposition of the two descriptions of Elmer's acts as 'robbery' and 'foolishness' (line 13) corresponds with the text of the police report, except for the fact that the term 'robbery' is reported as representing the police interrogator's talk, not Elmer's (excerpt 29, line **30**). It also differs from the talk in the police interrogation, as the interrogator's term 'robbery' followed instead of preceded Elmer's description of his acts as 'fooling around'. As it stands, the quote suggests that Elmer defended himself against the interpretation of his acts as a 'robbery', whereas originally his 'fooling around' was uttered after a prolonged discussion about his motives. It was produced as mitigating response to the interrogator's suggestion of 'pestering' (see excerpt 11), and was followed by the interrogator's explanations about the legal definition of Elmer's acts as 'street robbery' (excerpt 12). The fact that the interrogator's reported actions have been filtered out of the judge's quote creates the impression that Elmer volunteered this part of his statement (cf. Eades, 2008a: 323).

The third and fourth quotes (lines 13 and 25) seem to be in the direct reported speech style, but this time they are introduced by the quotatives 'you said like' (line 12) and 'you say like' (line 25). It has been observed that the quotative 'like' blurs the boundaries between direct and indirect reported speech (cf. Clift and Holt, 2007: 5), because the quote has the form of direct reported speech but allows for a lesser claim to faithful reproduction of the original speech (Lamerichs and Te Molder, 2009: 403). In these quotes the judge shows a specific shift in footing (Goffman, 1981). The lack of correspondence between the quotes and Elmer's reported talk in the police report, and the prosodic features of the judge's talk in line 13 (the prolongation of the vowel in 'Yea::h' followed by a slightly rising intonation, the emphasis in 'robbery' and 'foolishness') show the judge's relationship to the texts he utters: he is 'enacting' (Holt, 2007) or 'animating the voice' of Elmer (Galatolo, 2007). In doing this, he highlights Elmer's position as committed to mitigating or denying the charge of robbery.

The actions that are being accomplished by the judge's quoting practices can be understood by considering their substance, design and their sequential environments. The judge's selection of items to be quoted shows his preparation of the trial and his understanding of the two most salient elements of the case: the fact that Elmer confesses to having taken away the money but contests the interpretation of this as a robbery. So the first action accomplished by these quotes is drawing attention to the core of the business at hand; the fact that these utterances are presented as quotes makes Elmer accountable for them.

As the first substantive action in the trial is the prosecutor's presentation of the charges, the subsequent interaction between the judge and Elmer is framed within a context of accusations. In response to the accusation as formulated in the indictment Elmer defends himself by downplaying (lines 3, 5–6) and denying the charges (line 8). The sequential placement of the judge's initial quoting activities makes them recognisable as transforming Elmer's prior mitigation and denial of the charges into a confession and a mitigation (lines 10–13). The judge's references to the case file serve as verification or confirmation of Elmer's stance in court, as ratification as a piece of evidence, and as potential substance of further questioning.

This can be seen in the interaction that follows. The judge takes Elmer's expression just quoted ('it was just foolishness', line 13) and points out its discrepancy with the fact that Dan filed a complaint (lines 16–17). At the same time, the judge retains his appearance of neutrality by his references to the case file: by repeating the reported words or actions of Elmer and by explicitly mentioning the official source of his information he avoids taking a position himself (Holt, 1996; Matoesian, 2000). He refers to the victim's apparent evaluation of the events rather than to his own, and he invites Elmer to draw his own conclusions (lines 16–19).

In the episode that follows the judge asks Elmer to clarify the reported description of his acts as 'foolishness':

(37)
29. J: But if it was foolishness why didn't you give it back right away.
30. S: °Because we would go out again later on°.
31. J: Because?
32. S: We would go out again later on.
33. J: Ah. (2)
34. J: But just imagine right,
35. that everyone who feels in somebody else's pocket right
36. for ▼ that's what you say you did,
37. and ▲ uh everyone who then- those other ▼ boys right-
38. for you also say uh
39. You ask me if we closed in on that boy,
40. Yes that is right.
41. Right,
42. You ask me if it is right that I had my hand
43. in his coat pocket and took 5 Euros.
44. Yes that is right.
45. ▲by the way you confessed to have seen those keys,▼
46. did you ▲or didn't you take those keys. (1)
47. You say keys, I haven't done that=
48. S: =No.
49. J: Just those five Euros. (1)▼▲
50. S: °Yes°.

After Elmer's somewhat cryptic reply (line 32) the judge embarks on a new project. He invites Elmer to imagine his actions as something that everyone might do (lines 34–6) but he does not finish his line of reasoning. He checks himself mid-sentence (line 37) and then starts reading aloud from the case file (lines 39–44). He introduces this with: 'for you also say uh' (line 38). The references to Elmer's authorship of his reported talk (lines 36 and 38) provide the judge with accountability for what he is about to quote. This accountability is reinforced by the judge's gaze direction. He looks down at the case file when he starts referring to Elmer's statement (line 36), looks up again when he continues with his line of reasoning and down again when he starts reading (line 37). Similar examples of the judge's shifts of gaze direction are in lines 45–6 and 49. In those instances when the judge does not read aloud texts from the case file his glances at the documents may be taken, as we have seen before (lines 10–11), as pointing to his source of knowledge to show accountability for his current actions.

The quote (lines 39–44) is different from the ones we have discussed above, in that the judge is reading aloud the literal text of the police report (see excerpt **17**, lines **14–17**). It has been observed that direct reported speech lends the quotation an air of objectivity (Galatolo, 2007; Holt, 1996; Matoesian, 2000). This seems to hold even more so for quotations in the form of reading aloud written texts. In this example the judge does not only avoid taking a position by quoting Elmer's reported statement, he also dissociates himself from the content by his reading aloud a text, the artificiality of which makes it recognisable as police-report-style text. This identifies the judge's action as 'merely passing on' information, which underlines his officially neutral position (cf. Galatolo, 2007). Elmer does not respond to the judge's references to the police report, as the judge is evidently committed to producing an extended turn at talk (Licoppe, 2014). The judge ends this episode with an aside, marked by his 'by the way' (line 45). Apparently the judge misread or did not remember Elmer's reported expression 'I saw no keys' (excerpt 24, line **17**), but he clears up the confusion by asking Elmer about the keys and by verifying his answer (lines 46–50).

In spite of the obvious stylistic differences between the police report and ordinary talk the judge treats the quoted text as authored by Elmer (line 38). However, a comparison with the original talk in the police interrogation has shown that what Elmer actually answered was: 'We stood in front of the supermarket' instead of 'Yes that is right' (line 40), and 'yes', 'yes' instead of 'yes that is right' (line 44; see excerpts 23a and 24a). As discussed before, these differences are related to the practical circumstances of the typing and undetectable for readers of the police report.

The design of the quote suggests that the judge is ratifying the evidence by reading aloud those reported utterances that amount to Elmer's confession. The sequential position of the quote is ambiguous; it follows the judge's observation of a discrepancy between Elmer's reported description of his conduct as 'foolishness' and the delay in the return of the money (line 29), and is introduced by what appears to be a hypothetical case but that is abandoned on the way. This ambiguity is solved in the judge's following talk, as he resumes the earlier project, starting with 'just imagine' (see: excerpt 37, line 34):

(38)
51. J: Just imagine that everyone would say
52. and would have done that right,
53. you meet someone,
54. you close someone in,
55. you feel in his pockets,
56. you take away 5 Euros,
57. and you don't give it back right away,
58. and later on he starts telling the court here
59. we::ll, it was foolishness that was a joke.
60. (3)
61. Do you understand what I mean?
62. S: °Yes°
63. J: Hmyes anyone can say that it is a joke
64. but in any case that boy has not experienced it that way.
65. (1.5)
66. Right uhm any questions about this offence
67. ((looks at judges to his right and to his left, then to the prosecutor)).

The judge develops the line of argument he started before. In retrospect, the prior reading aloud of Elmer's statement to the police (lines 39–44) can now be understood as factual support of the hypothetical situation that the judge outlines (lines 53–9). He summarises the events written down in the police report and presents the summary as part of an incipient argument. His emphasis on that (line 52) seems to accentuate the seriousness of the events, which is further exhibited in the enumeration of the different actions involved in that (lines 53–7). Lines 58 and 59 reveal the grounds for this enumeration: to set up a contrast with what this person, referred to as 'everyone' (line 51), 'you' (lines 53, 54, 55, 56), 'he' (line 58), and 'anyone' (line 63), has done and how he later belittles it in court.

The emphasis that the judge puts on the wrongness of Elmer's actions may seem exaggerated in this case of 'theft' of a small amount of money that was returned afterwards. However, the fact that this is not the only offence for which Elmer stands trial places the case discussed here in a different light: a trivial offence can now be seen as part of Elmer's history of robberies and as evidence of his behavioural problems.

The contrast between *doing* and *saying* is mentioned in the beginning of the argument (lines 51 and 52) and actualised in its sequel. The contrast between the proposed severity of the *doing* and the belittlement of it in the *saying* culminates in lines 58 and 59. The judge's lexical choice in line 58 ('he starts telling the court here') and the prosodic features of the following enactment in line 59 (especially the drawn out we::ll), emphasise this contrast. As a result the impression is created of an indifferent or irresponsible suspect who does not take responsibility for the wrongness of his actions.

The judge's presentation of the argument as a generalised hypothetical situation, without specifying a particular actor, invites Elmer to take the perspective of an outsider, and to observe the actions of 'people-who-do-bad-things-and-then-belittle-them-in-court'. Moreover, as the judge does not spell out how to evaluate this contrast between the *doing* and the *saying* he invites Elmer to draw his own conclusions. He underlines this first by leaving a three-second pause after the completion of his enactment of Elmer's stance (lines 59–60) and then, when Elmer does not respond, by asking him whether he understands what he, the judge, means (lines 60–1).

Elmer's confirmation of this then gives the judge an opportunity to spell it out (lines 63–4). Whereas the judge previously inferred the alleged victim's position from his filing a complaint in a tentative way (lines 16–17) he now claims epistemic priority about the boy's experiences and feelings ('apparently', line 16, has become 'in any case', line 64). As he presents this view as conclusion of his summary of the facts that Elmer confessed to, and as he elicits Elmer's expression of understanding of the import of this summary, he makes Elmer retrospectively accountable for understanding the position that he now takes. The judge's concern is no longer to verify and establish Elmer's stance in court but, without losing sight of his own neutrality, to invite Elmer to take responsibility for his actions.

5.4.3 Summary

The epistemic domains that inform the exchanges between the judge and Elmer are Elmer's knowledge of the events, the judge's knowledge of the case file, and common-sense knowledge of typical conduct. The judge has to rely on his knowledge of the case as reported in the case file, knowledge about events that are also known by Elmer. The primacy of this source of knowledge for the judge's actions in court is exhibited by his references to the case file rather than to what Elmer tells him on the spot. Elmer's first-hand knowledge of the case gives him epistemic priority but, as he contests the interpretation of the events rather than the events themselves, he opens the door for the judge to question these interpretations on the basis of common-sense knowledge about why people press charges and about how people produce a 'normal' joke.

There are several ways in which the judge refers to the police report: he quotes it in different formats (directly: 'you say ...', indirectly: 'you say that ...' and 'mixed': 'you say like...'; he reads from it (e.g. 'you ask me if we closed the boy in'), he summarises it (e.g. 'you meet someone, you close someone in ...') and he enacts it (e.g. 'we::ll, it was foolishness that was a joke'). The judge does different things with these quotations. His first quotes draw the attention to the core elements of Elmer's stance in court. With the 'reading quote' the judge ratifies the evidence so that it can be used in the verdict, while he takes an officially neutral point of view as someone who is just passing on what is in the case file. A summary of this reading quote is then deployed as component of a line of argument that may serve to undermine Elmer's position. In enacting Elmer's statement the judge inserts a certain evaluation, which makes Elmer look indifferent or unwilling to take responsibility for his actions. So, by his quoting from the case file, by his generalising, and by his presenting the point of view of the alleged victim, the judge suggests what ought to be Elmer's moral stance in this case, while avoiding to take a position himself.

5.5 Conclusion

I have traced the 'career' of Elmer's oral statement, elicited in interaction with the police interrogator, through different stages of the criminal law process. This has illuminated the conditions of the construction of his written statement, their effects on the resulting text, and the affordances of this text for the judge's management of the case.

The construction of Elmer's written statement by the reporting officer is contingent on the 'typeability' and the 'recordability' of the talk, on the unwieldiness of the recontextualised monologue style, and on the impact of the text already written down on the texts to come. As the typing and the talk are produced simultaneously, the reporting officer has to deal with the constraints of time caused by the differential pace of the talk and the typing, and with the problems of listening to current talk while writing down a recordable selection of prior talk. As a result, the text of the report contains only a small selection of the talk.

Apart from the impact of the practical circumstances of the typing on the text, the reporting officer's performance also depends on the requirements of creating a text that can serve as piece of evidence in the further criminal law process. This is materialised by the selection she makes of what to write down and what to leave out, by the coherence she imposes on the emerging text on the screen, and especially by juxtaposing what turns out to be the central question of the case: whether Elmer's conduct should be interpreted as foolishness or as a street robbery.

As the text is written in the RM style, readers acquire some insight into the interactional basis of the suspect's written statement. However, the relative absence of interactional detail in the police report results in a monologisation of the text that foregrounds the informative elements of the suspect's statement and that makes Elmer appear more talkative and cooperative, and the interrogator less adversarial than they actually were. Although readers can get a sense of Elmer's confession to the taking away of €5 and his interpretation of his conduct as 'foolishness', they remain unaware of the interrogator's attempts to elicit recordable answers from Elmer's reluctant or evasive responses, and of Elmer's attempts to defend himself against the more harmful implications of the interrogator's questions and interpretations.

In court, the judge's understanding of Elmer's written statement is not only based on the text in the police report but also on the other documents in the case file, and on the case files of the other offences for which Elmer stands trial. The availability of the report of the complaint allows the judge to confront Elmer with a different version of the events, and the case files of the other offences lead the judge to treat the temporary taking away of €5 as a serious offence. The police report has put the judge on the track of what has been made the core problem of the case, by juxtaposing Elmer's description of his actions as 'foolishness' and the police interrogator's definition of it as a street robbery. The judge's references to the case file enable him to take a counter position and to argue his point of view without losing sight of his neutrality. By reading aloud, quoting, summarising or enacting parts of Elmer's written statement to the police, the judge performs a number of actions that serve to ratify the evidence, to verify and corroborate Elmer's confession, and to persuade Elmer to admit to the wrongness of his acts.

The career of Elmer's statement can be illustrated by tracing the changes of meaning and uses of Elmer's description of his actions as 'fooling around'. In the police interrogation Elmer uses this expression after some discussion. When first asked about his motives he claims he cannot tell anything about it. When asked a second time he gives an evasive answer, after which the two police officers persist in eliciting an answer, the interrogating officer by offering suggestions for possible motives, the reporting officer by questioning the voluntariness of the return of the money. Finally, after the interrogator's suggestion of 'pestering', Elmer says that 'it was just fooling around', produced as a downgrade of a potentially harmful description. This is reported as 'it was foolishness' twice, first as part of the answer to the reported question about his motives, and second as response to the interrogator's reported description of Elmer's acts as a street robbery.

In court Elmer repeats the words 'fooling around' as description of his actions, but the judge consistently refers to it as 'foolishness', the formulation in the police report. This becomes a central term for the judge's actions in court. He uses it to highlight the contrast between 'robbery' and 'foolishness', to set it off against the position of the alleged victim ('not . . . foolishness'), to create a contrast between 'foolishness' and the delayed return of the money, and to create a contrast between doing bad things and then belittling it as 'foolishness' in court. Thus, at each stage in the process Elmer's 'fooling around' changes meaning and gains importance. In the police interrogation Elmer utters it once; in the police report it is changed into 'foolishness' and reported twice; and in court the judge cites it four times. From Elmer's reluctant and cautious defence against the interrogator's suggestion of 'pestering' it has become a tool for the judge to question Elmer's position and to make him draw the appropriate moral conclusions.

Whatever the form or content of the judge's quotations, he addresses Elmer as 'speaker' and as 'author' of his statement to the police. This illustrates how the police report has 'forgotten' most of its interactional origins and has taken on a life of its own.

6 Conclusion and Discussion

The aim of this book was to acquire insight into the interactional and documentary foundations of the Dutch criminal law process by following the 'career' of the suspects' statements through different phases in the criminal law process. The analyses have shown how the talk in the police interrogation is transformed into the text of the police report, how this text is tailored to fit legal and institutional requirements and how the police report, as part of the completed case file, enables judges, prosecutors and defence lawyers to perform their institutional tasks in court. The examination of how suspects' statements are constructed, read and used has provided a deeper understanding of how 'context' is invoked and created through talk and writing in different settings. Although the criminal law process is predicated on the professional participants' active efforts to deal with crime and offenders, the investigation of the fine details of the practices through which the professionals carry out their tasks has shown the pervasiveness and significance of the unnoticed and unintended effects of entextualisation processes.

6.1 Summary of the Findings

6.1.1 The Police Interrogation

The impact of practical circumstances on the construction and on the substance of the police report should not be underestimated. The most noticeable of these is the contemporaneousness of the interrogators' dual tasks of truth finding and statement taking. Whether the interrogation is conducted by one or two police officers, solutions have to be found for the question of how to coordinate the talk and the typing. A related problem is that decisions have to be made about what to write down and what to leave out. Two forces are at work here. Police reports are meant to represent what the suspect told the interrogator 'as much as possible in the suspect's own words', but they are also drawn up to accommodate the needs of future readers. Thus, items may be drawn up in the colloquial language of suspects, or items may be left out, added or highlighted for their relevance to future readers. The result is a document written in a hybrid style that reveals an uneasy compromise between what future readers need to know, what reporting officers are willing to show, and what suspects are willing to tell.

Other practical circumstances that affect the construction and the substance of the police report are the number of interrogators, the degree of adversarialness of the interrogation, the writing styles used, and the requirements of coherence of the text-under-construction. All of these conditions have their specific constraining and enabling effects on the typing and on the text. In 'solo' interrogations the interaction is relatively simple. The interrogator asks questions, the suspect answers them, and when there is 'enough relevant answer' the interrogator types it up. So the routine episodes of 'solo' interrogations are characterised by a question–answer-typing organisation, resulting in relatively lengthy periods of typing during which the suspects usually wait for the interrogator to finish the typing and ask the next question. For the interrogators these conversational breaks do not necessarily disrupt the substance of the interrogations, as the emerging text on the screen informs the talk and the text to come. Because the suspect has limited opportunities for volunteering additional information during the typing, the recursive nature of the Q–A-T structure reinforces the interrogator's position of initiative and control.

However, because the interrogator decides when 'enough relevant answer' is given, there may be periods of unreported discussion or argument. In the more adversarial episodes of the interrogations the intensity of the interrogators' investigative questioning may interfere with the typing. Moreover, as the reporting of an answer suggests its acceptance and 'recordability', interrogators may convey their non-acceptance by not writing the answer down. And, finally, police officers may be wary of disclosing their interrogation tactics or putting their adversarial actions on display. As a result, the more adversarial episodes in the interrogations are underreported.

When interrogators work in pairs the interaction is less affected by the typing when one of the police officers acts as interrogator and the other as reporting officer. On the other hand, the interaction is potentially more complex, as there are also opportunities for interaction between the two police officers and between the reporting officer and the suspect. As the reporting officer's typing overlaps the talk between the interrogating officer and the suspect, he or she has to cope with the differential pace of the talk and the typing. To aid the writing process interrogators sometimes produce typing-facilitating actions such as leaving pauses for the typing, summarising or repeating the suspect's answers, and sometimes even telling the reporting officer what to write. However, when interrogating officers leave pauses for the reporting officer after a 'recordable' answer of the suspect, these pauses are usually not sufficient to complete the reporting of prior talk. As a result, the reporting officers are still occupied with the typing of previous talk when current question–answer sequences are already under way. This makes for a more complex writing task than in the 'solo' interrogations, as the reporting officers have to remember and write up past talk, see to it that the text of current writing is in line with the text already on the screen, and at the same time listen to current talk for future 'recordables'. When reporting officers do not understand or hear what has been said, they must put in a greater effort to accomplish repair, as they have to 'break in' on the interrogation. Weaknesses in teamwork may result in communication problems or incorrect reporting. In contrast, interrogators who work alone can set their own pace and solve their own communication problems.

In both the 'solo' and the 'duo' interrogations the 'typeability' of the talk is affected by the writing style adopted. The monologue style is more writer-friendly than the question–answer (Q–A) style, and the recontextualised monologue (RM or the 'you ask me') style is the least writer-friendly. As a result, the police reports written in the Q–A and especially in the RM style contain only part of the questions asked. As follow-up questions or questions that are asked when suspects' answers are deemed inadequate are the most likely to remain unreported, police reports underestimate the more hostile episodes and overestimate suspects' voluntariness and cooperation.

A contingency of interrogators' dual tasks of truth finding and statement taking is that the talk is produced in certain 'directions' and oriented to different aims. '*Talk for the truth*' looks back to the criminal events and is aimed at inducing the suspect to give an account of 'what happened'; *talk for the typing*' is orientated to police officers' current tasks of drawing up the police report; and *talk for the record* looks forward to the possible uses of the police report by its future readers. Thus, the police report does not only look backward as representation of prior talk, and forward in anticipation of its future uses, but it also reflects the current moment, which exhibits the police report as product of the practical circumstances of its construction.

6.1.2 The Police Report

Goffman's concept of 'footing' has been adapted to examine the reporting officers' perspectives and alignments to the texts they write. Next to their speaking roles, reporting officers adopt various 'writing roles' that show their alignments to the texts they write. Reporting officers' production of the anonymous texts that introduce and conclude the police report displays their role as 'form-filler'; their own professional texts that introduce the suspects and describe the accusations for which they are questioned display their perspective of 'writer-author'; and their rendition of the suspect's statement exhibits their role as 'reporter' of the suspect's statement. Each of these 'writing roles' affects the understanding of the suspect's written statement. The anonymous texts place the suspect's statement within the appropriate bureaucratic and institutional environments and make the police report recognisable as an official document drawn up according to the relevant and required practices. Reporting officers' own texts display their institutional identities, their professional tasks and their authorship of the document, in which the suspect's reported talk is presented as a quotation. Thus, the suspect's statement, as the substantive core of the police report, is surrounded by other texts that express the official, legal status of the document and its authenticity and accuracy.

A comparison of the texts of the police reports with the corresponding talk in the interrogations shows the kind and degree of their transparency. Differences between the talk and the text are especially noticeable in the routine texts immediately surrounding the suspects' statements. These texts overstate suspects' voluntariness, cooperation and conversational initiative. The suspect's written statement contains a specific selection of the talk, motivated in part by its assumed usefulness for the professional readers who will deal with the case. Other differences can be attributed to differences between talk and the conventions of writing and, as discussed above, to the practical circumstances of the typing. Typically, the police report offers factual representations of the suspect's narrative and understates the more emotional and personal elements of the interrogations.

It is the interaction rather than the substance of the interrogations that differs most from the written texts of the reports. Generally speaking, the police reports overstate the cooperation of suspects and understate hostilities. Each of the three reporting styles discussed here modifies the representation of the interactional organisation of the interrogation. The *monologue style* police reports overstate the suspects' voluntariness and understate the adversarialness of the interrogations as they give little or no insight into the interrogators' actions. *Question–answer-style* police reports make the suspects' reported talk recognisable as answers to questions but, as most of the interrogator's questions are not reported, the difference with the monologue-style reports is blurred. Moreover, question–answer-style reports do not accommodate the reporting of the interrogators' responsive actions that convey how they have understood the suspects' prior talk, such as comments or evaluations. Hence, the format of the Q–A-style reports discourages the reporting of the more antagonistic exchanges. As the *recontextualised monologue style* can incorporate the reporting of the interrogators' responsive actions it may offer a broader sense of their investigative or hostile actions. However, perhaps as a result of the 'writer unfriendliness' of the RM-style reports, even fewer interrogator actions are reported than in the Q–A-style reports, which results even more in a 'monologisation' of the reported talk.

In spite of the relative lack of interactional transparency of the police reports, the written texts contain some clues that suggest unreported utterances or actions of interrogators, such as unsolicited denials, narrative incoherence or details that a person would not volunteer. But, although readers may be able to reconstruct some understanding of what has been said and done in the police interrogation, they get limited insight into the conditions under which 'the suspect's statement' has come about, or into the effects these conditions may have on the text.

6.1.3 The Case File and the Trial

When the case comes to court the police report forms part of the completed case file, which allows the legal professionals who deal with the case to compare the suspect's reported statement with other documents. The case file also enables them to prepare, perform and display their professional tasks in the courtroom. Judges draw on the case file to manage the organisation of the trial, to verify and to ratify the evidence, and to question the suspect (and, if felt necessary, witnesses); the case file serves prosecutors and defence lawyers for arguing their case by comparing the suspect's statement with other written statements and with common-sense knowledge about typical features of offences, offenders and innocent people. All the professionals in court treat the suspects as accountable for their written statements, even when the interrogator's or reporting officer's input is clearly recognisable.

The discussions in court about the case rest on three epistemic domains: first-hand knowledge of 'what happened', second-hand knowledge of what is written about it in the case file and common-sense knowledge of the world. Of these, the knowledge about the case as written down in the case file takes a central place in the judges' questioning of the suspect in court. As against the primacy of the suspects' alleged first-hand knowledge of the events, the case file contains more information and can thus be used to compare the suspects' versions with those of others. An effect of the 'second-handness' of the information in the case file is that it allows judges to contradict or evaluate the suspect's talk while maintaining an appearance of objectivity, on the basis of the claim that they are 'merely passing on' what others have said. Moreover, the case file has 'first-hand' accessibility: it is ready for use, lying on the desk in front of the judges, a material object that can be drawn upon both for initiating the judges' actions and for responding to the suspects' answers. Whereas the cogency of the suspects' position rests on their alleged first-hand knowledge of the events, the cogency of the judges' position rests on the authoritative status, the immediate presence and the verifiable character of the case file.

The legal requirement that judges read aloud those passages from the case file that they need to base their verdict on, may lead to episodes of the judges' monologic reading aloud. The quoted passages from the case file may then serve judges as topics for further questioning. Seen from an interactional perspective, the judges' reading aloud may be a first-position action, that is, an initial action for launching requests for confirmation, elaboration or clarification of the texts just read aloud. The case file is also quoted in a third position, as response to the suspects' answers. In these cases the suspect's answer may be treated as a 'version' that can be set off against other versions. Thus, the actions performed by quoting from the case file are recognisable by the sequential position of the judges' quoting: first-position quoting makes relevant the judges' requests for information and confirmation, whereas third-position quoting may exhibit the judges' dissatisfaction with the suspect's prior answer and may lead to cautious confrontations and to more adversarial episodes.

The simultaneous relevance of the judges' tasks of ratifying the evidence and questioning the suspect may result in interactional ambiguities. Much of the turn taking between judges and suspects in court is unequivocal; when judges ask questions the suspects are encouraged to respond and when judges read aloud from the case file suspects are discouraged from responding. On the other hand, the kind of texts that judges read aloud may trigger the suspect's defensive responses, and the kind of questions that judges ask may occasion the suspect's defensive non-response. To fend off the suspect's unasked-for contributions, the judges may continue with reading aloud from the case file, through which they avoid discussion and retain the initiative. To encourage the reluctant suspect's participation judges may bring into play an array of more or less subtle invitations to talk that may gradually increase the pressure on the suspect to answer the question.

Thus, the invocations of the case file by the professionals in court, especially by the judges, show that the case file is more than just a representation of something else; it is a reality in its own right, with its own affordances and its own practical uses.

6.2 The Entextualisation Process

The examination of the career of a suspect's statement from the police interrogating room through to the courtroom has revealed the workings of the *entextualisation* process, which involves a *decontextualisation* of the real-time, lived experience of the interaction in the police interrogation and its *recontextualisations* as the fixed material reality of the text of the police report and as resource for the legal professionals' performance of their institutional tasks. Each of these recontextualisations of the suspect's statement exhibits and creates new contexts, which involves transformations of meanings and meaning potentials (Linell, 1998: 145). If we consider 'context' as related to those circumstances that affect the meaning of utterances, actions and texts, we can specify our understanding of 'context' by way of an inspection of the changes of meaning that the suspect's statement undergoes in the course of its 'career'. This is not to say that the 'contexts' involved in the de- and recontextualisations of the suspect's statement are mutually exclusive and separate entities, but rather that they form part of a configuration of contexts that may be relevant, to a greater or lesser extent, at the same time (cf. Cicourel, 1992). An examination of the conversational and textual details of the police interrogations, the police reports and the trials shows processes of recontextualisation that I shall list and discuss below.

First, the talk in the police interrogation is recontextualised as a text on a piece of paper, a material object that can be taken out of its setting to be shipped off to the desks of the professionals who will deal with it in the further criminal law process. It is a text that is meant to be understandable for readers independently of the circumstances of its construction. This stage of the entextualisation process comprises changes in accessibility and participation: from a real-time, emergent and negotiable interaction between one or two police officers and a suspect it has become an immutable written statement, accessible to a select group of professional readers; talk has become text and participation has become privileged readership. The recontextualisation of the talk into a document that can be distributed among the professionals who deal with the further case draws attention to the *institutional context* of the suspect's statement, which involves attentiveness to the anticipated institutional aims and uses of the document.

Second, the text of the suspect's statement in the police report is recontextualised by three kinds of surrounding texts, written from the perspectives of the suspect and of the reporting officers, and from an anonymous bureaucratic perspective. The suspect's statement is first recontextualised by the routine sentences immediately surrounding it, displaying what appear to be the suspects' expressions of acceptance, voluntariness, and conversational initiative. It is surrounded by quotation marks, which draws the attention to the suspects' authorship of their statements, and to the interrogators' reporting role. Next, the suspect's statement is surrounded and recontextualised by the personal texts of the reporting officers as 'writer-authors' of the accounts of their current professional identities, tasks and activities. Finally, the anonymous texts that introduce and complete the police report recontextualise the suspect's statement as drawn up according to the proper bureaucratic routines. These '*textual contexts*' of the suspect's statement display the interrogators' adherence to proper procedures and the suspects' acceptance and cooperation, as they transform the suspect's statement into a legally adequate piece of evidence.

Third, the interactional organisation of the talk in the police interrogation is recontextualised by the format and style of the police report. Generally speaking, the police officer's and the suspect's talk have been transformed into writing with its concomitant changes in style, structure and vocabulary, often resulting in texts that people would never articulate. More specifically, the suspect's talk-in-interaction has been recontextualised by the adoption of a particular writing style of the police report. As the suspect's reported utterances can be understood by reference to the preceding and following sentences, the reorganisation of the reported interaction may transform the talk of interrogators and suspects into actions different from the original. As the three writing styles underreport the interrogators' questions or comments, many of the suspect's answers (and in monologue-style reports all of them) are recontextualised as volunteered expressions, and many of the interrogator's hostile actions have disappeared from view. These recontextualisations illuminate the transformations of the *interactional and sequential contexts* of the talk in the interrogation into the reported talk of the suspect's written statement.

A fourth type of recontextualisation results from the combination of the police report with the other documents of the same case or with the documents of other offences of which the suspect has been accused. These other documents allow for a comparison of the suspect's statement with other written statements or with other pieces of evidence, which leads judges, prosecutors and defence lawyers to treat the suspect's statement as 'a version' that may or may not be corroborated by other versions. The case file may also contain documents pertaining to the suspects' criminal records, and documents drawn up by expert witnesses pertaining to the suspects' mental condition. The legal professionals' knowledge of these documents may affect their perception of the 'person' of the suspect as, for example, 'crime-prone' or 'mentally disturbed'. These *documentary contexts* afford police interrogators, judges, prosecutors and defence lawyers opportunities for confrontation and evaluation.

Finally, the suspect's statement is recontextualised in court as a number of actions that display and perform the institutional tasks of the professionals, exhibiting their 'professional reading' as constitutive of the *institutional and professional contexts* of the trial. Prosecutors and defence lawyers refer to the suspect's statement and to other texts of the case file as part of their arguments and conclusions that support their professional tasks in court. The judges' invocations of these texts cover a wider spectrum of actions, including the organisation of the trial, the ratification of the evidence and the questioning of the suspect. In particular, the judges' reading aloud or summarising the suspect's reported talk as written down in the police report exhibits the force of the *interactional and sequential contexts* of their quotes for the production and interpretation of their actions in court.

This discussion shows that 'the suspect's statement' changes its meaning at every step in the entextualisation process as different kinds or elements of context are produced, emerge or fade away. First, it changes from talk to text, and thus becomes a piece of paper that can be used in the further management of the case; second, the text of 'the suspect's statement' becomes part of an official document that is designed to serve as a piece of evidence; third, the original interaction is changed into a written monologue or into a different or simplified reported interaction, which overestimates the suspect's voluntariness and underestimates the adversarial episodes; fourth, the document is incorporated in the case file, which enables 'the suspect's statement' to be read as 'a version' that can be compared with other pieces of evidence, and which informs the professionals about the suspect's mental state or criminal tendencies; and finally the suspect's statement becomes part of the interaction in the courtroom, through which what is treated as the 'talk' of the suspect to the police is used to perform the actions of the legal professionals in court. Thus, 'the suspect's statement' is an emergent product, transformed through a sequence of interactions and written reports that reflect the changing relevancies of 'the suspect's statement' for different phases of the criminal law process.

6.3 Scope of the Findings

In the course of this study I became increasingly aware of the similarities between the topics I studied and the procedures I used for studying them, as these procedures depend on similar entextualisation practices (Slembrouck, 2001). Like the police detectives, I transformed the talk in the interrogations into writing; like the prosecutors, defence lawyers and judges, I selected parts of the written materials (my transcriptions) to investigate and make a point; like the prosecutors, defence lawyers and judges, I treated the written materials as the original talk; and finally I took the police interrogations and trials out of their context and inserted them into other contexts, such as publications and conference presentations. I shall discuss these similarities and their possible consequences below.

The *transformation of talk into writing* allows for the transportation of the resulting written texts to other readers who may use these texts in the performance of their professional tasks. As this is a crucial element of professional practices, this holds for the professionals in the criminal law process but also for the professionals in other institutional settings, such as academics who study transcriptions of talk. In fact, the transformation of talk into writing is one of the basic tools of conversation analysis, as transcription is the instrument for making talk in interaction available for inspection, reproduction and publication. Although the transcriptions made in conversation-analytic studies are obviously constructed to be more accurate and complete representations of the talk-in-interaction than the police reports analysed in this study, the principle is the same: talk is transformed into written materials that are easier to manage than live talk because they are fixed and transportable, so that they can be made accessible to a particular readership to serve specific ends.

In Chapters 4 and 5 I have shown how the professionals' *selection of quotable items* in court stems from practical and substantive considerations; as it is unnecessary and impractical to quote the whole police report, they only quote those items that are relevant for the performance of their institutional tasks in court. My selection of excerpts to be presented is based on similar considerations. The materials analysed in Chapters 2 to 4 were selected for their pertinence to the specific issues discussed in each section. A difference with the selection of quoted items by the professionals in the criminal law process is that they presumably know what they are looking for, whereas my categories and selections emerged as I familiarised myself with the materials. I selected the case of the theft of €5 (Chapter 5) for exhibiting the career of the suspect's statement because it is a simple case with a short police interrogation, a short police report and a short treatment in court, so that I could present the case almost in its entirety. However, to save space and avoid repetition I summarised the parts that consisted of items that had already been analysed. Thus, similar to the effects of the selectivity of reported talk in the police reports, my selection of excerpts has understated the repetitiousness of some of the more adversarial episodes in the interrogations (see also Komter, 2003: 465).

Another feature of entextualisation is the *treatment of reported or transcribed talk as talk.* I have shown that there are systematic differences between the talk in the police interrogations and the texts in the police reports. As my analyses taught me to be alert to these differences, I took pains to describe the texts in the police reports as: 'the suspect's reported talk' instead of 'the suspect's talk' (Chapter 3), in spite of the stylistic awkwardness due to the repetitiveness of these phrases. On the other hand, I treated the text of my transcripts as the talk it is meant to represent. For example, when I announced that I compared the talk in the police interrogations with the text of the police report, what I actually did was to compare the texts of my transcripts with the texts of the police reports.[1] Similar to the treatment of the suspects' reported talk by the professionals in court, it is common practice in conversation-analytic work to refer to the transcripts as 'the talk', and to those whose talk has been transcribed as the 'speakers' of their – transcribed – talk.

When talk is transformed into a written text it can be lifted out of its interactional setting and recontextualised in another setting, which affects its original meaning. My experiences of presenting my materials and analyses at conferences or lectures made me aware of the nature of the *de- and recontextualisations* of my materials as part of my own professional practice. Initially

[1] But I consulted the recordings of the original talk whenever I thought I needed to.

I presented the audio recorded police interrogations by playing fragments only of the recorded talk, leaving out the periods of typing. When I realised the impact of the typing on the interrogations and on the police reports I started playing the recorded talk together with the breaks in the talk and the sounds of the typing. At these moments the audience usually started to laugh. When asked, people said they laughed because they did not expect these typing sounds, nor these lengthy breaks in the interrogations; a police officer said she laughed because it sounded so familiar. Whatever the reason for their laughter, it made me realise that this was an element of the entextualisation process: I had extracted a recording of the police interrogation from its interactional setting and recontextualised it in a setting of academic exchange, with the alienating effects mentioned above.

These similarities between professional work in different institutional settings suggest that my findings may be relevant for the study and understanding of a number of other settings where documents are drawn up and referred to as expression and production of the participants' institutional tasks.

6.4 Relevance of the Findings

This study has illuminated the effects of the practical circumstances of the simultaneous tasks of typing and interrogating on the text of the police reports, the origins and nature of systematic differences between the text and the talk, the effects of the writing style of the police report on its interpretation, and the scope of the practical uses of the written documents by the professionals in court, especially by the judge. The articulation of these features sheds light on the operation of a criminal law process where texts travel from one setting to another, where they serve as the basis for decisions that may have a profound effect on the lives of suspects, and where boundaries between right and wrong are marked, established and maintained.

As in the criminal law process the stakes are higher than in most other institutional settings, the possible consequences of the operation of the entextualisation process require serious consideration. Although my analyses have not been motivated by the wish to solve problems of the transparency of the criminal law process or of the quality of police reports, it might be worthwhile to consider the possible relevance of my findings to the practitioners in the field. This study has revealed that the systematic differences between the interaction in the police interrogation and its representation in the police report result in a relative lack of transparency of the police report.[2]

[2] In the UK the differences between the original talk in the police interview and the resulting text of the transcript (or ROTI) have even been described as 'contamination' of the evidence (Haworth, 2010: 169). See also: Van Oorschot, 2014b).

This would suggest that the operation of the entextualisation process could create vulnerabilities in a criminal law system that depends heavily on written documents.

The ultimate consequence of this could be that the reliance on written documents of dubious transparency may result in miscarriages of justice or wrongful convictions (cf. Brants, 2012). The introduction of the suspect's right to be assisted by a lawyer during police interrogations, the mandatory audiovisual registration of police interrogations and the increased use of question–answer-style police reports are the measures introduced to help counter a lack of transparency of police reports (see Chapter 1). Moreover, the availability of audiovisual recordings of police interrogations can work as a safeguard against faulty interpretations of the police reports, because it gives the professionals a chance to inspect and monitor the original interrogation on which the police reports are based (Malsch et al., 2015).

The assumptions behind discussions about miscarriages of justice are that they result from errors or from conscious efforts to manipulate the evidence to secure a confession rather than find the truth. Such a description does not take into account that, as my materials show, many of the differences between the talk in the police interrogation and the text of the police report are the unnoticed and unintended effects of the entextualisation process rather than errors or conscious misrepresentations of the talk. If that leads to unjustifiable judgements, the effects will be all the more intractable, as it is more difficult to solve problems that result from unnoticed or unintended events than from recognisable errors or from conscious misrepresentations.

One of the effects of entextualisation processes is a loss of interactional detail in the police reports that affects the readers' insight into the interactional origins of the suspect's written statement and that may thus colour their interpretation of the events (cf. De Keijser et al., 2012). As mentioned before, in the courtroom the suspects' written statements are understood and taken by judges, prosecutor and defence lawyers as the suspects' own individual production for which they can be held accountable, irrespective of the circumstances under which these statements were elicited and irrespective of the interrogators' contributions. Hence, a 'professional reading' of the case file by the professionals in court encourages them to focus on those substantive items in the case file that further their professional tasks, and to disregard the interactional origins of police reports. This is related to the wider context of 'referentialist' linguistic ideology. Under the 'referentialist' ideology meaning is located exclusively in linguistic forms irrespective of the social and interactional context in which those forms occur (Ehrlich and Eades, 2016: 6; see also: Eades, 2010; Matoesian, 1999: 910; Slembrouck, 1992). The pervasiveness of this 'referentialist' ideology can be inferred from the tolerance for the use of written evidence in court, in the face of the requirement that the evidence must be presented in court in its most original form.[3] This is not to say that the professionals' approach is 'wrong' or short-sighted, but that it is a fundamental feature of the entextualisation process and of the way in which we do and see things (cf. Smith, 1974: 266).

The following excerpt is an example of how a judge, as part of her questioning of the suspect, quotes his statement from the – monologue-style – police report. The suspect has confessed to having snatched handbags from old ladies. In the passage that the judge reads aloud the suspect is reported to describe in great detail how he grabbed the handbag from one of his victims, suggesting that he had carefully considered and planned his modus operandi:

1. J: Leo rode his bicycle in front and I rode behind you say to the police, (2)
2. he just passed the woman, rode on slowly, when I saw that Leo did not do anything
3. I passed the woman on the left and jerked the handbag from her hand. (3)
4. I jerked (1) by giving a short pull downwards.
5. As a result, one lets go of the bag at once. I do that in order to make everything easier.
6. If I were to do it slowly, she will hang on to it and then it would not succeed.
7. It all sounds a little professional right? (1)
8. S: °Yes. I don't know.° (1)
9. J: Or do you think if you do it you'd better do a good job.
10. It uh sounds a bit scary for someone reading it. (2)

(30, O)

It is a monologue-style police report that relates how the suspect robbed a woman of her handbag, while riding past her on his bicycle. The judge introduces her quotation as representing the suspect's talk ('you say to the police', line 1), after which she reads aloud a detailed account of the suspect's 'modus operandi' and considerations (lines 3–6). The judge's conclusion that the suspect's conduct was 'a little professional' (line 7) and 'a bit scary' (line 10) suggests that her 'professional reading' is based on her training to look for 'the facts' rather than for the possible interactional basis of this passage. As judges are prohibited from expressing judgments in court this judge presents her conclusion not as her individual interpretation but as something that 'any reader' may see (line 10). Although it will not lead to a wrongful conviction as the suspect has confessed, the judge's interpretation of the suspect as a 'professional' and her description of his actions as 'scary' show her assessment of 'the person' of the suspect, and may thus increase the measure of punishment that the court will decide on.

[3] Other legal examples of the disregard of the significance of interaction for the interpretation of talk are the suspect's right to silence (an invocation of which will provoke inferences of 'having something to hide'), and the requirement that the police report must contain 'as much as possible the suspect's own words' (as if the police interrogator's words are of no importance).

However, as the passage read aloud contains a number of details that people would not tell of their own account, it is safe to assume that the suspect did not volunteer the descriptions of his modus operandi, and that the passage is constructed on the basis of a combination of the interrogator's unreported questions and the suspect's answers.[4] Thus, it is likely that the judge's apprehension about the suspect's state of mind during the robbery is an artefact of the police officer's questioning and reporting style; and that her failure to notice a discrepancy between the text of the police report and the unreported interaction underlying this text is a sign of her 'professional reading' and a 'normal' effect of the entextualisation process.

I do not want to create the impression that the entextualisation processes as I described and analysed them necessarily lead to flawed judgments that disadvantage suspects. There is nothing wrong with police reports that consist of good summaries of the suspects' talk. And the professionals who deal with the case need not necessarily know all the details of the interaction in which the suspect's statement was elicited (cf. Clayman, 1990: 82). But if a lack of transparency of police reports leads to undesired and undesirable interpretations of the suspect's statement this could be avoided by developing a sensitivity for alternative readings of the texts. My analyses of the sequential organisation of the texts of the police report have been based on interpretations of the text that 'any reader' would be able to make. I proposed that, although readers of the police report are offered little insight into the interactional origins of the suspect's statement, there are some indications that may lead them to infer unreported questions or other interrogator actions, such as the use of unsolicited denials, sentences or details that one would not volunteer, or incoherent successions of sentences (see Chapter 3). However, as illustrated above, there are no indications that the professional participants in the courtroom are oriented to these signs of possible unreported interrogator actions.

This study may then contribute to help the professionals deepen their understanding of the entextualisation process and sensitise their alertness to the possible effects of unreported actions of police interrogators on their understanding of the police report. Hence, my materials and analyses could be helpful for training purposes – both for those who write and for those who read the police reports – for developing an understanding of how to detect possible unreported interrogator actions and of how the practical circumstances and the writing styles of the reports can affect the construction and interpretation of its contents.

When I started on this project I could not foresee what it would entail. My efforts to satisfy my original curiosity about what was concealed behind the

[4] I do not have access to the police report for this case.

judges' references to the suspects' statement generated other questions about the construction and character of the police report, the analysis of which led to questions about the relations between the construction, character and use of the suspect's statement. As mentioned before, entextualisation processes are central to the operation of many institutions. My findings suggest that the practical circumstances of the transformation of talk into writing, the removal of the written text from the setting of its production and its insertion into other settings, the selection of items to be reported or quoted, and the tendency to treat the written texts as straightforward representations of the talk, are practices inherent to entextualisation processes, whatever their settings. So what this study has revealed about the interactional and textual foundations of the Dutch criminal law process may also hold for other judicial systems or for other institutional settings where documents are produced to serve the institutional professionals as a basis for their decision-making. A research orientation that covers more than single interactions, that includes documents that link one interaction to a next and that considers 'cases' in addition to 'conversations', affords insights into how institutions are not only 'talked into being' but also 'written into being'.

LICE AMSTERDAM - AMSTELLAND
STRICT 7
EA TEAM Fledder Laan

lice report nr. : 2008123456-3

POLICE REPORT
of suspect interrogation

Reporting officer 1
Henk Walter Bloem, (12345), police sergeant, district 7 detection office and
Reporting officer 2
Fiona Balken, (67890), senior police officer, area team Fledder Laan

---

On Wednesday the 4th of March 2008, around 12.00 hrs, we, reporting officers, questioned a man, in the police station Fledder Laan 48 in Amsterdam, as suspected of violation of section 312/2/2 Criminal Code juncto section 310 Criminal Code.
The suspect stated to us to be named:

Name	: Martina (man)
Christian names	: Elmer
Place of birth	: Amsterdam
Date of birth	: 03/05/1991
Country of birth	: The Netherlands
Nationality	: Dutch
Address	: West Dreef 18
Place	: 1002 BK Liemen
Telephone number	: 061234567
ID in accordance with	: register of residents
Age	: 16
School	: vocational education
Name school	: Regional Education college

The suspect stated that the address given by him is also the postal address for correspondence in criminal cases.

After we informed the suspect that he was not obliged to answer questions and about what we wished to hear him he stated: "

"I understand that you wish to hear me and that I am not obliged to answer questions.

You ask me if I consent to having the interrogation recorded for study purposes. I consent.

You tell me that you wish to question me about a robbery of 5 Euros on the 7th of February at Bloemhof in Liemen. Tha complainant is called Dan.
You ask me if I want to tell something about that.
No I do not want that.

You read to me from the report of the complaint that the complainant is being closed in by a group, that I had my hand in his pocket. Took 5 Euros from that and that his father fetched the money back

a day later.
That is right.

You ask me with whom I was that day.
I do not want to tell that.

You ask me if it is right that Jairo addressed that boy.
Yes that is right.

You ask me if we closed in on that boy.
Yes that is right.

You ask me if it is rigt that I had my hand in his coat pocket and thook 5 Euros.
Yes that is right. I saw no keys. I took 5 Euros.

You ask me why I did it.
I cannot say. I do not understand why someone files a complaint wh you already got your 5 Euros back. It was foolishness. We were goi to give it back.

You ask me when that complainant's father came to visit me.
The next day. My cousin was also present. That father said a numbe of things. He also threatened me. He was going to rip off my hand. told him that he should do that.
I do not know that boy. That Dan has heard where I live in the neighbourhood.
We were going to give it back at the community centre. We did give it back didn't we?

You explain to me that it is still a street robbery.
It was foolishness. I don't understand that.

You ask me who the other boys were with whom I was.
Jairo and two or three others. I am not going to give names. There were some other people that I know from the street, they were with us, but we did not hang around with them.

I have nothing further to state."

After the suspect had read through his statement, he persisted in and signed it.

Elmer Marti

(suspec

This report has been drawn up by us on oath of office and promise office respectively, finalised and signed in Amsterdam on the 4th c March 2008.

The reporting officers,

Henk Bloem (12345) (oath)

F. Balken (67890) (promise)

References

Anderson, T. J. (1999). The Netherlands Criminal Justice System: An audit model of decision-making. In: Malsch, M. and Nijboer, J. F. (eds.), *Complex cases. Perspectives on the Netherlands criminal justice system*. Amsterdam: Thela Thesis.

Atkinson, J. M. (1981). Ethnomethodological approaches to socio-legal studies. In: Podgórecki, A. and Whelan, C. J. (eds.), *Sociological approaches to the law*, pp. 201–24. London: Croom Helm.

Atkinson, J. M. and Drew, P. (1979). *Order in court: The organisation of verbal interaction in judicial settings*. London: Macmillan.

Atkinson, P. and Coffey, A. (2004). Analysing documentary realities. In: Silverman, D. (ed.), *Qualitative research. Theory, method and practice* (2nd edn), pp. 56–75. London: Sage.

Bauman, R. and Briggs, C. L. (1990). Poetics and performance as critical perspectives on language and social life. *Annual Review of Anthropology* 19: 59–88.

Beach, W. A. (1993). Transitional regularities for casual 'okay' usages. *Journal of Pragmatics* 19: 325–52.

(1995). Conversation analysis: 'Okay' as a clue for understanding consequentiality. In: Sigman, S. J. (ed.), *The consequentiality of communication*, pp. 121–61. Hillsdale, NJ: Erlbaum.

Beach, W. A. and Dixson, C. N. (2001). Revealing moments: formulating understandings of adverse experiences in a health appraisal interview. *Social Science and Medicine* 52: 25–44.

Beach, W. A. and LeBaron, C. D. (2002) Attending to personal problems and reported sexual abuse during a medical encounter. *Journal of Communication* 52/3: 617–39.

Benson, D. and Drew, P. (1978). "Was there firing in sandy row that night?": some features of the organisation of disputes about recorded facts. *Sociological Inquiry* 48/2: 89–100.

Blommaert, J. (2005). *Discourse: A critical introduction.* Cambridge: Cambridge University Press.

Brants, C. (2012). Wrongful convictions and inquisitorial process: The case of the Netherlands. *University of Cincinnati La Review*. 80/4: 1069–1114.

Bucholtz (2000). The politics of transcription. *Journal of Pragmatics* 32: 1439–65

Cicourel, A. V. (1968). *The social organization of juvenile justice.* New York: Wiley.

(1992). The interpenetration of communicative contexts: examples from medical encounters. In: Duranti, A. and Goodwin, C. (eds.), *Rethinking context: language as an interactive phenomenon*, pp. 310–91. Cambridge: Cambridge University Press.

Clayman, S. (1990). From talk to text: newspaper accounts of reporter–source interactions. *Media, Culture & Society* 12: 79–103.

(2001). Answers and evasions. *Language in Society* 30: 403–42.

Clayman, S. and Heritage, J. (2002). *The news interview. Journalists and public figures on the air.* Cambridge: Cambridge University Press.

Clift, R. and Holt, E. (2007). Introduction In: Holt, E. and Clift, R. (eds.), *Reporting Talk. Reported speech in interaction*, pp. 1–15. Cambridge: Cambridge University Press.

Coulthard, R. M. (2002). Whose voice is it? Invented and concealed dialogue in written records of verbal evidence produced by the police. In: Cotterill, J. (ed.), *Language in the legal process*, pp. 19–34. Basingstoke: Palgrave.

Coulthard, M. and Johnson, A. (eds.) (2010), *The Routledge Handbook of Forensic Linguistics*. London/New York: Routledge.

De Boer, M. (2014). 'Ik zal het in die bewoordingen op papier zetten'. De verschillen tussen politieverhoren en processen-verbaal. ['I shall put it on paper in those words'. The differences between police interrogations and police reports]. NSCR report.

De Keijser, J. Malsch, M., Kranendonk, R. and de Gruyter, M. (2012). Written records of police interrogation: differential registration as determinant of statement credibility and interrogation quality. *Psychology, Crime & Law* 18/7: 613–29.

Depperman, A., Schmitt, R. and Mondada, L. (2010). Agenda and emergence: contingent and planned activities in a meeting. *Journal of Pragmatics* 42/6: 1700–18.

D'hondt, S. (2014). Defending through disaffiliation: The vicissitudes of alignment and footing in Belgian criminal hearings. *Language & Communication* 36: 68–82.

D'hondt, S. and Van der Houwen, F. (2014). Quoting from the case file: How intertextual practices shape discourse at various stages in the legal trajectory. *Language & Communication* 36: 1–6.

Drew, P. (1992). Contested evidence in courtroom examination: The case of a trial for rape. In Drew, P. and Heritage, J. (eds.), *Talk at work: interaction in institutional settings*, pp. 470–520. Cambridge: Cambridge University Press.

(1998). Complaints about transgressions and misconduct. *Research on Language and Social Interaction* 31/3 & 4: 295–325.

(2006). When documents 'speak': Documents, language and interaction. In: Drew, P., Raymond, G. and Weinberg, D. (eds.), *Talking research: Talk and interaction in social research methods*, pp. 63–80. London: Sage.

Drew, P. and Heritage, J. (eds.) (1992a). *Talk at work. Interaction in institutional settings*. Cambridge: Cambridge University Press.

Drew, P. and Heritage, J. (1992b). Analyzing talk at work: An introduction. In: Drew, P. and Heritage, J. (eds.) *Talk at work. Interaction in institutional settings*, pp. 3–65. Cambridge: Cambridge University Press.

Drew, P., Raymond, G. and Weinberg, D. (eds.) (2006). *Talk and interaction in social research methods*. London: Sage.

Dupret, B., Lynch, M. and Berard, T. (eds.) (2015a). *Law at work. Studies in legal ethnomethods.* Oxford: Oxford University Press.
Dupret, B., Lynch, M. and Berard, T. (2015b). Introduction: law at work. In: Duprez, B., Lynch, M. and Berard, T. (eds.) *Law at work. Studies in legal ethnomethods*, pp. 1–24. Oxford: Oxford University Press.
Eades, D. (2000). I don't think it's an answer to the question: Silencing Aboriginal witnesses in court. *Language in Society* 29: 161–95.
(2008a). *Taken for a ride: courtroom talk and neo-colonial control.* The Hague/Berlin: Mouton de Gruyter.
(2008b). Telling and retelling your story in court. *Current Issues in Criminal Justice*: 209–30.
(2010). *Sociolinguistics and the legal process.* Bristol/Tonawanda/Ontario: Multilingual Matters.
(2012). The social consequences of language ideologies in courtroom cross-examination. *Language in Society* 41: 471–97.
Edwards, D. (2008). Intentionality and mens rea in police interrogations: The production of actions as crimes. *Intercultural Pragmatics* 5/2: 177–99.
Ehrlich, S. (2012). Text trajectories, legal discourse and gendered inequalities. *Applied Linguistics Review* 3/1: 47–73.
Ehrlich, S. and Eades, D. (2016). Introduction. Linguistic and discursive dimensions of consent. In: Ehrlich, S., Eades, D. and Ainsworth, J. (eds.), *Discursive constructions of consent in the legal process*, pp. 1–20. Oxford: Oxford University Press.
Ericson, R. V. (1981). *Making crime. A study of detective work.* Toronto: Butterworths.
Frankel, R. (1989). 'I wz wondering – uhm could RAID uhm effect the brain permanently d'y know?': Some observations on the intersection of speaking and writing in calls to a poison control center. *Western Journal of Speech Communication* 53: 195–226.
Franken, A. A. (2010). Regels voor het strafdossier [Rules for the criminal case file]. *Delikt en Delinkwent* 40/4: 403–18.
Frers, L. (2009). Space, materiality and the contingency of action: A sequential analysis of the patient's file in doctor–patient interactions. *Discourse Studies* 11/3: 285–303.
Galatolo, R. (2007). Active voicing in court. In: Holt, E. and Clift, R. (eds.), *Reporting talk: reported speech in interaction*, pp. 195–220. Cambridge: Cambridge University Press.
(2015). Reporting talk when testifying. Intertextuality, consistency, and transformation in witnesses' use of direct reported speech. In: Dupret et al. (eds.), *Law at work. Studies in legal ethnomethods*, pp. 139–62. Oxford: Oxford University Press.
Galatolo, R. and Drew, P. (2006). Narrative expansions as defensive practices in courtroom testimony. *Text & Talk* 26/6: 661–98.
Garfinkel, H. (1967a). *Studies in ethnomethodology.* Englewood Cliffs, NJ: Prentice-Hall.
(1967b). What is ethnomethodology? In: Garfinkel, H., *Studies in ethnomethodology*, pp. 1–34. Englewood Cliffs, NJ: Prentice-Hall.
(1967c). Common sense knowledge of social structures: The documentary method of interpretation in lay and professional fact finding. In: Garfinkel, H., *Studies in ethnomethodology*, pp. 76–103. Englewood Cliffs, NJ: Prentice-Hall.

(1967d). Some rules of correct decisions that jurors respect. In: Garfinkel, H., *Studies in ethnomethodology*, pp. 104–15. Englewood Cliffs, NJ: Prentice-Hall.
(1967e). Good organizational reasons for 'bad' clinic records. In: Garfinkel, H., *Studies in ethnomethodology,* pp. 186–207. Englewood Cliffs, NJ: Prentice-Hall.
Glenn, P. and LeBaron, C. (2011). Epistemic authority in employment interviews: Glancing, pointing, touching. *Discourse and Communication* 5/1: 3–22.
Goffman, E. (1970). *Strategic interaction.* Oxford: Basil Blackwell.
(1981). Footing. In: *Forms of talk*, pp. 124–59. Oxford: Basil Blackwell.
González Martínez, E. (2000). La 'déclaration' dans le cadre d'une procédure pénale ou la constitution d'un 'je' multiple et rassembleur. *Schweitzerische Zeitschrift für Soziologie* 26/3: 591–614.
(2006). The interweaving of talk and text in a French pretrial hearing. *Research on Language and Social Interaction* 39/3: 229–61.
Goodwin, C. (1981). *Conversational organization: Interaction between speakers and hearers.* New York: Academic Press.
(1994). Professional vision. *American Anthropologist* 96: 606–33.
(2000). Action and embodiment within situated human interaction. *Journal of Pragmatics* 32: 1489–1522.
(2007) Interactive footing. In: Holt, E. and Clift, R. (eds.), *Reporting talk: Reported speech in interaction*, pp. 16–46. Cambridge: Cambridge University Press.
Goodwin, C. and Duranti, A. (1992). Rethinking context: An introduction. In: Duranti, A. and Goodwin, C. (eds.) *Rethinking context: Language as an interactive phenomenon*, pp. 1–42. Cambridge: Cambridge University Press.
Greatbatch, D., Luff, P., Heath, C., Campion, P. (1993). Interpersonal communication and human–computer interaction: An examination of the use of computers in medical consultations. *Interacting with Computers* 5/2: 193–216.
Greatbatch, D., Heath, C., Luff, P. and Campion, P. (1995a). Conversation analysis: Human–computer interaction and the general practice consultation. In: Monk, A. F. and Gilbert, G. N. (eds.), *Perspectives on HCI. Diverse approaches* pp. 199–222. London: Academic Press.
(1995b). How do desk-top computers affect the doctor–patient interaction. *Family Practice* 12/1: 32–6.
Halldorsdottir, I. (2006). Orientations to law, guidelines, and codes in lawyer–client interaction. *Research on Language and Social interaction* 39/3: 263–301.
Hanks, W. H. (2012). Evidentiality in social interaction. *Pragmatics and Society* 3/2: 169–80.
Harper, R. H. R. (1998). *Inside the IMF. An ethnography of documents, technology and organisational action.* San Diego: Academic Press.
Haviland, J. B. (1987). Fighting words: Evidential particles, affect, and argument. *Proceedings of the Thirteenth Annual Meeting of the Berkeley Linguistics Society*: 343–54.
(1996). Text from talk in Tzotzil. In: Silverstein, M. and Urban, G. (eds.), *Natural histories of discourse*, pp. 45–78. Chicago: University of Chicago Press.
Haworth, K. (2010). Police interviews in the judicial process. Police interviews as evidence. In: Coulthard, M. and Johnson, A. (eds.), *The Routledge handbook of forensic linguistics*, pp. 169–181. London/New York: Routledge.

Hayano, K. (2012). Question design in conversation. In: Stivers, T. and Sidnell, J. (eds.), *The handbook of conversation analysis*, pp. 395–414. Hoboken, NJ: Wiley-Blackwell.

Heath, C. and Luff, P. (1996). Documents and professional practice: 'Bad' organisational reasons for 'good' clinical records. *Proceedings of the Conference on Computer Supported Cooperative Work*, pp. 354–63. Boston: ACM Press.

(2012). Embodied action and organizational activity. In: Stivers, T. and Sidnell, J. (eds.), *The handbook of conversation analysis*, pp. 283–307. Hoboken NJ: Wiley-Blackwell.

Heffer, C., Rock, F. and Conley, J. (eds.), *Legal–lay communication. Textual travels in the law*. Oxford: Oxford University Press.

Hepburn, A. and Bolden, G. B. (2012). The conversation analytic approach to transcription. In: Stivers, T. and Sidnell, J. (eds.), *The handbook of conversation analysis*, pp. 57–76. Hoboken, NJ: Wiley-Blackwell.

Heritage, J. (1984a). *Garfinkel and ethnomethodology.* Cambridge: Polity Press.

(1984b). A change-of-state token and aspects of its sequential placement. In: Atkinson, J. M. and Heritage, J. (eds.), *Structures of social action. Studies in conversation analysis*, pp. 299–345. Cambridge: Cambridge University Press.

(2012a). Epistemics in action: Action formation and territories of knowledge. *Research on Language and Social Interaction* 45/1: 1–29.

(2012b). The epistemic engine: Sequence organization and territories of knowledge. *Research on Language and Social Interaction* 45/1: 30–52.

Heritage, J. and Raymond, G. (2005). The terms of agreement: Indexing epistemic authority and subordination in talk-in-interaction. *Social Psychology Quarterly* 68/1: 15–38.

Heritage, J. C. and Watson, D. R. (1979). Formulations as conversational objects. In: Psathas, G. (ed.), *Everyday language. Studies in ethnomethodology*, pp. 123–62. New York: Irvington.

Holt, E. (1996). Reporting on talk: The use of direct reported speech in conversation. *Research on Language and Social Interaction* 29/3: 219–45.

(2000) Reporting and reacting: Concurrent responses to reported speech. *Research on Language and Social Interaction* 33/4: 425–54.

(2007). 'I'm eyeing your chop up mind': Reporting and enacting. In: Holt, E. and Clift, R. (eds.), *Reporting talk. Reported speech in interaction*, pp. 47–80. Cambridge: Cambridge University Press.

Holt, E. and Johnson, A. (2006). Formulating the facts. Paper presented at the International Conference on Conversation Analysis (ICCA-06), Helsinki.

Horselenberg, R., Vredeveldt, A. and van Koppen, P. J. (2016). Nederlandse politieverhoren in de praktijk [Dutch police interrogations in practice]. *Nederlands Juristenblad (NJB)* 43: 3185.

Houtkoop-Steenstra, H. (2000). *Interaction and the standardized survey interview: The living questionnaire*. Cambridge, UK: Cambridge University Press.

Iversen, C. (2012) Recordability: Resistance and collusion in psychometric interviews with children. *Discourse Studies* 14: 691–709.

Jefferson, Gail (1983). Issues in the transcription of naturally-occurring talk: Caricature versus capturing pronunciational particulars. *Tilburg Papers in Language and Literature*, 34, 1–12. Tilburg: Tilburg University.

Johnson, A. (2013). Embedding police interviews in the prosecution case in the Shipman trial. In: Heffer, C., Rock, F. and Conley, J. (eds), *Legal–lay communication. Textual travels in the law*, pp. 147–67. Oxford: Oxford University Press.

Jönsson, L. and Linell, P. (1991). Story generations: From dialogical interviews to written reports in police interrogations. *Text* 11/3: 419–40.

Jörg, N., Field, S. and Brandts, C. (1995). Are inquisitorial and adversarial systems converging? In: Harding, C. et al. (eds.), *Criminal justice in Europe. A comparative study*, pp. 41–56. Oxford: Clarendon Press.

Kameo, N. and Whalen, J. (2015). Organizing documents: Standard forms, person production and organizational action. *Qualitative Sociology* 38: 205–29.

Kessler, M. (2016). *Audiovisuele verslaglegging in een gemoderniseerd Wetboek van Strafvordering* [Audiovisual reporting in a modernised Code of Criminal Procedure]. Oratie [inaugural lecture], Universiteit Leiden.

Kidwell, M. (2009). *What happened?*: An epistemics of before and after in 'at the scene' police questioning. *Research on Language and Social Interaction* 42/1: 20–41.

Komter, M. L. (1995). The distribution of knowledge in courtroom interaction. In: P. ten Have and G. Psathas (eds.), *Situated order: Studies in the social organization of talk and embodied activities,* pp. 107–28. Washington, DC: University Press of America.

(1998). *Dilemmas in the courtroom. A study of trials of violent crime in the Netherlands*. Hillsdale, NJ: Lawrence Erlbaum.

(2001) La construction de la preuve dans un interrogatoire de police. *Droit et Société* 48: 367–93.

(2002). The suspect's own words: The treatment of written statements in Dutch courtrooms. *Forensic Linguistics. The International Journal of Speech, Language and the Law* 9/2: 168–92.

(2002–3). The construction of records in Dutch police interrogations. *Information Design Journal + Document Design* 11, 2/3: 201–13.

(2003). The interactional dynamics of eliciting a confession in a Dutch police interrogation. *Research on Language and Social Interaction* 36/4: 433–70.

(2005). Understanding problems in an interpreter-mediated police interrogation. In: S. Burns (ed.), *Ethnographies of law and social control. Sociology of crime, law and deviance*, vol. VI, pp. 203–24. Amsterdam: Elsevier.

(2006a). Introduction. Special issue: Talk and text: The relationship between spoken interaction and written documentation in legal settings. *Research on Language and Social interaction* 39/3: 195–200.

(2006b). From talk to text: The interactional construction of a police record. *Research on Language and Social interaction* 39/3: 201–28.

(2006c). The interactional antecedents of 'recontextualisation phrases' in police records of suspect interrogations. Paper presented at the International Conference on Conversation Analysis (ICCA-06), Helsinki.

(2012a). The career of a suspect's statement: Talk, text, context. *Discourse Studies* 14/6: 731–52.

(2012b). Conversation analysis in the courtroom. In: Sidnell, J. and Stivers, T. (eds.) *The handbook of conversation analysis*, pp. 612–29. Hoboken, NJ: Wiley-Blackwell.

(2013). Travels of a suspect's statement. In: Heffer, C., Rock, F., Conley, J. (eds.), *Legal–lay communication. Textual travels in the law*, pp. 126–46. Oxford: Oxford University Press.

Komter, M. L. and Malsch, M. (2012). The language of criminal trials in an inquisitorial system: The case of the Netherlands. In: Tiersma, P. and Solan, L. (eds.), *The Oxford handbook of language and the law,* pp. 408–20. Oxford: Oxford University Press.

Labov, W. and Fanshel, D. (1977). *Therapeutic discourse: Psychology as conversation.* New York: Academic Press.

Labov, W. and Waletzky, J. (1967). Narrative analysis: Oral versions of personal experience. In: Helm, J. (ed.), *Essays on the verbal and visual arts*, pp. 12–44. Seattle: University of Washington Press.

Lamerichs, J. and Te Molder, H. F. M. (2009). 'And then I'm really like. . .': The role of fuzzy self-quotations in adolescent talk. *Discourse Studies* 11/4: 401–19.

Lerner, G. (2003). Selecting next speaker: The context-sensitive operation of a context-free organization. *Language in Society* 32: 177–201.

Levinson, S. C. (2012). Action formation and ascription. In: Stivers, T. and Sidnell, J. (eds.), *The handbook of conversation analysis*, pp. 103–30. Hoboken, NJ: Wiley-Blackwell.

Licoppe, C. (2014). Two modes of referring to the case file in the courtroom: The use of indirect reported text and text-as-addressed speech in case summaries. *Language & Communication* 36: 83–96.

Linell, P. (1998). Discourse across boundaries: On recontextualizations and the blending of voices in professional discourse. *Text* 18/2: 143–57.

Linell, P. and Jönsson, L. (1995). Suspect stories: perspective-setting in an asymmetrical situation. In: I. Marková and K. Foppa (eds.) *Asymmetries in dialogue*, pp. 75–100. New York: Barnes & Noble.

Llewellyn, N. and Hindmarsh, J. (2010), Work and organisation in real time: An introduction. In: Llewellyn, N. and Hindmarsh, J. (eds.), *Organisation, interaction and practice. Studies in ethnomethodology and conversation analysis*, pp. 4–15. Cambridge: Cambridge University Press.

Lynch, M. (2015). Turning a witness: The textual and interactional production of a statement in adversarial testimony. In: Duprez, B., Lynch, M. and Berard, T. (eds.), *Law at work. Studies in legal ethnomethods*, pp. 163–89. Oxford: Oxford University Press.

Lynch, M. and Bogen, D. (1996). *The spectacle of history: Speech, text, and memory at the Iran–Contra hearings*. Durham, NC: Duke University Press.

Malsch, M. and Nijboer, J. F. (1999). Conclusions and recommendations. In: Malsch, M. and Nijboer, J. F. (eds.) (1999). *Complex cases. Perspectives on the Netherlands criminal justice system*, pp. 228–39. Amsterdam: Thela Thesis.

Malsch, M., de Keijser, J., de Gruijter, M., Komter, M. L. and Elffers, H. (2012). *Het opmaken van proces-verbaal van een verdachtenverhoor: ervaringen en oordelen van verbalisanten* [Drawing up police reports of suspect interrogations: experiences and evaluations of reporting officers]. NSCR publication (Netherlands Institute for the Study of Crime and Law Enforcement).

Malsch, M., Kranendonk, R., de Keijser, J., Elffers, H., Komter, M. L. and de Boer, M. (2015). *Kijken, luisteren, lezen. De invloed van beeld, geluid en schrift op het oordeel over verdachtenverhoren.* [Look, listen, read. The influence of image, sound and writing on assessments of suspect interrogations]. Politie & Wetenschap, NSCR publication.

Manzo, J. F. (1997). Ethnomethodology, conversation analysis, and the sociology of law. In: Travers, M. and Manzo, J. F. (eds.)., *Law in action. Ethnomethodological and conversation analytic approaches to law*, pp. 1–15. Aldershot: Ashgate.

Maryns, K. (2013). 'Theattricks' in the courtroom: The intertextual construction of legal cases. In: Heffer, C., Rock, F. and Conley, J. (eds.), *Legal–lay communication. Textual travels in the law*, pp. 107–25. Oxford: Oxford University Press.

Matoesian, G. (1993). *Reproducing Rape: Domination through talk in the courtroom* Chicago: University of Chicago Press.

(1999). Intertextuality, affect, and ideology. *Text* 19/1: 73–109.

(2000). Intertextual authority in reported speech: production media in the Kennedy Smith rape trial. *Journal of Pragmatics* 32/7: 879–914.

Maynard, D. and Schaeffer, N. (2006). Standardization-in-interaction: The survey interview. In: Drew, P., Raymond, G. and Weinberg, D. (eds.). *Talk and interaction in social research methods*, pp. 9–27. London: Sage.

Meehan, A. J. (1986). Record-keeping practices in the policing of juveniles. *Urban Life* 15/1: 70–102.

Moerman, M. (1988). *Talking culture. Ethnography and conversation analysis.* Philadelphia: University of Pennsylvania Press.

Mondada, L. (2007). Commentary: Transcript variations and the indexicality of transcribing practices. *Discourse Studies* 9/6: 809–21.

Moore, R. J., Whalen, J. and Cabell Hankinson Gathman, E. (2010). The work of the work order: Document practice in face-to-face service encounters. In: Llewellyn, N. and Hindmarsh, J. (eds.), *Organisation, interaction and practice. Studies in ethnomethodology and conversation analysis*, pp. 172–97.

Park, J. S and Bucholtz, M. (2009). Introduction. Public transcripts: entextualization and linguistic representation in institutional contexts. *Text & Talk* 29/5: 485–502.

Philips, S. U. (1986). Reported speech as evidence in an American trial. In: Tannen, D. and Alatis, J. E. (eds.), *Languages and linguistics: The interdependence of theory, data, and application*, pp. 154–70. Washington, DC: Georgetown University Press.

Pollner, M. (1975). 'The very coinage of your brain': The anatomy of reality disjunctures. *Philosophy of the Social Sciences* 5: 411–30.

(1987). *Mundane reason: Reality in everyday and sociological discourse.* Cambridge: Cambridge University Press.

Pomerantz, A. (1984a). Agreeing and disagreeing with assessments: Some features of preferred/dispreferred turn shapes. In: Atkinson, J. M. and Heritage, J. (eds.), *Structures of social action: Studies in conversation analysis*, pp. 57–101. Cambridge: Cambridge University Press.

(1984b). Giving a source or basis: The practice in conversations of telling 'how I know'. *Journal of Pragmatics* 8: 607–25.

Pomerantz, A. and Denvir, P. (2007). Enacting the institutional role of chairperson in upper management meetings: The interactional realization of provisional authority. In: Cooren, F. (ed.), *Interacting and organizing. Analyses of a management meeting*, pp. 31–52. Mahwah, NJ: Lawrence Erlbaum.

Puchta, C., Potter, J. and Wolff, S. (2004). Repeat receipts: A device for generating visible data in market research focus groups. *Qualitative Research* 4/3: 285–309.

Raffel, S. (1979). *Matters of fact: A sociological inquiry*. London: Routledge & Kegan Paul.

Ravotas, D. and Berkenkotter, C. (1998). Voices in the text: The uses of reported speech in a psychotherapist's notes and initial assessments. *Text* 18/2: 211–39.

Raymond, G. (2006). Questions at work: Yes/no type interrogatives in institutional contexts. In: Drew, P., Raymond, G. and Weinberg, D. (eds.), *Talk and interaction in social research methods*, pp. 115–34. London: Sage.

Raymond, G. and Heritage, J. (2006). The epistemics of social relationships: Owning grandchildren. *Language in Society* 35/5: 677–705.

Robinson, J. D. and Stivers, T. (2001). Achieving activity transitions in physician–patient encounters from history taking to physical examination. *Human Communication Research* 27/2: 253–98.

Rock, F. (2001). The genesis of a witness statement. *Journal of Forensic Linguistics* 8/2: 44–72.

(2007). *Communicating rights. The language of arrest and detention.* Basingstoke: Palgrave Macmillan.

(2013). 'Every link in the chain'. The police interview as textual intersection. In: Heffer, C., Rock, F. and Conley, J. (eds.), *Legal–lay communication. Textual travels in the law*, pp. 78–103. Oxford: Oxford University Press.

Rossano, F. (2012). Gaze in conversation. In: Stivers, T. and Sidnell, J. (eds.), *The handbook of conversation analysis*. Hoboken, NJ: Wiley-Blackwell, pp. 308–29.

Sacks, H. (1978) Some technical considerations of a dirty joke. In: J. Schenkein (ed.), *Studies in the organization of conversational interaction*, pp. 249–69. New York: Academic Press.

(1995). *Lectures on conversation* (Parts I and II). Edited by G. Jefferson with an introduction by E. Schegloff. Oxford: Blackwell.

Sacks, H., Schegloff, E. A. and Jefferson, G. (1974). A simplest systematics for the organization of turn-taking for conversation. *Language* 50/4: 696–735.

Sanders, W. B. (1977). *Detective work. A study of criminal investigations*. New York: The Free Press.

Sandlund, E. (2014). Prescribing conduct: Enactments of talk or thought in advice-giving. *Discourse Studies* 16/5: 645–66.

Sarangi, S. (2009). Editorial: Entextualizing the institutional. *Text and Talk* 29/5: 481–4.

Sarangi, S. and Brookes-Howell, L. (2006). Recontextualising the familial lifeworld in genetic counselling case notes. In: Gotti, M. and Salager-Meyer, F. (eds.), *Advances in medical discourse analysis: Oral and written contexts, linguistic insights. Studies in language and communication* 45, pp. 197–225. Bern: Peter Lang.

Scheffer, T. (1998). Übergänge von Wort und Schrift: Zur Genese und Gestaltung von Anhörungsprotokollen im Asylverfahren. *Zeitschrift für Rechtssoziologie*, 20/2: 230–65.

(2006). The microformation of criminal defense: On the lawyer's notes, speech production, and a field of presence. *Research on Language and Social interaction* 39/3: 303–42.

(2010). *Adversarial case-making. An ethnography of English crown court procedure.* Leiden/Boston: Brill.

Scheffer, T., Hannken-Illjes, K. and Kozin, A. (2010). *Criminal defence and procedure. Comparative ethnographies in the United Kingdom, Germany, and the United States.* London: Palgrave Macmillan.

Schegloff, E. A. (1972). Notes on a conversational practice: formulating place. In: Sudnow, D. (ed.), *Studies in Social Interaction*, pp. 75–120. Glencoe, IL: The Free Press.

(1987). Between micro and macro: Contexts and other connections. In: Alexander, J., Giesen, B., Munch R. and Smelser, N. (eds.), *The micro–macro link*, pp. 207–34. Berkeley/Los Angeles: University of California Press.

(1991). Reflections on talk and social structure. In: Boden, D. and Zimmerman, D. H. (eds.), *Talk and social structure,* pp. 44–70. Cambridge: Polity.

(1996). Some practices for referring to persons in talk-in-interaction: A partial sketch of a systematics, in: Fox, B. A. (ed.), *Studies in anaphora*, pp. 437–85. Amsterdam: John Benjamins.

(2000). Overlapping talk and the organization of turn-taking for conversation. *Language in Society* 29: 1–63.

Schegloff, H. and Sacks, H. (1973). Opening up closings. *Semiotica*, 7: 289–327.

Shuy, R. (1998). *The language of confession, interrogation, and deception.* London: Sage.

Sidnell, J. (2012). Declaratives, questioning, defeasibility. *Research on Language and Social Interaction* 45/1: 53–60.

Slembrouck, S. (1992). The parliamentary Hansard 'verbatim' report: The written construction of spoken discourse. *Language and Literature* 1/2: 101–19.

(2001). Explanation, interpretation and critique in the analysis of discourse. *Critique of Anthropology* 21/1: 33–57.

Sliedrecht, K. Y. (2013). Formulations in institutionele interactie: de praktijk van 'samenvatten' in het politieverhoor, sollicitatiegesprek en journalistieke interview [Formulations in institutional interaction: The practice of 'summarising' in the police interrogation; job interview and news interview]. PhD dissertation, VU University, Amsterdam.

Smets, L. and Ponsaers, P. (2011). Het proces-verbaal van een verdachtenverhoor: Een bron van informatie? [The police report of a suspect interrogation: A source of information?] *Cahiers Politiestudies* 2011/4: 123–42.

Smith, D. (1974). The social construction of documentary reality. *Sociological Inquiry* 44/4: 257–68.

(1990a). The active text. In: Smith, D. *Texts, facts, and femininity: Exploring the relations of ruling*, pp. 120–58. London: Routledge.

(1990b). Textually mediated social organization. In: Smith, D. *Texts, facts, and femininity: Exploring the relations of ruling*, pp. 209–24. London: Routledge.

(2001). Texts and the ontologies of organizations. *Studies in Cultures, Organizations and Societies* 7/2: 159–98.

Sneijder, P. (2014). The embedding of reported speech in a rhetorical structure by prosecutors and defense lawyers in Dutch trials. *Text & Talk* 34/4: 467–90.

Steensig, J. and Drew, P. (2008). Introduction: Questioning and affiliation/disaffiliation in interaction. *Discourse Studies* 10/1: 5–15.

Stivers, T. (2011). Morality and question design: 'Of course' as contesting a presupposition of askability. In: Stivers, T., Mondada, L. and Steensig, J. (eds.), *The morality of knowledge in conversation*, pp. 82–106. Cambridge: Cambridge University Press.

Stivers, T. and Heritage, J. (2001). Breaking the sequential mold: Answering 'more than the question' during comprehensive history taking. *Text* 21/1–2: 151–85.

Stivers, T., Mondada, L. and Steensig, J. (2011). Knowledge, morality and affiliation in social interaction. In: Stivers, T., Mondada, L. and Steensig, J. (eds.), *The morality of knowledge in conversation*, pp. 3–24. Cambridge: Cambridge University Press.

Stivers, T. and Rossano, F. (2010). Mobilizing response. *Research on Language and Social Interaction* 43: 3–31.

Stivers, T. and Sidnell, J. (eds.) (2012). *The handbook of conversation analysis.* Hoboken, NJ: Wiley-Blackwell.

Stokoe, E. and Edwards, D. (2008). 'Did you have permission to smash your neighbour's door? Silly questions and their answers in police-suspect interrogations. *Discourse Studies* 10/1: 89–111.

Sudnow, D. (1965). Normal crimes: sociological features of the penal code in a public defender office. *Social Problems* 12/3: 255–76.

Van Charldorp, T. (2011). From police interrogation to police record. PhD dissertation, VU University, Amsterdam.

(2013). The intertwining of talk and technology: How talk and typing are combined in the various phases of the police interrogation. *Discourse & Communication* 7/2: 221–40.

(2014). 'What happened?' From talk to text in police interrogations. *Language & Communication* 36: 7–24.

Van der Houwen, F. (2013). Reported writing in court: Putting evidence 'on record'. *Text & Talk* 33/6: 747–69.

Van Oorschot, I. (2014a). Seeing the case clearly: File-work, material mediation, and visualizing practices in a Dutch criminal court. *Symbolic Interaction* 37/4: 439–57.

(2014b). Het dossier-in-actie: vouw- en ontvouwpraktijken in juridische waarheidsvinding [The dossier-in-action: folding and unfolding practices in judicial truth finding]. *Sociologie* 10/3: 301–18.

Wartna, B. S. J., Beijers, W. M. E. H. and Essers, A. A. M. (1999). *Ontkennende en bekennende verdachten* [Denying and confessing suspects]. Den Haag: Ministerie van Justitie, WODC.

Watson, D. R. (1990). Some features of the elicitation of confessions in murder interrogations. In: Psathas, G. (ed.), *Interaction competence*, pp. 263–95. Washington, DC: University Press of America.

Watson, R. (2009). *Analysing practical and professional texts: A naturalistic approach.* Farnham: Ashgate.

Whalen, J. (1995). A technology of order production: Computer-aided dispatch in public safety communication. In: ten Have, P. and Psathas, G. (eds.), *Situated order. Studies in the social organization of talk and embodied activities*, pp. 187–230. Washington, DC: University Press of America.

Zimmerman, D. H. (1969). Record-keeping and the intake-process in a public welfare agency. In: S. Wheeler (ed.), *On record: Files and dossiers in American life*, pp. 319–54. New York: Russell Sage Foundation.

(1992). The interactional organization of calls for emergency assistance. In: Drew, P. and Heritage, J. (eds.), *Talk at work*, pp. 418–69. Cambridge: Cambridge University Press.

Author Index

Subject Index